YOU ARE
WHAT YOU SEE

Watching Movies Through a Christian Lens

Scott Nehring

RIGHTLINE

Unless otherwise noted, all Scripture taken from The English Standard Version (ESV). The Standard Bible Society. © 2005-2010. Available at www.ESV.com.

Scriptures noted (NASB) taken from The NEW AMERICAN STANDARD BIBLE®. Copyright © 1960,1962,1963,1968,1971,1972,1973,1975,1977,1995. The Lockman Foundation. Used by permission. Available at www.BibleGateway.com.

Scriptures noted (NIV) taken from The HOLY BIBLE, NEW INTERNATIONAL VERSION®. Copyright © 1973, 1978, 1984. Biblica. Used by permission of Zondervan. All rights reserved. Available at www.BibleGateway.com.

Unless otherwise noted, all word and phrase definitions are taken from Webster's Third New International Dictionary, Unabridged. Merriam-Webster. 2002. http://unabridged.merriam-webster.com. Accessed throughout 2009 until May 2010.

DISCLAIMER:

I. The opinions and references in this book are the sole property of Scott Nehring and/or Right Line Publishing and do not imply any support for or connection with any producer, distributor, actor, writer, or other entity.

II. Unless specifically, explicitly stated, any reference to any film, movie, book, character, writer, director, producer, or anyone or anything connected with any film, movie, or book referenced within this work is not a recommendation of that particular film, movie, or book. All references are for instructional purposes only and only within their respective context within this work. By referencing any particular work I am not advocating the viewing of that work nor am I condoning or supporting all or any part of that work, its writers, producers, directors, actors, or any others involved in its production.

ISBN NO. 978-0-9844395-2-2

Library of Congress Control Number: 2010921387

Printed in the USA

This book is dedicated to four women:

For my dear wife, Andrea,
Through you the Lord has done His work in my life.

For my mother, Helen Nehring,
who always encouraged me to write a book.
Thank you for my love of story and for the better parts of my nature.

And for Dolores Gaffaney and Pat Turonie,
Thank you for pointing the way to my salvation
and showing me how we live our faith.

We have come from God
and inevitably the myths woven by us, though they contain error,
will also reflect a splintered fragment of true light,
the eternal truth that is with God.
— J. R. R. Tolkien

CONTENTS

SECTION TWO   The Structure of Film: Seeing What's Right in Front of You

SECTION THREE   Watching Film:
The Right Way to Sit There and Do Something

* — denotes an original concept

YOU ARE WHAT YOU SEE

Sometimes You Have to Die Before You Can be Reborn

THE EVENING OF FRIDAY, SEPTEMBER 21, 2007, MY WIFE AND I SAT through the movie *Premonition*. The film's synopsis is simple: Linda (Sandra Bullock) is an unsatisfied suburban housewife. One morning the sheriff arrives with news that her husband, Jim (Julian McMahon), died in a car accident the previous evening. Throughout that day Linda wallows in grief and faces telling her daughters of their loss until, emotionally spent, she finally falls asleep.

When she wakes, Linda finds it is not the next day but several days in the past. Jim is still alive, things seem normal, and that terrible day is a memory that has yet to happen. Linda does all she can to repair her relationship with Jim and to squeeze real life out of their final days together. In the end, Linda

---

Epigraph—Humphrey Carpenter. *J.R.R. Tolkien: A Biography*. Mariner Books. 1977 by George Allen & Unwin (Publishers) Ltd. 151. Reprinted by permission of Houghton Mifflin Harcourt Publishing Company. All rights reserved.

1. C. S. Lewis. *The Great Divorce*. MacMillian. 1973. 75. Used by permission. The C. S. Lewis Company Ltd. Dorset, UK.

recalls something her priest said, "It's never too late to realize what's important in your life—to fight for it."[2]

I intended to analyze *Premonition* for my movie review blog, Good News Film Reviews, but for days had avoided watching it—I knew it was not going to be my kind of film. As far as I was concerned, a movie about a wife whose husband dies then comes back to life sounded tedious with a side order of corny, but my wife and I settled in that Friday evening, worn ragged from a week of work and parenting. We spoke little, did not even bother to snuggle together—she sprawled out on the loveseat, I slumped in my chair on the other side of the room.

The next morning, I died.

Saturday morning, September 22, 2007, I stopped at the bank to cash in some change before I headed to the bakery to buy donuts. I never made it to the donut shop. While standing at the change machine in the bank, I suffered a devastating heart attack and croaked right on the spot. There I was, a thirty-eight-year-old corpse cooling on the tile floor of Wells Fargo. I had a blockage and arrhythmia—a combination known to medical personnel as The Widow-Maker. Only four percent of people who experience that type of heart attack will survive. Those lucky few who do make the cut rarely come out the other side unscathed.

The Lord was generous. He had me keel over one block from the local EMTs. They reached me in time. They brought me back from the dead.

The coincidence should be apparent. On the very evening before I died and came back to life, my wife and I watched a film about a husband who dies and appears to come back to life. The irony certainly has not been wasted on us, but this strange coincidence is not the only oddity that surrounded my death experience. As my family and I pieced together facts from the months which led up to that Saturday morning in the bank, a number of strange coincidences revealed themselves.

> On Saturday mornings, I *always* spend the whole morning alone in my basement office writing—but, for some odd reason, not that day.

> My wife and oldest son recently had a notion to take up coin collecting; they collect change and search for old coins as a way to spend time together.

> The coin collecting led me to drive to the bank that morning to turn in the change. I never, **never** go to the bank. I hate going to the bank—more now than I did before.

---

2. Bill Kelly. *Premonition.* Tri-Star Pictures. 2007.

I did not take either of my sons with me that morning, which was perhaps one of only a handful of times that has happened. I enjoy my children's company whenever I can get it.

I parked my car in the parking lot then looked at the long walk between the parking space and the building. Being lazy, I decided to pull around and park on the street.

I made it inside the bank and dropped to the floor in front of the change machine, mere feet away from the tellers.

I did not have my heart attack in my basement, alone.

I did not have my heart attack in my car, alone.

I did not have my heart attack in that large, empty parking lot, alone.

I did not drop on the near-empty sidewalk.

I died in front of a crowd of people only one block from emergency responders.

The EMTs who found my cooling corpse chose to roll the dice and try a newly acquired, previously untested (by them) method of resuscitation. It worked perfectly.

For a year prior to that Saturday, my wife fed me fish oil supplements and beta-blockers—"just in case." Without those, either the EMT's efforts could have been fruitless or I could have returned physically or mentally impaired.

My wife was notified by telephone of my condition. For moments she was lost in fear. What was she going to do with our children? At that moment a woman from our church happened to walk by our house and was free to babysit.

Though there was no reason for me to suspect my impending doom, I had recently begun to outline my dying wishes to my wife— something she had found to be more than a little morbid. For example, I requested my headstone read: "Scott Ellery Nehring, ~~beloved~~ tolerated husband and father."

The list above is not all-inclusive and it does not delve into the numerous other strange synchronicities I witnessed during my journey into the Light of Christ.

I know God was directly involved both in the events that unfolded that day and in the time that led up to them. Some may argue otherwise, but from my perspective I know He was, and I know another thing: when you see a coincidence in your life, pay attention. Coincidence is God's way of being obvious.

While I certainly would never recommend it, to nearly die was a clarifying experience, a great filter for the rest of life. On that Saturday morning, everything in existence was shoved through the lens of death. The world fell into two categories: *important* and *meaningless*. It was totally clear that decisions on how to spend my remaining time were simple: stick with what is important and completely ignore the meaningless.

The ability to continue with my life after that experience, as well as my new perspective, are great gifts from my Creator. Yet it is common for those who have a near-death experience to fall into deep depression. I succumbed to one that lasted for months. The reason is simple: when you have a moment of such brilliant clarity where the world is so easily parsed, it becomes clear that we waste a great deal of our existence on nonsense.

Also, the clarity fades over time. We were pulled from the muddy mire of this existence and exhilarated by the freedom. Slowly we begin to sink back into the muck of daily life and are once again muddied by the slop around us. That brief moment of clarity eventually succumbs to a return to the old way of life.

But there is the haunting memory of our clear thinking, so we return to our life tainted with a constant reminder that most of what we do amounts to nothing. Our greatest achievements are no more than cosmic burps in an endless universe. That perspective makes it a little difficult to get out of bed in the morning.

> **Coincidence is God being obvious.**

I look at this experience as though God gave me a firsthand account of Ecclesiastes. I have lain on my death bed so I can tell you with absolute certainly that nearly everything our culture values as important is actually and utterly meaningless. The world of celebrity plus all the films, books, television shows, and video games are all puffs of sweet air in a wind tunnel. They are nothing.

Instead of spending an evening of meaningful, quality time with the love of my life, God's gift to me, I nearly spent the last night of my existence on earth in numbed silence as we stared at a Sandra Bullock movie—not the kind of thing I want written in my obituary.

Since God intervened on that Saturday morning, I am alive. But I am not only alive, I am a reborn man. My death experience renewed my love for my family and my dedication to being a worthy husband and father. It also solidified my faith in Jesus Christ and His truth, and it prompted me to finish the book you now hold in your hands.

My turn toward Jesus Christ had occurred several years earlier. I can be a very stubborn and stupid man. It took me a long while to realize a few things, like the fact I really could be forgiven by other people, let alone God, and that they would be there for me to help me rebuild my life.

During that time I had attended church and Bible classes, had even begun to teach a Sunday morning film class which became the groundwork for this book. I was a Christian and I had things pretty well under control. Then I found out that I did not control anything.

I had given my life to Christ, I had just forgotten the part where I actually handed it over to Him. You see, when you hand your life over to Christ, you cannot keep a bit of it hidden in the other hand behind your back. He knows what you are up to, and you will look like a dope when He calls you on it.

I may have become a "Christian" before my Saturday morning on the Wells Fargo tile, but I still was not following in Christ's steps. I was just another dead man walking. My death experience ended the first meaningful test of my faith, and I failed horribly—not because I did not have faith in Christ but because I did not take that faith seriously. I had cobbled together a faith that looked good but could never weather even a moderate storm. From my point-of-view, God killed me so that I could begin again from scratch, as if He had said, "Nice try kid; now do it again, and this time let's put some work into it."

In the mobster parody *Oscar*, Connie (Chazz Palminteri) is asked by mob boss Oscar (Sylvester Stallone) to unload all his weapons and place them on a table. Connie proceeds to cover the top of the table with guns and knives of every assorted size and shape that come from more pockets and hidden places than clothes could ever have. He even unloads a few sticks of dynamite, a bottle of poison, a mace, and a meat hook. When Connie is finished, Oscar asks, "Is that all?" Connie sheepishly reveals he is still holding a one-shot pistol in his sock. Exasperated, Oscar exclaims, "This is disarming Germany!"[3]

That was me surrendering my life to Christ. I placed my negative behaviors before Him, but I still had a gun in my sock. That final step was a spiritual one, and it was the one I could not or would not take. God has to be very overt with me—and very patient. He loves me enough to say, "Next time I let you drop, I'm not picking you up again."

My death experience gave me the opportunity to begin anew. I was forced to reconsider my life and my relationship with God. Every aspect of my life

---

3. Michael Barrie and Jim Mulholland. Based on the play by Claude Magnier. *Oscar*. 1991. Silver Screen Partners IV and Touchstone Pictures.

needed to be re-evaluated and assessed. God gave me a glimpse at what was important and what was nonsense. It was time to remove the pistol from my sock.

When faith fails, it is not God's fault. It is ours. He has given us the instruction manual. He has even gone so far as to give us a clear example in Jesus on how to live. It is not His fault if we are idiotic enough to try shortcuts and rabbit trails.

Confessions of a Film Geek

I am a film geek. I have loved movies since childhood. For better and worse, movies have consumed most of my life. At any given moment, thousands of films and television references swim around in my mind. Ask me what I think of a film and I will offer opinions until you plead for me to stop. Prior to becoming a Christian I watched almost everything a person could see on screen, from the most insufferably self-important adaptation of a Jane Austin costume drama to a straight-to-video slasher movie.

My love for film goes beyond just watching movies. As a small child I was fascinated with how films were made. I devoured books, scoured magazine articles, and sat mesmerized by television shows on anything to do with films and their creation. At the age of twelve I wrote my first screenplay, *Battle of the Rebels*. At the time I thought it was brilliant and fancied myself the next George Lucas. In truth, it was even worse than Lucas' scripts.

Later, my studies included Lajos Egri's *The Art of Dramatic Writing*, Syd Field's *Screenplay: The Foundation of Screenwriting*, Christopher Vogler's *The Writer's Journey: Mythic Structure for Writers*, and works on mythology by intellectuals such as Joseph Campbell (*The Hero of a Thousand Faces*) and Otto Rank (*The Myth of the Birth of the Hero*). I also read scripts by the best screenwriters—William Goldman, Billy Wilder, the Coen Brothers. Throughout the years I learned the structure and design of stories.

I felt I had a secret knowledge only a handful of people could understand because I could identify act structure, see character archetypes, and place movies in the context of film history. I came to understand that films were a mode of communication, and I could translate their meaning.

To know how something works thrills geeks like me. It has been explained to me, however, that freely sharing these details actually annoys everyone else on earth.

While dating, I took my future bride to see a murder mystery. Ten minutes into the film I grumbled loudly enough for her to hear, "His wife did it." I almost did not get another date.

For years my longsuffering wife listened to me ramble about story structure and film. I may as well have yapped about lawn care and fertilizer. Actually, she would have preferred the fertilizer—we might have grown something in our yard besides brown scrub. Yet week by month by year I compulsively prattled on about act breaks and character arcs. My wife settled back, resigned to accept my blathering as another sacrifice required to have me in her life.

We avoided divorce by setting a rule that I raise my hand and wait to be called on before I expose surprise endings. Now, after almost two decades of marriage, I have learned not to point out every tiny detail in a movie. And something else in our lives also changed and changed big. I became a Christian.

Today, I often feel my purpose in life is to be an example of how far God will go to save His creation. My conversion to Christ Jesus took a long time and I did not come willingly. I was a deeply materialistic, immoral, and corrupt man-boy for much of my life. I believed in what I could touch, and I had no room for God. Why did I need an invisible control freak pushing me around? I had enough people in my life telling me what to do.

Throughout my adventures in bad living, I denied God and openly mocked Christians—the normal reaction of an atheist toward faith.[4] To trust in Jesus Christ was not a flash of inspiration or a quick revelation. I came pitching a fit every step of the way. God called me; I said no. God asked again; I told Him I was busy. God kicked me in the gut and called one final time, and then I relented. And before long I was dealing with conversion issues such as old friends not talking to me anymore.[5]

I also encountered a number of difficult internal tasks. New adult believers must maneuver through mine fields of their own pasts, define their new relationship with God, and figure out their place in the world. To learn to walk by faith in Jesus Christ can feel like a move into a new neighborhood where everyone has a completed house. We show up at an unfinished lot and God has laid out all of the materials along with a note that reads, "Get to building. Call if you have questions." The neighbors help, but we still have to figure out how to build the home.

Some people build faster and create sturdier structures than others. In my case, I often feel like I am the dork with the Spanish hacienda on a street

---

4. In their defense, I do not blame atheists for attacking God's faithful. Let me explain. I am color blind. The green paint on my living room walls appears purple to me. My wife's brilliant blue eyes are, to me, a soothing green. Surprisingly, I had no idea how impaired my vision was until I was in my thirties—had spent years studying art and making decisions based on my ability to choose proper colors. While I thought that what I saw was real and true, I was blind. Nothing in my vision was as it was meant to be, yet I belligerently insisted others were not paying attention. It never occurred to me I was the one not seeing correctly. Atheists are blind. I did not say evil. I did not even say wrong. They are blind and they do not know it.

5. Someone can be a friend for a decade, but tell them you have become a Christian and there is no predicting how they are going to react.

lined with ornate Victorians. It is functional and I can live in it, but everyone walking down the street points at it and asks, "What the heck is this guy doing?"

When I talked with other Christians, I found them swamped with concerns about things I never thought twice about—guilt from watching a television show or seeing a film. One grown man beat himself up because he kissed a girl when he was a teenager. I wondered, *Have I dropped into a faith that transforms grown men into whimpering sissies without sufficient defenses to handle the slightest bump in the road?*

I also noticed that Christian brothers and sisters thoughtlessly switched from plain English into "Christianese." They talked about "worldview," being "discerning," or how "convicted" they were.

I constantly doubted my conversion. I attended what I knew to be a great church led by one of the best pastors in the country. I assumed the disconnect had to be my fault. Perhaps my faith was too thin. Maybe I was too coarse, too cynical to settle into a Christian lifestyle. I felt as though God had invited me to a dinner party but failed to introduce me to the other guests.

I stuck with the church and God stuck with me. I attended Bible classes. One class was called The Drama of the Bible and was based on the book *God's Big Picture: Tracing the Storyline of the Bible* by Vaughn Roberts.[6] The subject matter covered the narrative structure of the Bible, examined the larger storyline of Scripture, and revealed how the Bible, taken as a whole, tells a fuller story than most people realize.

The overarching story of the Bible is the identification of the New Adam. After the fall of Adam and Eve, God promised to rebuild paradise; He provided a means for His creation to become Eden again. Throughout the Old Testament, great leaders arose: Abraham, Moses, King David. Each appeared to be the one who would save mankind—or at least the Jewish people. Each one failed to be the New Adam of God's promise. Then Jesus of Nazareth arrived as the Christ and the New Adam. He provided mankind with the one and only way to redemption from sin. The Bible tells this arcing story of grace.

During the class on The Drama of the Bible, I looked at the Bible's grand narrative and an epiphany descended upon me. A shaft of light stabbed down from the heavens and shone upon my brow. Music swelled. Angels appeared. Well, okay, I may be overstating things. It was more like I raised my eyebrow and said, "Hmm, will you look at that."

My years of babbling about story structure and film found a context. My wife's years of patient listening became worthwhile. I looked at the story of the Bible and saw the structure I had talked about my whole adult life.

---

6. InterVarsity Press. 2003.

Soon other things fell into place and I became able to see how God could make Himself known even in something as seemingly frivolous as a movie. From there I launched into seeing possibilities for a Biblical approach to film.

God reveals Himself in the Arts,[7] and that includes movies. This may not make sense reading it here, but I hope it will before we finish. This book you are reading will explain how film influences us and will provide the tools needed to judge whether a movie is good or bad. We will look at the structure of film-story and see how film can be used to display the Lord's true majesty. From the lessons in this book, you will become a better audience member, one who can make informed demands of actors, directors, and producers.

Be warned: These concepts can radically change the way you watch a movie. My brother-in-law watched movies like most people do: sit down, absorb whatever is on screen, then move on. As an unwilling participant in my endless blathering about story structure and film, his movie-viewing was revolutionized.

He likened the change to *The Matrix*. The hero of that film, Neo, is told that the world is an illusion created by computers. Morpheus, Neo's mentor, offers him a chance to break the illusion and see the world as it actually is, in all of its gritty detail. Morpheus dramatically holds out two pills, one blue and one red. Take the blue pill and the illusion continues and Neo is never the wiser. Take the red pill and the truth will be revealed but his comfortable world will melt away. My brother-in-law says he took the red pill. Now he has two sets of films he has seen—the films before I showed him how things work and those he has seen since.

Take the red pill. Join me to look at the world that hides behind the illusions on screen.

---

7. In this book, 'the Arts' refers to wide-ranging forms of expression, from painting to drama to interpretive dance. I default to the term since it conjures the image of haughty, solemn works seen on PBS but can be extended to include the frivolous, crude efforts of MTV and the gamut of creative and culturally relevant possibilities in between.

2

The Rise of the VCR Generation

"If the education of our kids comes from radio, television, newspapers——
if that's where they get most of their knowledge from, and not from the schools
——then the powers that be are definitely in charge because
they own all those outlets."[1] —— Maynard J. Keenan

WHEN I WAS A KID, MY MOM AND DAD WERE NOT THE ONLY parental figures in our home. Like many households who raised Generation–X-ers, my parents never knew they shared their authority, never knew the morality they tried to instill in my spongy little mind was always opposed by another voice.

They would say, "Two wrongs don't make a right," and the other voice would whisper, "Revenge feels so good." They would try to teach me to be responsible; the other voice would advise me to follow my heart. I would hear my parents claiming, "Honesty is the best policy," but it was no match for "All truth is relative." For every point my parents made, the counterargument was delivered in a fantastically alluring package.

My other parent was the VCR.

Baby-boomers may have been the first generation raised on television, but my generation, Generation-X, was the first raised on the video cassette recorder (VCR). The effect of the VCR was immense due to its singular convenience: choice.

---

1. Kurt Loder. Maynard James Keenan: Not Yet a Legend, Not Yet Dead. MTVNews. January 2004. http://www.mtv.com/bands/a/a_perfect_circle/news_feature_040122/. Last accessed November 2009.

Before the introduction of the VCR, if Suzy Q. Public did not see a film in the theatre, she did not see the movie at all. She might eventually see a heavily-edited version on network television, but had no control over what was available or when.

With the introduction of the VCR, we could choose what we wanted to see and when we would see it—we only had to find it on videotape. For the first time the average person could buy copies of their favorite movies and watch them at their leisure. Soon the lowered price of VHS tapes allowed people to buy movies they only marginally enjoyed. No longer were audiences forced to drag themselves to the cinema, they could enjoy the pleasure of film from their couches without commercial interruption and completely unedited.

While cable television and video games may seem to be heavier cultural influences (and I will not reduce their importance), it was the VCR which changed Western civilization. Until the late 1980s, cable television was not available to large areas of the country and still did not allow the audience to choose what or when they would watch. It was, fundamentally, network television with swearing and skin. Video games were, in general, the passion of the young. The VCR, however, served multiple generations and nearly all socio-economic groups.

> The freedom of choice the VCR offered allowed people to become more adventurous in their tastes and opened whole new avenues of cinema for the general public.

VCRs could be plugged in anywhere a television could be found, and the affect on my generation was pervasive. As long as we waited for VHS tapes to hit the market, or found a bootlegged copy, we could have the world of cinema at our beck and call. The images that flowed from Hollywood grew from a constant drip to a raging torrent. Major studio production schedules went into overdrive; independent film producers cashed in. The industry expanded from one-shot theatre runs to films that pulled in millions from additional videotape sales. And many people in my generation were more than willing to consume whatever came our way.

Conversely, this freedom also meant that, for the first time in history, mainstream Americans watched films with strong language, nudity, and violence while seated in the privacy of their family rooms. A few stalwarts maintained strict control over what was watched, but many parents did not know or care. Across the country, parents and children sat side-by-side to watch R-Rated films—*The Road Warrior, Animal House, Stripes*. How many teens from the 1980s suffered both embarrassment and the erosion of God-given modesty via a sex scene or flash of nudity while their mother or father sat mere feet away?

Crafty folks in the pornography industry were also at the forefront of the VCR boom. As with R-Rated films, adult films (referred to as X-Rated at the time) had only been seen in movie theatres—and theatres that would play porn films were not in the nicest neighborhoods. The pornography industry knew that expansion of their product line to include porn-on-the-go through videotapes could be a huge business. They were right. The porn industry mushroomed. The VCR turned homes into pornography theatres.

The casual appearance of harsh content in films changed us as a people. Combined with the corrosive effects of cable television and an industry willing to produce increasingly harsher material, we ingested content and ideas we had shunned only a decade before. And we consumed these films voraciously.

The VCR in the American home was the birth of the frantic, pornography-crazed, on-demand society we live in today. It was the first in a long line of modern technologies created to enhance our leisure time.

Today's abundance often overwhelms us with trivialities and the extraneous yet leaves us empty and hungry with no knowledge of where to find what will satisfy. In 1985, media critic Neil Postman, in his landmark book *Amusing Ourselves to Death*, explained that while we waited for the evil overlords of George Orwell's *1984* to sap our freedoms, it was more likely that the oppressors from Aldous Huxley's *Brave New World* were the ones we should have worried about. In his Foreword, Postman explained:

> What Orwell feared were those who would ban books. What Huxley feared was that there would be no reason to ban a book, for there would be no one who wanted to read one. Orwell feared those who would deprive us of information. Huxley feared those who would give us so much that we would be reduced to passivity and egoism. Orwell feared that the truth would be concealed from us. Huxley feared the truth would be drowned in a sea of irrelevance. Orwell feared we would become a captive culture. Huxley feared we would become a trivial culture, preoccupied with some equivalent of the feelies, the orgy porgy, and the centrifugal bumblepuppy. As Huxley remarked in Brave New World Revisited, the civil libertarians and rationalists who are ever on the alert to oppose tyranny 'failed to take into account man's almost infinite appetite for distractions.' In 1984, Huxley added, people are controlled by inflicting pain. In Brave New World, they are controlled by

inflicting pleasure. In short, Orwell feared that what we hate
will ruin us. Huxley feared that what we love will ruin us.[2]

Postman's warning has become a reality in our on-demand society. We
get what we want, when we want it, and if it does not come there will be
hell to pay. This impulse-demand mindset is promoted by corporate
marketing campaigns that intrude into our daily lives. The continual
stream of marketing from the entertainment industry looks down at us
from billboards and calls to us from magazine covers, television commercials,
and movie trailers. News programs, owned by the same parent companies
that distribute the movies, actively promote films by announcing box office
statistics and celebrity gossip as if it were newsworthy. National attention is
diverted from real life issues such as war, poverty, and political corruption
and guided toward starlet divorces and celebrity drug abuse scandals.

All of this comes to us in a frantic turnstile of daily and weekly news cycles
that change the national debate so quickly nothing actually gets said. We
are distracted by the constantly churning culture, and many of us want to
believe the projected images rather than the hard-earned wisdom of previous
generations. We have developed a disposable culture based on the whimsical
direction of an entertainment industry that produces works with shorter shelf
lives than bread. We have perverted the most vibrant and powerful culture
in human history into the cultural equivalent of a Blue-Light Special. The
flashing light flares, we rush to grab the deal, then wander away no richer
for the experience.

It is not a surprise, given our lack of historical perspective and prevalent
post-modern self-referencing, that the film industry now remakes the movies of
our childhoods (*A Nightmare on Elm Street, Red Dawn, Charlie and the Chocolate
Factory, Texas Chainsaw Massacre, Friday the 13th*). In a culture where Self is
paramount, we look to our experiences for wisdom. Raised on film, films
become the legacy we leave our children. How sad.

When we want to immortalize something we make a movie about it. Instead
of carving memorials in stone to stand forever, we flash lights on a screen
that last only seconds. Even with issues we deem vital we are helpless to do
more than make them passing fancies to distract us (*Pearl Harbor, Saving
Private Ryan, United 93*).

If we have not already taken the turn, Western society is certainly in the
process of becoming a reflection of those written about in Romans 1:18–25:

> For although they knew God, they did not honor him as God
> or give thanks to him, but they became futile in their thinking,
> and their foolish hearts were darkened. Claiming to be wise,

2. Neil Postman. *Amusing Ourselves to Death: Public Discourse in the Age of Show Business.*
    Penguin Books. 1985. Foreword. Used by permission of Viking Penguin, a division of Penguin
    Group (USA) Inc.

they became fools, and exchanged the glory of the immortal God for images resembling mortal man and birds and animals and reptiles. Therefore God gave them up in the lusts of their hearts to impurity, to the dishonoring of their bodies among themselves, because they exchanged the truth about God for a lie and worshiped and served the creature rather than the Creator, who is blessed forever! Amen.

And Christians are conflicted. As the culture frantically tells us new releases and vacuous movie stars are worth our interest, that being famous is more important than being important, Christ-followers know it is God alone who is worthy of our full attention. The seduction of constant distractions, the flash and bang of commercials, trailers, music videos, and movies, plus all the nonsense online, make dedication to faith and godliness like trying to thread a needle while a swarm of wasps buzzes around our heads.

But we *can* change our direction. We can still steer away from our self-indulgence and turn toward becoming a culture worthy of handing over to the generations that follow.

The question before us is: How do we change this lost culture?

> Our culture is no longer on the road to hell—it is flying down the off ramp and pulling into town.

The first thing we must change is ourselves. Our status quo is not an option. Recognizing that fact is a critical step in making meaningful change.

Christian filmmakers create products well-intentioned but poorly crafted. These movies are sanitized to meet the restrictive requirements of the Christian subculture. On the other side of the screen, and thanks to decades of assaults in the cinema, Christian audiences are instinctively wary of film. Some shy away from the medium altogether. Others consider that to view a PG-13 or R-Rated film is to bring instant jeopardy to the soul.

There is another way. Through education and artistry we can create an alternative voice. Our artists can produce change, but this movement must begin with us, the audience, not the filmmakers.

The audience is the consumer—that gives us far more power than we realize. We buy the tickets and DVDs, therefore we ultimately decide which productions are successful and which fade into oblivion. As obvious as it sounds, if the audience does not show up, the film industry dies. Yet we are most often treated as if it were the other way around. Hollywood pretends they do not need us. The truth is they do.[3]

An educated and discerning audience will make demands on those who want to cater to them. When Christian audiences become both savvy and more organized, they can call upon filmmakers to create works that are truly meaningful and worthy of viewing.

An audience with high moral standards will lead to artists with moral standards. This symbiotic relationship offers the fertile ground of true creativity and beauty that our culture desperately needs.

Let us start changing the culture by changing ourselves. We must start by altering how we look at what we see in the cinema.

---

3. It is easy for Christians to take an "Us vs. Them" policy toward Hollywood or anyone in the entertainment industry. We should remember that the reason the industry promotes such salacious material is because it is populated by lost souls, people just like you and me, and they need Christ just as much as we do. I strongly suggest looking into groups like MasterMedia International, The Hollywood Prayer Network, or XXX Church to find ministries that are working with and praying for those who create entertainment.

Standards of Indecency: Welcome to Our Culture

3

Keeping an Eye on What You Watch

"Participant [Media] believes that a good story well told can truly make a difference in how one sees the world."[1]

MOVIES MATTER. THEY HAVE MEANING IN OUR LIVES. IF YOU TAKE nothing else from this book, you must understand: Movies matter and they absolutely have a deep impact on all of our lives.

This reality may run counter to all your preconceptions about watching movies, after all, our society considers them innocuous timewasters—something to do after work or on a weekend. To believe that is to be like a fly who tells itself the spider's web is no more than a cozy place to hang out.

Life can be an irritating affair and the escape from daily life is a natural desire. Today that escape is often accomplished through the medium of film. We sit before a flickering screen and allow the lights and sounds to fill our heads. Our burdens melt away—at least for two hours.

Each time we participate in this seemingly mundane task, we allow ourselves to be somewhat hypnotized. Have you ever gotten lost in a movie? The characters seem so rich and meaningful, the plot so surprising and original that you lose track of time? Have you been swept away to another land, involved in the on-screen struggles? This harmless escape from reality is actually a form of hypnosis. Merriam-Webster defines *hypnosis* as "A trance-like state that resembles sleep but is induced by a person whose suggestions are readily accepted by the subject."

---

1. Opening sentence from the mission statement of Participant Productions, producers of *An Inconvenient Truth, Good Night and Good Luck, North Country,* and *Syriana.* http://www.participantmedia.com/company/about_us.php. Last accessed May 2010.

Instead of looking at film as a means of entertainment, consider what it actually is: a mode of communication. Screen images are more than flashing pictures blended together to give the illusion of movement. These pictures are composed and edited to make statements.

The filmmaker intentionally molds sequences of images to manipulate your conscious and subconscious. You are not a passive lump of meat in front of a screen. You are a vibrant, active soul created to experience Story, and you react as the filmmaker plays with your emotions. We loathe the villain as he guns down the hero's friend then cheer as the hero blows away the villain's bodyguard. Both acts involve killing, but we chose sides because a gifted director or storyteller used our innate understanding of Story to influence our thought process.

The medium of film relies on direct manipulation of the audience in order to succeed. Cinema magic is not based on logic, it is based in the heart. We rarely expect or enjoy having our intellects touched directly. No one goes to the cinema to watch abstract mathematical concepts being explained. We need an emotional hook to grab us, to engage us, so we can feel and not think. Explanations of complex mathematical equations require the mathematician to be a debilitated, hallucinating genius (*A Beautiful Mind*), then people are interested. We want to be manipulated into that slightly hypnotic state and have the director caress our emotions.

Because film speaks to us through our emotions rather than our logical mind, we run the risk of prolonged manipulation that extends well beyond our time in that darkened room. Film is a hypodermic needle through which either a venom or its antidote is injected into the social body. The toxin or cure which is delivered is known as worldview.

A Worldview to Call Your Own?

Worldview is what it sounds like: a view of the world, how one recognizes and defines existence. Where do we come from? Where do our values come from? What is life anyway? Every one of us has a way in which we view and interpret the world around us.[2] Every filmmaker does too, as evidenced by this statement by James Cameron, writer, producer, and director of *Avatar, Titanic, Aliens,* and *The Terminator*:

> "I think that with large scale movies that are going to reach a lot of people, when you construct the film, what you're always trying to do is tap into people's view of the world we live in."[3]

2. For more information, see Ravi Zacharias's *Jesus Among Other Gods* or David Noble's *Understanding the Times.*

3. David Chen. *The Filmcast Interview: James Cameron, Director of* Avatar. December 18, 2009. http://www.slashfilm.com/2009/12/18/the-filmcast-interview-james-cameron-director-of-avatar. Last accessed December 2009.

And every film reflects aspects of its maker's worldview. In the climactic scene of *Raiders of the Lost Ark,* Indiana Jones and his friend, Marian, are saved when they close their eyes as the Ark of the Covenant is opened. Greedy Nazis watch as the ark is opened and they are smitten by God. The film promotes the concept that God exists and that He is powerful. He punishes those who do evil and spares the good. The worldview of *Raiders of the Lost Ark* is Judeo-Christian at its core and demands the audience believe a higher order of right and wrong.

The worldview of Christians is well known. Christians see things as created and managed by a single, personal, loving God who established this universe for His purposes. Through the failure of sin, we are unworthy to be in His presence. To rectify this imbalance, God sent His Son, Jesus Christ, to pay the price for our sin. This sacrifice is God's greatest gift and, if we choose to accept it, our eyes are opened, we are purified from said sin, and are enabled to freely stand before Almighty God.

Most films do not present this worldview. They do not, for that matter, even present the concept of sin. Granted, most films are not meant as a treatise on Romans 3:23 or a debate over the doctrine of election. We do not go to the theatre to witness a sermon. However, the role of faith—and Christian faith in particular—is most often completely ignored or misused. If one was to identify the prominent worldview of the past fifty years[4] it would be existentialist philosophy often in the form of its derivative, post-modernism,[5] which in turn manifests itself in secular humanism.[6]

Existentialism, at its core, is a belief that God does not exist. The universe is a blob of random, meaningless events. We, as humans, are mere accidents who find fortune in a random universe without value. This means we have no worth beyond what we decide is valuable. Social rules, knowledge, and hope are little more than our false constructions used to apply meaning to

---

4. For a simple but well-written listing of common philosophies in film I suggest reading Brian Godawa's *Hollywood Worldviews: Watching Films With Wisdom & Discernment.* Available at http://www.covenantbookstore.com/howobybrgo.html or at Amazon.com: http://tinyurl.com/yb5gsvy.

5. When examining this world it is good to keep a healthy amount of skepticism. Post-Modernism is what happens when you keep an unhealthy amount of skepticism on hand. While Post-Modernism has a broad range of definitions, my usage keeps with the contemporary line that grew in post-1960s America. In the Arts, Post-Modernism relies heavily on irony, deconstruction, and winking self-references—think Quentin Tarantino—which all work to underline a lack of verifiable truth, honor, or understanding. It is all the fun of working in the Arts without that pesky need to create something of value.

6. Secular humanism is a worldview defined by its complete denial of religious dogma and institutions. In a nutshell, it is the belief that we humans are alone in the universe and must rely on our own power of reason and compassion to get by. In other words, it is the worship of science because, as we all know, scientists are never compelled to fudge their findings and never make stuff up.

that which means nothing. From my experience, existentialists tend to not be the happiest people.[7]

Existentially-minded cinema is a mushy place where the antiques of honor, service, and loyalty are ignored in favor of the hollow notions of following one's heart and achieving one's desires.

In an existential universe where man is alone without God, self-serving attitudes and situational ethics will rule. The decadence found in a majority of modern films aligns with the logic of an existential worldview—because truth evaporates when removed from the hand of God, and where there is no truth there can be no morality.

Generally speaking, we as a culture have tried to remove the planks of logic, history, and natural law from the platforms of public discourse, including from the Arts. The resulting vacuousness must then be filled with the only thing we know: our personal experiences, and those are precarious substances upon which to build the foundations of human understanding. To do so, we must rely upon our own, transitory feelings rather than follow moral truth as directed by divine will. We construct *truth* from our passing inclinations rather than from an identifiable code of morality guaranteed to last from one second to the next. When we follow this existential worldview, everything quickly begins to lose all sense.

All films demand the audience take on the perceptions of the filmmakers. Films as wide-ranging as *Sands of Iwo Jima, 300,* and *Steel Magnolias* share this requirement. We see the universe through the filmmaker's eyes, through their worldview. They intend to persuade us toward their way of thinking— which is what artists mean when they say they want to express themselves. Their expression is their explanation of their worldview.

The Arts are a valuable gift from God that Christians should cherish. As with any tool, however, the Arts—and film in particular—can be used for myriad purposes. Film can promote and speak truth, and it can be used to disseminate lies. Viewing films not created through the prism of the Christian worldview is similar to reading a non-Biblical religious text—and it is wise to approach film with this in mind.

Like many boys of my generation, *Star Wars* transformed my life. The excitement of a new world where good and evil do battle with cool laser swords awed me and every other boy I knew. I spent my childhood pretending to be Han Solo (no cool kid wanted to be Luke Skywalker, he was a whiner) and drawing pictures of Chewbacca, Darth Vader, and Boba Fett. The influence

7. Some existentialists may complain that my definition of the philosophy is sophomoric and watered down. As reply to these complaints, I will remind existentialists you are indeed existentialists and therefore do not believe in a definable truth. Therefore, I am free to do as I please in your chaotic universe and define your philosophy as I choose. If you want to pretend the universe has no identifiable truth, then this is how you should expect things to work out. Your rules, not mine.

of George Lucas' classic series of films sent me on a lifelong path of film study and storytelling. I would not be the man I am today without Lucas and his original trilogy.

Others have been influenced by films such as *The Green Berets,* which led boys to be soldiers. Oliver Stone's indictment of capitalism, *Wall Street,* ironically consoled the greedy nature of a generation of stock brokers. Mel Gibson's film *The Passion of the Christ* led many to belief in Jesus Christ for salvation while it directed others to confess their sins and crimes. Conversely, a film such as Martin Scorsese's *Taxi Driver* starred a twelve-year-old Jodie Foster as a whore who is saved by a budding presidential assassin and is tied to John Hinckley's decision to attempt the assassination of President Ronald Reagan.[8]

But not all of cinema's influences on our world are that obvious—they are normally far less perceptible but equally impactful. Catch phrases, hair styles, fashion, even social morality are dictated by the flashing light of cinema.

When Steven Spielberg produces a film, he makes detailed decisions regarding what to have on screen, what sounds will accompany the images, and which words his actors will say. He orchestrates grand productions devised to entertain but also to instruct his audience. When

> Those who manipulate a culture's images are the ones who direct its soul.

we watch one of his films, Mr. Spielberg literally plays with our emotions and manipulates our thinking. That is what we pay him to do. We want him to make us laugh and cry. We want to feel anything at all as long as it is not based in reality. We pay him to remove us from our daily lives and place us in an artificial one of his creation.

We can do this to some degree when we pick up a book or watch a play, yet film is somehow different. Film seeps deeper into our core than most books do. Movies' flashing lights precondition our subconscious to receive more shifts in perception than we would experience during a theatrical play. Film's flickering images can hook us faster and for longer periods of time than other modes of communication. Movies affect our minds.

Strong imagery can change how you perceive your world. Once you grasp that fact you will begin to understand that those who manipulate a culture's images are the ones who direct its soul.

How many people still feel exposed in the shower thanks to Hitchcock's *Psycho?* Or realize they are uneasy while swimming because of Spielberg's

---

8. http://www.law.umkc.edu/faculty/projects/ftrials/hinckley/jfostercommun.htm shows the letter written by Hinckley to Foster expressing his plans to assassinate the President. Last accessed April 25, 2010.

Jaws? How do we perceive the way Old West sheriffs did their job? We learned by seeing the *High Noon* standoff. What do we think of when the issues of the McCarthy Era or Hollywood blacklisting are mentioned? Who have become today's bigger bad guys—the Communist infiltrators or the U. S. Government?

Filmmakers want to use the power of film to change the way you think. They love to explain the world to you. Each time you watch a film, you give them that opportunity.

Not all filmmakers are out to do something nefarious; many simply, thoughtlessly attempt to tell a story and make a buck in the process. Of those with something to say, a number do support a basic Judeo-Christian worldview, albeit from a socially liberal viewpoint.

What about those who want to do harm, to dismantle current society and societal norms? To use an audience's vulnerabilities to alter perceptions and behaviors? To mislead for the sake of their agenda? What about those who do wish to influence people toward evil?

In 1934, Adolf Hitler commissioned the film *Triumph des Willens (Triumph of the Will)* from filmmaker Leni Riefenstahl. The film was a masterful work of propaganda which followed the proceedings of the Sixth Nuremberg Party Congress. The piece stands as one of the most haunting films ever created. It expounds the virtues of Aryan power and the righteousness of Adolf Hitler and his Nazi Party. This was not the first film to support the Nazi party line.

Works such as *Es Leuchten die Sterne (The Stars are Shining)* and *Das güldene Bäumchen (The Little Golden Tree)* were screened throughout Germany. These films promoted the image of Jews as thieving, subhuman scum. In *Der Ewige Jude (The Eternal Jew)*, images of Jews were intercut with images of rats—a clear implication to unsuspecting audiences that their Jewish neighbors were vermin.

Though an extreme example, the Nazis used the influence of the cinema to sell the worst of ideas. We do not need to rely on extremes, however, to know that what occurs in the cinema often translates to real life. This does not mean it always crosses over, but what we see definitely has the ability to spill into our reality—and that is when film places our minds in a precarious place.

As with television, film provides both young and old with a lens to view the world. As stated in *Growing Up With Television: The Cultivation Perspective Processes:*

> Those who spend more time 'living' in the world of television are more likely to see the 'real world' in terms of the images, values, portrayals, and ideologies that emerge through the lens of television.[9]

The cinema is a public mirage and many are lured into believing the optical illusion is real. In a media-drenched society we confuse the real with the unreal. When we watch a movie, just as when we watch television, we cast the real world aside for one presented on screen. This is the *escape* aspect of movie-going. But to delve too deeply into these false worlds or rely too heavily on their teachings leads us to internalize what we see.

All this sounds rather grave, so before you throw your DVD player out the window and barricade the cinema doors, allow me to explain. While it may sound like I am warming up to tell everyone to steer clear of the cinema or television, that is not my intention. What I suggest is we must understand the potential dangers of being led down the wrong path. We must tread fully aware of surrounding dangers.

What Gerbner, Gross, Morgan, and Signorelli intended in the quotation above was not to claim there is a confusion of literal worlds. No sane, mature adult believes the galaxy of *Star Wars* exists. Rather, the authors warn of spoiling our perception of *this* world, our world, as it actually is.

We have a God-given tendency to take what we experience in Story and graft it into our personal lives, whether that story was flashed on a wall or printed on a page. When moral issues are played out in that story, whether they occur in Middle America or Middle Earth, we mentally note the consequences of the characters' choices.

When we see Luke Skywalker and friends skip around the universe, we translate that to our lives on earth. When Han Solo is cornered by the bounty hunter in the cantina, we see him in a strange bar in a fictional spaceport, but we also observe someone confront a difficult situation.

This part of the scene is more subconscious in its delivery. Han distracts the bounty hunter until he has a chance to secretly pull out his blaster and shoot the green menace. In our minds we see a semi-heroic figure confirm the moral right of self-preservation. While this lesson does not mean we will all shoot the people who confront us, it does, on a subconscious level, reaffirm acceptance of self-defense with lethal force when necessary. Now apply this concept to all the times you have seen a hero dispatch someone in self-defense. We collect those viewings into one big mental-moral concept that confirms it must always be okay to kill in self-defense.

9. George Gerbner, Larry Gross, Michael Morgan, and Nancy Signorelli. Growing Up with Television: The Cultivation Perspective. In *Media Effects: Advances in Research and Theory.* J. Bryant and Mary Beth Oliver, editors. Routledge. Hillsdale, New Jersey. 2008. 17–41.

Conversely, when we see a constant string of movies and movie scenes which show crime without moral consequence (*Ocean's 11, True Romance, A Fish Called Wanda, Snatch*), we weaken our convictions that theft or other immoral behaviors are wrong.

Our casual relationship with the stories of our day has consequences. As our media has become more violent and cruel, our society has likewise become more violent and cruel.

Watching movies is often a social activity. It is common to watch movies in a theatre or with friends or family. You are not alone when you watch a movie in the theatre, so the social aspects of film-viewing can deepen the effects of cinema on an individual.

If we are in the middle of a crowded theatre when something questionable is presented, we are not in the best circumstance to defend ourselves. The crowd is engaged with whatever is on screen. At that point, we are influenced by crowd dynamics to dispense with our personal inhibitions.

To complain about the content of a film while the credits roll leads to shrugs or scorn from those unwilling to be confronted by such talk. These social constraints placed upon an individual's thought processes teach us to be passive audience members. We turn off our brains and allow a film to sweep us away—and we set ourselves up for a potentially dangerous ride.

A passive mind is a weak mind and is easily led astray. Ponder what is whispered to your soul while you are under the influence of a cinematic trance.

4

Befoul Western Civilization Once, Shame on You—Befoul It Twice, Shame on Me

"But the one thing you should not do is to suppose that
when something is wrong with the arts,
it is wrong with the arts ONLY."[1]

—— Ezra Pound

IN 2006, THE CATHOLIC CHURCH COMPLAINED ABOUT RON HOWARD'S adaptation of Dan Brown's *The Da Vinci Code*. The film claimed Jesus and Mary Magdalene were married and had children and ever since then the Catholic Church has been involved in a murderous plot to conceal it from the public.

In response to complaints, the film's star, Tom Hanks, claimed:

> If you are going to take any sort of movie at face value, particularly a huge-budget motion picture like this, you'd be making a very big mistake.[2]

---

1. Ezra Pound. Zweck or the Aim. In *Guide to Kulchur: Volume 257*. New Directions Publishing Corp. 1970. 60. Emphasis in the original. Used by permission. All rights reserved.
2. Tom Teodorczuk and Mike Goodridge. Hanks Blasts *Da Vinci* Critics. London Evening Standard. November 5, 2006. Available at http://www.thisislondon.co.uk/film/article-22582687-hanks-blasts-da-vinci-critics.do Last accessed October 2009.

If Mr. Hanks believes a "huge-budget motion picture" should not be taken at face value, why did he bother to make message movies and memorial films like *Philadelphia, Saving Private Ryan,* or *Band of Brothers*? And why, in 1994, did Mr. Hanks give the following answer in response to a question about the effect of his Oscar-winning performance as a homosexual attorney suffering from AIDS (*Philadelphia*)? His response:

> Almost everyone I've met has already come to some conclusion about AIDS. They already have in their mind that either dark or light image of what it is. But because I'm the guy that's in the movie, the first thing that comes out of the people who have talked to me about it is their incredible emotional response.[3]

In other words, it was a good thing people were affected by his movie. Apparently some films' messages are more equal than others. Perhaps we should defer to Mr. Hanks to find out which of his productions we need to take seriously and which ones we should dismiss.

Tom Hanks and others within the film industry understand their actions have consequences. They know they have the power to influence the way audience members view a wide array of subjects.

Mr. Hanks had followed the accepted rhetoric of promotional speaking when he addressed only the single production he wished to advance; he, thereby, ignored the collective insulting of Christians by the film industry as a whole.

Even if we ignore *The Da Vinci Code* and its blatant attack on Christ and His followers, we still must contend with a large number of films that portray flagrant anti-Christian storylines. Allow me to name just some of them: *Stigmata, Dogma, The Saint, Priest, Footloose, The Pope Must Die, Carrie, The Godfather III, Kinsey, The Basketball Diaries, The Magdalene Sisters, Primal Fear, The Last Supper, Mission Impossible III, Hannibal, 2012, Contact, Hudson Hawk, Crimes of Passion, The Last Temptation of Christ, Quills, Saved!, The Order, The Seventh Sign, Sleepers, Jeffrey, The Third Miracle, [REC], The Omen 666, Will Penny, Jesus Camp, Mystic River* —I will stop before the printer runs out of ink. The list of films expands greatly if we include productions which promote a morality not overtly contemptuous of Christianity but which still promote anti-Christian doctrines, beliefs, or morality.

Productions created to provoke a response (*Tropic Thunder, The Golden Compass, The Assassination of a President*) often result in the industry's expenditure of almost as much energy to defend their product as they did to produce it. Filmmakers continue to release "socially responsible" films about

---

3. Chewing the Fat About the Green Mile. http://video.barnesandnoble.com/search/Interview. asp?CTR=132138. Last accessed August 2009.

global warming, McCarthyism, and frustrated homosexual sheepherders[4] while—when their audiences balk—they maintain that films are without consequence.

Film leads unsuspecting audiences to take the world of fantasy and translate it to redefine reality. Filmmakers such as Quentin Tarantino, Takashi Miike, Paul Verhoeven, and David Lynch have built careers by pushing us to question our morals and by shocking our senses to get our attention. When directors or actors push too far, they often defend themselves by dismissing the charges. An embattled actor or filmmaker claims the insult was unintended or unwarranted, as reflected in these statements from Verhoeven and Lynch:

> People seem to have this strange idea that films can influence people to be violent, but in my sincere opinion film only reflects the violence of society.[5]   and   There is a fear about sex in motion pictures, as if sex would undermine morality.[6] — Paul Verhoeven, director of *RoboCop, Total Recall, Basic Instinct, Showgirls, Starship Troopers, Hollow Man,* as well as a new movie, *Jesus of Nazareth,* currently in pre-production at the time of this writing

> I'm not sure what these people are saying. Is it that if you depicted no graphic violence, the world would calm down and there would be less violence? Or is it that if you sense certain things about violence and then portray those things in a film, does that make the violence go to another level? Or is the violence in films a way to experience something without having to do it in real life?[7] — David Lynch, director of *Mulholland Drive*, producer of *Eraserhead, Twin Peaks, Hugh Hefner: Once Upon a Time, Darkened Room*

Why do filmmakers constantly argue that their actions have no impact? Because if they continue to get their audiences to deny the industry's influences on everyday life, then filmmakers can remain detached from responsibility for the movies they release. Their argument is no different than that of a cigarette executive who claims no one has definitive proof smoking causes lung cancer. After all, non-smokers get lung cancer, too.

"Sure, a number of teens have committed murder while wearing a mask from the *Scream* films. Big deal. They were probably going to stab those

---

4. This refers to *Brokeback Mountain,* an award-winning film about two sheepherders who "fall in love" while tending their flocks. If you had to read this to know what I was referring to, you should be proud.

5. Home page of http://www.paulverhoeven.net. Last accessed March 2010.

6. The Paul Verhoeven Fan Page. http://ghosts.org/verhoeven/quotes.html. Last accessed March 2010. Also available at http://www.imdb.com/name/nm0000682/bio.

7. Mikal Gilmore. Trent Reznor Takes David Lynch's 'Lost Highway.' In *Rolling Stone* Magazine. Issue 755. March 6, 1997.

people anyway." Do not believe that hype. While filmmakers cannot control reactions to their work, they do understand that their actions leave a wake.

Movies Are Intentional

Part of the beauty of film is that everything appears spontaneous. When film is done correctly, we lose all sense of the presentation. We forget that the on-screen car chases, sex scenes, and humorous quips are components of an organized, scripted production created to deliver a message.

When we see two stunningly attractive stars passionately kissing, we think they are truly in the moment, ardently focused only on each other. Surely the couple is deeply in love or, as is more commonly shown, in lust. Their well-lit moment of carnality must be the result of two young lovers meeting in the night. We never see that three feet away from the those two beautiful actors, just outside the view of the lens, slumps a disinterested crewmember sipping stale coffee from a Styrofoam cup as he waits for the shot to be done so he can take down the lighting rigs.

The illusion of spontaneity is just that, an illusion. The illusion of spontaneity offers cover for both artist and audience. The artist can shield himself from any criticism by the dismissal of his work as nothing more than a movie. The audience, when presented with indecent material, can likewise claim it is just a movie and, thereby, give themselves permission to ignore their own consciences. For the sake of the entertainment, both sides agree to ignore the 500-pound worldview gorilla in the room.

When you watch a film, you must understand that everything from what shirt an actor wears, to what hangs on the wall behind him, to what words come out of his mouth are all precisely planned—and planned for effect. Obviously, in historical pieces (*Shakespeare in Love, Tombstone, Troy*) the sets and costumes must match the story's time period. It would break the suspension of disbelief if Achilles charged the beaches of Troy wearing running shorts and a fanny pack. But even in contemporary pieces, what is chosen to go on screen is intended to give the illusion that we see real people perform real actions in a real environment. That illusion enables us to believe the story we are told.

Once we grasp the reality that movies are well-organized events, we begin to more clearly comprehend the decisions made by filmmakers. The multitude of choices made for even small movies completely removes the filmmaker's defense that 'It's just a movie.' Consider the intensity of Tarantino toward his movie projects:

> Movies are my religion and God is my patron. I'm lucky enough
> to be in the position where I don't make movies to pay for my
> pool. When I make a movie, I want it to be everything to me;
> like I would die for it.[8]

When a filmmaker creates something foul and then attempts to deny culpability, it should strike us just as ludicrous as an artist who points to his latest portrait and exclaims, "I've no idea how that person got in my painting!"

Intentionality proves that movies are more than just random events. The filmmaker's choices make a statement, whether unconsciously or by design. Every detail of a film is the result of a decision. It falls to us to see not only the end result but to see the motivations behind the filmmaker's choices.

Product Placement

In *Mission Impossible III*, Tom Cruise's character, Ethan Hunt, must break into the Vatican. What does he use as cover? Cruise dresses up as a DHL delivery man complete with official company van. The bright yellow van with its big red logo is prominently displayed in a prolonged scene leading to Hunt's successful infiltration of Catholic headquarters. What does the presence of this DHL truck have to do with anything in the plot? It served no actual purpose within the storyline.[9]

DHL and Paramount struck a deal which led to Tom Cruise appearing on screen with a DHL truck. When marketing for the film hit the airwaves, DHL's company tag line changed to "Accepting Impossible Missions Daily."

And DHL's involvement was hardly unique. In *Mission Impossible III* you can also find product placements for 7-Eleven, Acura, Baby Ruth, Belstaff, BMW, Budweiser, Casio, Chips Ahoy, Chris Craft, Cisco Systems, Coca-Cola, Dell, Ford, Heckler & Koch, Heinz, Kodak, Lamborghini, Land Rover, Lay's, Lincoln Navigator, L'Oreal, Mazda, Mercedes, Miller, Motorola, Nokia, Oreo, Oxford University, PayDay, Philips, Prada, Ritz, Sama, Sharpie, Snapple, Sprite, Star Magazine, Triumph, Volkswagen Beetle, and Volvo. All share the stage with the diminutive international superstar.

Film producers understand their ability to alter the minds of their viewers —a fact supported by these actions. Studios and producers work hard to secure

---

8. Empire Magazine. *The Directors Of Our Lifetime: In Their Own Words, #5 Quentin Tarantino.* Unknown Author/Editor. http://www.empireonline.com/magazine/250/directors-of-our-lifetime/5.asp. Last accessed March 2010.
9. One might argue that he dressed up like a DHL delivery man so he could blend into the environment. On its face this may appear reasonable, but would it not have made more sense to don the garb of a local Italian business?
   The use of products in films often appears to have a logical function, but it still remains that any product, including fake ones, would usually work just as well. The choice to use an identifiable brand almost always results from a product placement agreement.

deals for advertisements in their films. Product placement, also known as "product integration," is a serious part of today's filmmaking business.

Product placement is exactly what it sounds like: The willful placement of a particular product in a film for advertising purposes. A company pays for that screen time either by traditional methods or by trading services.

Why do this? Why do we see strange relationships such as the one between The National Frozen and Refrigerated Foods Association (NFRA) and Fox Filmed Entertainment, makers of the children's film *Ice Age: The Meltdown*?[10] The reasons are simple: fistfuls of money and a nation's attention. In fact, an entirely new industry was created to concentrate on the coordination of placements of client products within feature films and television shows: The Entertainment Resources and Marketing Association (ERMA).

Product placements within film are scarcely-concealed commercials meant to influence our buying habits no differently than the ads played during the Super Bowl. Most of us are skeptical about the claims made in commercials. We know we are being marketed to and the people on screen have an agenda —yet, commercials work. It is not the single exposure that influences you to buy that car, it is the cumulative effect that alters your behavior. Films are no different, so be on your guard when you watch movies. Not only do filmmakers slip commercials into their productions, they often slip in political messages and other manipulative elements, as well, as James Cameron explains:

> Our culture evolves through all of its various influences, and major films, major TV shows, celebrities, whatever. If you hear it enough times, it does start to generate an interest."[11]

What do his words say about the rest of the content available at the multiplex?

The industry concedes that when an audience sees Jennifer Aniston hold a bottle of apple juice, people are influenced to buy that product. What would happen to the sales of a brand of apple juice if audiences saw Jennifer Aniston, Sarah Jessica Parker, and Anne Hathaway each hold and drink the beverage in a string of films viewed within the short span of a few months?

---

10. The National Frozen and Refrigerated Foods Association (NFRA) cross-marketed with the release of the film *Ice Age: The Meltdown* to promote their "Warm up to frozen food" campaign. The campaign's purpose was to simply promote frozen foods to consumers on behalf of such brands as Dole, Healthy Choice, Welch's, and Sara Lee. The campaign used images from the film in their promotional materials. From the documentation for the campaign, I was not able to find anything that would support the idea that viewing an animated woolly mammoth on the verge of extinction would prompt me to want to eat a Hot Pocket.

11. David Chen. *The Filmcast Interview: James Cameron, Director of* Avatar. December 18, 2009. http://www.slashfilm.com/2009/12/18/the-filmcast-interview-james-cameron-director-of-avatar. Last accessed December 2009.

The obvious answer is that sales would soar. The apple juice would have the endorsement of each of these leading ladies and be presented in the fun, lighthearted atmospheres of their films.

Now replace the apple juice with a behavior such as pre-marital sex. Would witnessing scenes of these attractive starlets involved in casual sexual behavior also have an effect on audience members? Each of these women did endorse premarital sex via its casual display in their films— *The Break-Up* (Aniston), *Failuwre to Launch* (Parker), and *The Devil Wears Prada* (Hathaway). All three films were released either in theatres or on DVD in June of 2006. Witness the loose sexual behavior of these women in film, then turn to Aniston and Parker's television series, *Friends* or *Sex in the City,* respectively (not respectfully), and get more of the same. The effect of this collection of images on the thinking of a populace is a pervasive, erosive drumbeat that promotes frivolous sexual immorality.

But the value of advertising reaches deeper than the moral issues of sex and violence. The promotion of worldview must concern us because the promotion of non-Christian worldviews is harder to identify. Even films that appear to have Christian underpinnings can ultimately deliver New Age or other non-Biblical messages (*What Dreams May Come, Bedazzled, Knowing*).

A film that includes content which at first appears Biblical does not mean it is promoting the truth of Scripture. In fact, it is these are the films of which we must be most wary since they attempt to use the impact of Scripture to their own ends and can more easily lead audiences away from the truth of Christ Jesus (*Book of Eli* [12]). In this respect, I would much rather watch a film that is agnostic in regard to the Almighty. The absence of the Lord in Art, I believe, is preferable to the attempts to pervert Him so that He matches our delusions and falsehoods.

We must apply critical evaluation to any film we choose to see. I will not urge you to over-analyze every DVD that enters your home, but it is wise to remember that more is going on in many productions than simple entertainment, particularly when the subject matter is controversial or inclined to advocate a specific message (*Dead Man Walking, Nixon, To End All Wars*).

It is also advisable, when someone from the entertainment industry denies the impact of their product, to remember a quote from the character Verbal Kint in the film *The Usual Suspects*: "The greatest trick the devil ever pulled was convincing the world he did not exist."[13]

---

12. *The Book of Eli* takes place in a post-apocalyptic America where a man, Eli, carries the last existing Bible in the world. Although the film retains a sense that Eli is being directed by God, the overall message equates the Bible with all other religious texts and avoids direct reference to God, Himself. All of this while Eli, who is versed in Scripture, shoots, cuts and bludgeons his foes—you know, just like Jesus did.

13. Christopher McQuarrie. *The Usual Suspects*. Polygram Filmed Entertainment. 1995.

LEARNING BY ROTE

To learn by rote is an educational method whereby a student repeats facts or data until the information becomes intuitive, second nature. Rote learning is quite useful when dealing with cold facts like mathematical formulas or historically important dates. It removes the cognitive elements and inserts the information into a more reflexive mode for the student. They know when to say "The Pilgrims landed in 1620" (well, students knew such facts until history class became merely 'social studies'), but when pressed, can rarely explain with much intelligence the importance of that event. This can also be known as cramming.

While cramming has negative connotations and can be considered a poor method of education, it does work—my high grades in Art History prove this. Cramming is useful for temporary situations.

But what happens when the cramming, the rote learning, does not stop? What consequences are faced when it continues for years? When it continues without our awareness that we are even being taught?

For most of American cinema history, movies were transitory events with short shelf lives. A movie would be in the theatre for a week, maybe two, then was gone—with never a VCR or cable channel to re-air it. Now, even the lousiest movies have not only long shelf-lives, they can practically be considered to have a half-life.

When a film is released into the cultural mainstream it is no solitary event. Before a film hits theatres a marketing campaign is released. Images, movie trailers, and celebrity interviews bombard the internet, television, and print media. Trailers, in particular, are played multiple times—some viewers may see the same trailer dozens of times. Often these trailers focus in the simplest terms possible on the central conflict of the story and are loaded with catch phrases and cheap jokes.

The film then arrives, generally to play for several weeks and quietly disappear only to reemerge months later on DVD. A lesser version of the original marketing campaign reappears to promote the DVD. Then comes distribution via cable television, on-demand services, Netflix, and, if its rating is low enough, it can be seen on the wall of televisions at WalMart or playing on screens at the checkout counter of your grocery store.

Combine the months-long presence of the average movie with its ability to sway our thinking and it is easy to see how even the most frivolous actions and ideas can have great influence. When we examine the full array of movies that bombard our daily lives and consider the messages delivered in their seemingly never-ending rotation, the power of the entertainment industry over our thoughts and perceptions cannot be denied.

5

Agenda, Inc.

"To mix culture with personal charm or advertisement
is to prostitute culture."
—Virginia Woolf[1]

IT IS PART OF OUR HUMAN NATURE TO MIMIC WHAT WE SEE. WE WITNESS amazing characters in fantastic adventures who live wonderful lives—of course we want to imitate these grand heroes. We want to be as tough as Indiana Jones, suave as James Bond, or mischievous as Jack Sparrow. Our heroes are great, and unconsciously we want to partake in their greatness.

Rooted in our need for acceptance is a natural desire to follow, seen in the son who parrots his father or in how his mother follows the latest trends. Even rebels usually rebel in prescribed and predictable ways. Travel to your local mall food court and see if all the disenfranchised youth are not dressed like Dracula's roadies.

The imitation of those we respect and idolize extends to our heroes on screen, so those who would hope to push social change look to on-screen, larger-than-life figures to promote their philosophies. Activists of any stripe can advance all manner of political, social, and even theological agendas. Many of these should make us choke, but since they are sweetened by delivery via Leonardo DiCaprio or Zoe Saldana, we smile and ask for more.

---

1. Virginia Woolf. *Three Guineas*. Harcourt, Brace, and Co. 1938. 150.

The idea is simple and nearly as old as film itself. Commercials plant a seed in your mind to encourage your purchase of that special brand of potato chips or car wax.[2] The same methods are used in film to encourage individual responses and stimulate emotional activity; that is, they implant thoughts within your mind which make you sympathetic to their messages, including controversial subjects.

It is not accidental that when a social movement gathers steam—be it homosexual rights, immigration, or global warming—we see a bevy of films in the multiplexes which promote the arguments of the movement *du jour*. This technique is known as social marketing, and film is an important part of their campaigns.

Social marketing is a tool used to alter your perception of reality and truth. This tool can be used for commercial purposes or for political ones. From run-of-the-mill secular humanists to cult leaders, many people use film to promote their social and theological agendas. Examine issues such as homosexuality (*Saved!, I Love You Phillip Morris, Infamous*), drug use (*The Wackness, Pulp Fiction, The Breakfast Club*), divorce (*Mrs. Doubtfire, Kindergarten Cop, Walk the Line*), and pre-marital sex (*Sideways, Wedding Crashers, Iron Man*). It takes little effort to find rivers of social marketing flowing through the film industry. Productions have points of view and, when melded with activists looking to shill agendas, the results can be devastating for an unaware public.

Most people have bought into concepts without ever realizing they have been sold something. They are oblivious to the fact that their minds have been changed for them.

Case Study No. 1: *After the Ball*

According to the list of the top 200 gay and lesbian films listed on boxofficemojo.com, an online box-office reporting service, only fourteen

2. Jon A. Krosnick, Andrew L. Betz, Lee J. Jussim, and Ann R. Lynn. Subliminal Conditioning of Attitudes in *Personality and Social Psychology Bulletin*. Vol. 18. No. 2. 152. doi:10.1177/0146167292182006. Their conclusion: "Most of the literature on attitude formation assumes that attitudes are the products of deductive integration of an individual's beliefs about an object's attributes. Two studies demonstrate that attitudes can develop without deduction from such beliefs and, indeed, without individuals' being aware of the antecedents of those attitudes. ... These findings demonstrate conditioning of attitudes without awareness of their antecedents." also Jim Brackin. Hypnosis and Subliminal Techniques are Commonplace in Advertising, But Do They Work? in *Hypnosis in Advertising*. February 7, 2008. http://bizcovering.com/marketing-and-advertising/hypnosis-in-advertising/. His study concludes: "Both ads use a number of well known and legal hypnotic and subliminal techniques to promote their products. This is by no means unusual. An analysis of the twenty most popular ads ever reveals that all of them use some form of hypnosis or subliminal techniques to sell their message. It seems that despite early attempts to ban it, the use of hypnosis and subliminals to increase market share are widespread in advertising."

notable gay or lesbian films were made prior to 1990.[3] Of those fourteen films, most portrayed homosexuals in a negative and violent light. It is safe to assert that negative portrayals of homosexuals are no longer shown. In fact, it is rare to find a homosexual character, let alone storyline, presented in anything but a glowing, positive manner. This is not because all homosexuals are peppy, helpful people. Perceptions were altered because the individuals driving the agenda want us to see homosexuals in that light.

Prior to the early 1980s, homosexual behavior was effectively a taboo topic in film. When it did appear, it was done in allusion.

In *Lawrence of Arabia* (1962), the military hero, Lawrence, keeps company with two bright-eyed boys as he travels the desert. Director David Lean provided sufficient inferences to make the point that Lawrence may have specific and intimate reasons for their company. It was also implied that another man brutally, sexually assaulted Lawrence during a torture sequence. These issues were handled with respect. Similarly, the film adaptations of *These Three* (1936) and *Suddenly, Last Summer* (1959) avoided the overt homosexual content found in the original stories. It is not a stretch to wonder how Lawrence would be handled by today's standards. Tact is not the first word to leap to mind.

What has changed? The audience's expectations, tolerances, and beliefs have been modified over the past few decades. Homosexuality is now considered acceptable by the majority in our society—or they no longer have any basis to think it unacceptable. Radical change did not occur because people decided one day it was okay for two men to shop for his and his bath towels. Agendas were unfurled and carefully applied to bring about this shift in social norms.

During a 1988 conference of homosexual activists, a series of purposeful actions were undertaken to normalize homosexual behavior and condemn anti-homosexual opinion. These items were laid out in a manifesto entitled *After the Ball: How America Will Conquer Its Fear & Hatred of Gays in the 90's*.[4] In their book, Marshall Kirk and Hunter Madsen demanded a continuous stream of homosexual discussion to flood the media markets. The idea was (and still is) that once the media was clogged with homosexual issues, the population would grow weary of being incensed by the subject. As they explain in the book, "If straights can't shut off the shower, they may at least eventually get used to being wet."[5] Furthermore the couple lays out examples of how to discredit "homohaters": "The best way to make homohatred look bad is to vilify those who victimize gays." And "The

---

3. http://boxofficemojo.com/genres/chart/?id=gay.htm. Last accessed August 2009.
4. Marshall Kirk and Hunter Madsen. *After the Ball: How America Will Conquer Its Fear & Hatred of Gays in the 90's*. Penguin Group. NY. 1989.
5. Ibid. Part I: Problems: The Straight and Narrow, Chapter 2: The Roots of Homophobia and Homohatred, Pushing the Right Buttons: Halting, Derailing, or Reversing the 'Engine of Prejudice,' 1. Desensitization. 149.

objective is to make homohating beliefs and actions look so nasty that *average Americans* are not 'homohaters.'[6] This was to be done by showing that those who believe Heather should not have two mommies are impulsive villains, such as:

> » Klansmen who demand that gays be slaughtered or castrated;

> » Hysterical backwoods preachers who drool with hate to such a degree they look both comical and deranged; and

> » Menacing punks, thugs, and convicts who speak coolly about the "fags" they have bashed or would like to bash.[7]

Through the continual use of social marketing, the homosexual agenda became normalized to the extent that some politically correct folks will be offended I dared to use it as an example in this book. Where homosexual activity was once considered something to be handled with discretion (as were all topics pertaining to sexuality), we now have its promotion at every level of society. Today, film is a primary standard-carrier of the rainbow banner. The influence of the homosexual agenda is one of the main reasons one of the biggest films involving cowboys in the 2000s is *Brokeback Mountain*.[8]

While it is not accurate to point to *After the Ball* as the sole voice at work to change society's views towards homosexuality, it was a touchstone for the movement at the time. Since the 1980s, the homosexual subculture has become accepted homosexual culture and a powerful force in the American social landscape. The power of film was leveraged to make this change occur.

Case Study No. 2: *Happy Feet*

Alan Horn, President and Chief Operating Officer of Warner Brothers, and his wife, Cindy, along with Lyn and Norman Lear, co-founded The Environmental Media Association (EMA). Their group's sole purpose is consultation with entertainment companies on how to insert environmental messages into their products.

---

6. Ibid. Part II: Driving the Wedge, Chapter 3: Strategy–Persuasion not Invasion, The Strategy of "Waging Peace": Eight Practical Principles for the Persuasion of Straights, Principle 8: Make Victimizer Look Bad. 189. Emphasis added. In other words, they acknowledge that ordinary Americans are not homohaters.

7. Ibid.

8. *3:10 to Yuma*, the only notable Western of the 2000s, has a worldwide gross of $70,016,220 (http://www.boxofficemojo.com/movies/?id=310toyuma.htm). *Brokeback Mountain* has a worldwide gross of $178,062,759 (http://www.boxofficemojo.com/movies/?id=brokebackmountain.htm). The comparison between the movies is not necessarily fair since *Brokeback Mountain* is not a Western but rather a homosexual love story set in the early 1960s. Where homosexuality was once considered to be taboo, it has been mainstreamed since the late 1980s to the extent that a film about two homosexual sheepherders was the 22nd highest grossing film of 2005. (http://www.boxofficemojo.com/yearly/chart/?yr=2005&p=.htm)

Here is an excerpt from their own description of their organization's actions:

> We regularly network with writers, directors and producers, helping shape plotlines that seamlessly incorporate environmental messages. The work that we have done for almost 20 years has helped inspire millions of people to reduce air pollution, ensure clean water for drinking and recreation, protect endangered species, preserve open spaces, minimize waste, promote a safe food supply (go organic!) and live more environmentally sustainable lives.[9]

Sounds innocuous. They only want to help entertainers get out messages about recycling. But I believe we should look at this a different way.

EMA and other organizations like it are not simply offering advertising campaigns to promote ideas. They are "weaving environmental messages within entertainment programming" and "helping shape plotlines." When we translate this, we discover the group is involved in social marketing.

Social agendas slip into films like Pepsi cans into movie stars' hands.

Happy Feet is a children's movie about a little penguin named Mumble who would rather tap dance than sing like the rest of the penguins. This seems like a charming story about self-acceptance. But is something else going on in the storyline besides a cute penguin who dances? Commercial fishermen cruelly robbed Mumble and his friends of their food. Mumble's friend, Lovelace, had his neck stuck in a plastic, six-pack can holder that strangled the poor guy like a noose. The penguins languished in a zoo where they almost lost hope. Bleak stuff for a children's movie.

The film's director, George Miller (*Mad Max, The Witches of Eastwick, Babe: Pig in the City*), intentionally inserted the global warming message into his film. He explained to *The Wall Street Journal*, "You can't tell a story about Antarctica and the penguins without giving that dimension."[10] I am sure it was just a coincidence, but *Happy Feet* was created in part through the auspices of Warner Brothers, again, whose COO is, you guessed it—Alan Horn, co-founder of EMA.

Christians appreciate the ozone as much as everyone else—or they should. We certainly do not argue against caring for our environment, quite the opposite. Inherent within our faith is the mandate to be conservationists, good stewards of God's creation. If the founders of EMA and their cohorts have their views projected onto the screen, who are we to argue?

---

9. *About EMA*. http://www.ema-online.org/about_us.php. Last accessed October 2009.
10. Kate Kelly. The New Animated Film 'Happy Feet' Doesn't Dance Around Serious Issues. *The Wall Street Journal Online*. November 17, 2006. Last accessed August 2009.

This is not a book on politics and certainly not one on environmental issues. I do not condemn EMA or any other similar group for their actions. EMA may be a wonderful organization with noble goals, but you must be aware that EMA and groups like it exist to promote use of film as a means of widespread behavior modification. On its site, the group proposes the use of social marketing techniques:

> As [could be] seen on TV … a family elects to adopt rather than have another child; a poster for "Zero Population Growth" appears in a teenager's bedroom; a couple decides to stop after having two children and debate[s] vasectomy vs. tubal ligation.[11]

Case Study No. 3: *What The #$*! Do We Know?*

What The #$! Do We Know?* is an entertaining pseudo-documentary about quantum physics and the role of humanity in the universe. Buttressed by interviews with scientists, spiritual leaders, and others, the movie reveals incredible secrets of existence. The production did rather well for a small budget, independent film and grossed over fifteen million dollars in worldwide distribution.[12] Add to that the DVD and auxiliary merchandise sales and the profits for this production were even higher. Viewers who were intrigued by the ideas forwarded by the "documentary" could visit a website[13] dedicated to education on quantum physics and self-improvement. The site, in turn, connected readers to other sites which offered additional products plus the philosophy of the filmmakers.

What does this have to do with anything? *What the #$*! Do We Know?* is connected with The Ramtha School of Enlightenment and professes the teachings of that organization. The Ramtha School of Enlightenment is a tightly knit group of folks who follow a philosophy of self-awareness formed by a woman called J. Z. Knight who claims to channel Ramtha, a 35,000-year-old spirit-warrior.[14] The two apparently met in Knight's kitchen in Tacoma one day and have been together ever since. No, I am not joking. Knight and her followers claim that we are all gods and have the ability to change the universe, down to the molecular level, with our thoughts. Let me know if this starts to get strange. *What the #$*! Do We Know?* is a starter kit promoting involvement in the group's belief system.

---

11. http://www.ema-online.org/about_us.php. Last accessed October 2009.
12. http://boxofficemojo.com/movies/?id=whatthe.htm. Last accessed, December 2009
13. http://www.whatthebleep.com. Last accessed August 2009.
14. http://www.ramtha.com/html/media/press-rels/97.stm. Last accessed August 2009.

According to boxofficemojo.com,[15] *What the #$*! Do We Know?*, with its nearly sixteen-million-dollar box office take and subsequent DVD sales, is more profitable than all but six Christian films: *The Passion of the Christ*, the two Narnia films, *Fireproof, The Nativity Story,* and *Jonah: A Veggie Tales Movie.*[16] Only these six films fared better than the small-budget movie that advocates the beliefs of a loon from the West Coast who channels a prehistoric brute she met next to her dishwasher. In fact, in most cases, you can take two of your favorite Christian films, add their profits together, and they still will not perform better than J. Z. Knight's ode to the power of happy thoughts over water molecules.

This does not mean that J. Z. Knight and company have the cultural power to threaten all of Christendom. It does illustrate the type of individuals who see the power of film and use it to their advantage.

Case Study No. 4: "You are the thought leaders"

On August 10, 2009, a conference call for artists was conducted by the White House Office of Public Engagement, representatives of the National Endowment for the Arts (NEA), and United We Serve. The event focused on how the Arts could assist in promoting the current administration's policy goals or, to put things more crudely, how the Arts could act as a propaganda arm for a political movement.[17]

Russell Simmons, co-founder of Def Jam Recordings, CEO of Rush Communications, and founder of Phat Farm, a national urban-focused line of upscale fashions and accessories, has deep influence on American culture, especially during the closing decades of the 20th Century. Michael Skolnik is political director for Russell Simmons. Mr. Skolnik was invited by the White House and the NEA to speak to the artists assembled on that August 10, 2009, conference call. Mr. Skolnik stated:

> You are the thought leaders. You are the ones that, if you create a piece of art or promote a piece of art or create a campaign for a company, and tell our country and our young people sort of what to do and what to be into; and what's cool and what's not cool. And so I'm hoping that through this group—and the goal of all this and the goal of this phone call—is through this group that we can create a stronger community amongst ourselves to get involved in things that we're passionate about as we did

---

15. http://boxofficemojo.com/movies/?id=whatthe.htm. Last accessed August 2009.
16. http://boxofficemojo.com/genres/chart/?id=christian.htm. Last accessed August 2009.
17. It should be noted that political movements throughout history have used artists to promote worldviews. This example is used because it is recent and relevant.

during the [Obama presidential] campaign, but continue to get involved in those things, to support some of the president's initiatives, but also to do things that we are passionate about and to push the president and push his administration.[18]

Mr. Skolnik sees everyone on that conference call as having the ability to mold public opinion through the use of Art as propaganda.

That the Arts can and should be utilized by artists to shape the public's view of the world is not unique to Mr. Skolnik, just as the confluence of artists and power-brokers is not unique to the NEA's conference call.

Agenda and the Church

Christians, likewise, use film to promote their views and objectives. We have our own genre dedicated to presentation of Christian ideals. This genre tends to keep to itself and does a poor job of reaching out to non-believers — partially due to the skepticism of most Americans, including American Christians, toward overt displays of Christian faith. Promotion of faith, though, is the central force behind the Christian film movement. Granted, Christian filmmakers seem to not be as skillful as other agenda-driven groups—and they usually come right out and tell you their agenda—but they are involved in social marketing just the same.

The growing chasm between Christian film and today's increasingly secularized audiences only permits wolves to flourish unhindered by any opposition which wields truth. The correct response to film's impact is not to bring movie watching to a screeching halt. No one stops crossing a street because they may get hit by a car. Instead, learn to look both ways before you step into traffic.

The proper response to film-driven social marketing is to learn to perceive the agendas and to protect yourself and your family from potential influences —from the "prostitution of culture," as Virginia Woolf called it. You have already made a huge step toward freeing yourself from movies' effects when you understand that messages are delivered to your subconscious mind. That simple awareness can prevent some of those messages from getting through unnoticed.

Never forget that when you watch a movie
you allow someone else
to explain your world to you.

18. Transcript of conference call. National Endowment for the Arts. August 10, 2009. 8.

ATTACKS ON CATHOLICS—
Just Because I Don't Follow You Doesn't Mean I Won't Back You Up

A cursory glance at film attacks on Christianity show a vast majority of the barbs are thrown at the Roman Catholic Church. I contend that even if you are not a Catholic it is vital that dogmatic disagreements be put aside and close observation made as to why Catholics are almost always the ones who get publically pummeled.

I can identify two main reasons for the negative attention. First, the Catholic Church has an international reach and deep influence on nearly every culture it touches. Catholicism's worldwide impact is undeniable and did not happen overnight but dates back to Biblical times. You cannot tell the story of mankind without talking a great deal about the workings of the Roman Church.

A second reason is because Catholics are so dang easy to spot. Priests, nuns, cardinals, and popes all wear easily identifiable uniforms. No one ever said, "Hey, I was down at Chuck E. Cheese and thought I saw the pope. Turned out it was Jerry." Even if Jerry likes to wear a large, bejeweled hat, the pope is still the pope.

So, if you are a filmmaker and want to make a point about Christianity, what do you do? How do you easily show a Baptist preacher? A guy with big hair and a bad sweater? Even then you must point out he is a Christian and not just a poorly dressed guy with a lot of opinions. For the sake of economy, it is far easier to slap a collar on the guy and give him an Irish last name.

When filmmakers take shots at Christians in general it causes an uproar. When the target of the insult is Catholic, the cries of foul are often much quieter, though with groups like The Catholic League (no, they're not a softball team) and well organized bloggers, few insults go unanswered.

For non-Catholics the attacks are usually treated as someone else's problem. If a Christian sees a cheap shot at a priest or views a story centered on the Roman church's misdeeds, whether real or imagined, and that Christian is not troubled, I believe there is a problem.

All Christians should react strongly when any of our brothers and sisters—even those we disagree with—are maligned. When filmmakers attack Catholics, more times than not their real intent is to attack ALL Christians: Catholic, Lutheran, Baptist, or anyone in between. The Christian faith is the target, not just one segment.

Films that specifically focus on Catholicism (*Elizabeth: The Golden Age* or *The Golden Compass*) should be studied for what they say. They usually do not attack just Roman Catholics but all of Christendom. Following Jesus Christ is the issue. If one can injure Christians and dismantle Scriptural faith, the vacuum created can then be filled with another belief system.

During an interview on The Today Show, actor Ian McKellen stated "I've often thought the Bible should have a disclaimer in the front saying this is fiction."[19] It should come as no surprise that McKellen, a proud hater of the Christian faith, has had ample opportunity to star in a number of films that are openly hostile to God (*The Da Vinci Code, The Golden Compass, For the Love of God*).

Those who loathe Jesus Christ and His teachings have a voice. They use it freely with full support of their industry. Do not fool yourself—those willing to tear down the Roman Catholic Church do not trouble themselves with distinctions between the pope and Billy Graham. When filmmakers throw cinematic eggs at the Vatican, they are intended to splatter on us all.

---

19. *Da Vinci Code* Actor: Bible Should Have "Fiction" Disclaimer. http://newsbusters.org/tnode/5402. Last accessed February 2010. For a clip of the interview please visit: http://newsbusters.org/media/20050-05-17-NBCToday.wmv (Windows Media Player Format) NBC Today Show broadcast date: May 17, 2006.

6

Hollywood's Lowercase God

"The first effect of not believing in God is to believe in anything."[1]
— G. K. Chesterton

IN DECADES LONG GONE IT WAS COMMON TO HAVE FILMS FRONTED BY strong, confident, admirable heroes such as Sidney Poitier's Virgil Tibbs (*In the Heat of the Night*, 1967) or Alan Ladd's Shane (*Shane*, 1953). Today, we can find those cinematic heroes, but they come few and far between.

The truly heroic hero has been overshadowed by today's shiftless slacker (*The Big Lebowski*). This new "hero" is sarcastic, emotionally stunted, and could not find a moral code if it were tattooed on the inside of his eyelids (Ben Stone in *Knocked Up*, Jackson Curtis in *2012*, or Sing in *Kung-Fu Hustle*).

The Golden Age of Hollywood supported moral behavior, embraced life, and encouraged happiness, but the film industry has spiraled downward to become a business intent on production of corrupting works which actively destabilize society. A review of release schedules for the past decades seems to verify that the days of thoughtful, uplifting productions are vestiges of the distant past. Major studios have become an aggressive carnival barker standing outside a Porta-Potty and loudly demanding we step right up to enjoy their latest cinematic deposit.

The film industry pushes their products into our lives through intrusive marketing campaigns that entice us to watch films which do little to improve our lives. They provide pornography on demand, advertise graphic violence to children, and reject traditional morality as antiquated. When the producers

---

1. Emile Cammaerts. *The Laughing Prophet* (a study of G. K. Chesterton). 1937. http://chesterton.org/qmeister2/any-everything.htm. Accessed May 2010.

and celebrities have peddled their inane wares, they hand out awards to each other and ask us to applaud.

During her acceptance speech for the 2007 Primetime Emmy Award for Outstanding Reality Program for her show *Kathy Griffin: My Life on the D-List*, Ms Griffin (*Shrek Forever After*) revealed the state of her soul:

> "A lot of people come up here and they thank Jesus for this award. I want you to know that no one had less to do with this award than Jesus. He didn't help me a bit. If it had been up to Him, Cesar Millan would be up here with that d*** dog. So, all I can say is 'Suck it, Jesus! This award is my god now!'"[2]

Our cinema, our culture, is disconnected from reality and is not serving us well. We are the most medically-advanced civilization known to mankind, but our culture has become putrid and is making us a sick society. In a time when we should be thrilled to be alive, anti-depressant industries thrive. We, theoretically, have one of the most educated populations in human history, but our generation feeds on a constant flow of cartoons and self-help books. We have the history of music, painting, and literature at our fingertips, yet the Arts have become backdrops for stuffy elites while the masses are taught to value pornography over Picasso. As a civilization, we should be awe-inspiring; as a people, we often seem to be a pathetic mess.

What caused our advanced society to collapse into this morass? What caused Western culture to slide into the sewer of our selfish desires? I believe it is the result of our attempt to remove God from the proceedings.

The trajectory of movies produced over the course of film history reveals a gradual separation from God as He has revealed Himself in Scripture.

This is not to say God is not shown in movies. From Morgan Freeman's bemused therapist version of God in *Bruce Almighty* and *Evan Almighty* to the cranky Heavenly Father who scolds King Arthur in *Monty Python and the Holy Grail*, God continues to make on-screen appearances. The problem is that the God presented by Hollywood is not the God revealed in Scripture. They say "God" when what they mean is "god."

---

2   http://www.youtube.com/watch?v=re-8MeEBUJ8. Last accessed May 2010.

Horror Films
and The Death of God Image

Rebellion against God is why a denial of God or of the church appears in many films. This is particularly true of horror movies. When the villain arrives, he (or it) kills a priest, destroys a church, or defiles another religious symbol.

What is the first thing blown up in Steven Spielberg's *War of the Worlds*? A church. Where does Jim, in *28 Days Later*, discover the zombies? In a church. And who is the first person Jim sees in zombie form? A minister.

Even in Wallace and Gromit: Curse of the Were-Rabbit, the first victim of the beast is the town reverend in the local, you guessed it, church.

This is what I call the Death of God image. The point of this imagery is to show evil placing itself in the void left by the absence of God. This establishes the basis for horror, for where there is no God there can be no hope.

With the death of God, the structure of the story's universe is transformed into hell itself. The prisoners have taken over the prison and this leaves the hero to fend for himself in a universe where evil is the supreme and tyrannical power.

A Useless Figurehead

The major film industry has removed the fullness of what God is and replaced Him with a filtered version polite enough to show the general public. He may be all-powerful but He is neither demanding nor sovereign; rather he is an Oprah-esque kind of god, more like Dr. Phil than the Almighty who obliterated Gomorrah.

When God does make an appearance on screen, it is usually an impersonal affair. He is shown as a passive bystander who watches silently as the devil does his bidding (*The Devil's Advocate*), an ominous but ultimately impotent booming voice (*Bill and Ted's Bogus Journey*), or a nude and soft-spoken Canadian chick (*Dogma*). With the exceptions of the wrathful God in *Raiders of the Lost Ark* or the silent but active version in *I Am Legend*, it is difficult to find images of the Almighty that come even close to His real power and glory.

To find God in the movies you need to look deeply. Many times God is shown on screen through a symbolic character in the story. When we find a character who is an overt, symbolic god, he is usually a portrayal of the Gnostic version of God. This is god as a faulty creator, god as a fool unable to control creation.[1]

The Wizard of Oz is a great example of this caricature. The man behind the curtain was a fumbling master who ineptly tried to control his kingdom. When cornered, he dispensed quasi-miraculous gifts upon his uninvited guests (Dorothy and friends).

In the Jim Carrey movie *The Truman Show,* Christof (Ed Harris), an all-powerful television producer, watched over the life of Truman (Carrey). Truman discovered his life had been spent inside a massive television studio and he was the focus of a reality show. Christof managed the fake world of Truman but found himself unable to control his creation once Truman discovered the universe beyond his protected world. Christof represents God and is shown to be a useless figurehead once we humans see past his self-serving plans for us.

Relevance and Relationship

God does not need to be at the forefront of every film. His direct presence should only be displayed when relevant to a story, and not all stories require

---

1. Gnostics believe Yahweh is a lesser god who was created when his mother, Sophia, created him without need of a male counterpart. Yahweh, known as Demiurge to the Gnostics, went forth and created mankind in his image. The Gnostics hold that Demiurge is a flawed, incomplete god and in turn infused his fallible nature into man. (See http://www.biblicalstudies.org.uk/pdf/ft/gospel-of-thomas_bruce.pdf.)

a heavenly cameo.[2] What is needed is a sense of His presence in the universe, His fingerprints of beauty upon His creation, a relationship between God and mankind.

Characters today are not shown to have any communication with God. He is a non-player in their lives. Common storylines at the multiplex call for heroes to suffer incredible physical attacks and emotionally draining tragedies, yet it is almost shocking to see anyone on the screen bend their knees and look to God for comfort or guidance. It does happen from time to time, like the trapped firemen's recital of The Lord's Prayer in *World Trade Center* or Robert Neville (Will Smith) hurriedly leading his wife and son in prayer in *I Am Legend*.

Often, when a relationship with God is shown, prayer is used to emphasize oppression (*Carrie*) or to express a character's desperation (*Million Dollar Baby, Mr. Brooks*) rather than reveal God's grace and love. Normal reactions to distress are for a character to "turn to the power within themselves" (*Field of Dreams, The Matrix, Bedazzled*). They resolve their issues alone, without the help of some pesky, external god.

This reduction in the providence of God is common and best noted in movies about the apocalypse. Many of these films drag out deity as a reference tool but fail to put the end of the world scenarios in any theological context. A series of terrible plagues will be halted or a mischievous antichrist will be dispatched, not by the loving intervention of Christ, Himself, but by the main character's self-

Without God there is no truth and therefore no morality.

sacrifice in the climactic scene (*End of Days, The Seventh Sign, Prince of Darkness*). The apocalypse is watered down to a series of natural disasters capable of being quelled by Demi Moore.

When we see a heroine send demons back to hell or defeat the machinations of the antichrist, it sends a message that we humans are capable replacements for God. Our good natures or ability to love are shown to be as potent as the protection of the Almighty.

This message erroneously minimizes God. Humans able to dispatch Satan without turning to God imply that He is an unnecessary bystander on the spiritual battlefield.

Separation of mankind from God is not a small concept. As we will discuss later, the main purpose of story is to reveal truth. When God's authority is removed from our stories the intellectual and metaphysical dominos

---

2. Who needs another rendition of the Almighty as a foul little imp who slobbered on a cigar (George Burns, *Oh God!*)?

fall. The hero works in a world where God has no role; the hero is left to his own devices. While this may appeal to a number of filmmakers as an appropriate situation—many filmmakers tend to be committed secularists —it profoundly affects how the world is presented.

Most heroes are required to literally save the world. When his world is without a higher being, the hero effectively takes on God's role, to operate under his own moral authority. The hero fights to rescue people from slavery, stop an evil corporation, or prevent an evil clown who lives in the sewers from eating the children. These actions are based only on the hero's ideals.

Without God involved at some level, any ideal proposed by the hero is meaningless, for without God there is no truth and therefore no morality. If God does not exist, all occurrences are coincidences of random events. In a random universe, truth cannot exist because nothing is stable enough to be deemed trustworthy.

THE USE OF THE CROSS IN FILM
— Getting to the Crux of When Others Use the Crucifixion

Pay attention when you see crosses and crucifixes in films. Crosses on walls, on actor's necklaces, or hanging from rearview mirrors have been placed there on purpose. Their presence is never an accident. Someone had to find that cross—the right-looking cross—and intentionally place it in just the right place for the camera angle or on the actor. Image and symbol are planned.

You can often see crosses in scenes where death is present. They are also common in scenes involving sacrifice. The image in the background of a shot will subconsciously connect the action on screen with the concept of Christian sacrifice.

In other instances, you may see the cross used for the opposite purpose. The cross may be in scenes of oppression and cruelty. An example of this is in the movie *Monster*. The heroine, serial killer Aileen Wuornos (Charlize Theron), and her lesbian lover are caught in bed together by her partner's racist, Christian mother. The scorn of the mother is buttressed by the ominous cross that rests above their bed. The vitriol of the Christian mother and the dark cross over the bed intentionally unite to contrast the lesbian lovers with the cruelty of the mother's dialogue.

The Christ Posers

We should all be familiar with the indelible image of Jesus on the cross—His arms outstretched with hands elevated higher than His shoulders, His legs crossed at the ankles. His head is usually tilted in repose. That image of Christ on the cross is a haunting, painful recollection of the horrors of His death, yet it is also an awe-inspiring reminder of His gracious gift to all who receive Him.

At Golgotha Jesus was offered in ultimate sacrifice for the sins of mankind. At that moment He exemplified the ideals of sacrifice, duty, and selfless love. It should come as no surprise, then, that film directors and producers want to use the image of Christ for their own artistic or financial gains.

When a character—be it the hero, the mentor, the herald, or even sometimes the villain—dies in a moment of sacrifice, stay alert. If the character is to assume a tone of self-sacrifice or honor they will take on the Christ Pose—an intentional posing of the body of a dying or dead character where they mimic the posture of Christ on the cross.

Sgt. Elias Grodin (Willem Defoe) offers this pose toward the end of *Platoon*. Grodin is left behind by the platoon during an Vietnamese offensive by his nemesis, Sgt. Bob Barnes, who announced that Elias was dead. The helicopters lift off and the platoon leaves the battlefield.

As the choppers fly over the jungle treetops, they break out into a clearing. Sgt. Grodin is seen running from a large number of enemy soldiers. Barnes lied, and Grodin would pay the ultimate price. As enemy bullets tear into Grodin, he drops to his knees. His only hope are the men flying above who have abandoned him. Grodin raises his hands in a final gesture—arms raised, head tilted back. Director Oliver Stone posed actor Willem Dafoe in a way that would recreate a 1968 photograph by Art Greenspon of a soldier who actually died in that fashion, but the image of Grodin's death is so impactful because his final moments reflect the death of Christ.

In the final moments of *Braveheart*, William Wallace (Mel Gibson) has been arrested and faces execution. He is tied to a wooden rack, arms outstretched, legs bound together. He is to be brutally tortured, and he knows he will be dying for his fight for freedom. Director Mel Gibson included a bird's-eye view of Wallace on the rack. The visual connection to Christ's sacrifice is obvious.

When you actively look for the Christ Pose, it is astonishing how many films and television shows utilize it. From animations—Mr. Incredible is hung in the pose while a prisoner of Syndrome, to superhero movies—in *4: Rise of the Silver Surfer*, the Silver Surfer strikes the pose when he sacrifices himself to save the earth, to hard-boiled crime dramas. In *Heat*, the criminals go to visit a colleague only to find him shot to death. In the hallway a large cross hangs on the wall. They turn the corner to find the corpse laying in the Christ Pose in a pool of blood. His death was not for nothing.

When you see a character don this pose you should take it very seriously. The director is copying Jesus Christ, Himself, which means he runs a huge risk. If the Christ Pose is used for nefarious motives, the director is maligning Jesus' death by using it to promote evil.

Anchors Aweigh Achieves Unmoored Morality

A hero in a godless universe has no moral anchor—there is no supreme arbiter of good and evil. Therefore, the heroes of those films must be amoral creatures who assume moral authority without any basis for doing so. Without a foundation for morality, conduct quickly reverts to a simplistic world of "might makes right." That is how we can have icons like Arnold Schwarzenegger or Bruce Willis slaughter hundreds of faceless bad guys in horrific ways then offer a smile and cute tagline to end the scene.

Ultimately it is only the presence of God, the Supreme Creator and Authority, who can distinguish right from wrong and enable truth to exist. Without the authority of God to establish truth, we are helpless to do anything but argue competing perspectives.

The attempt to separate mankind from God is neither new nor surprising; in fact, it could appear logical. It is an act consistent with our times. Modernists of the late 19th and early 20th Centuries argued against the concept of a loving, intruding God. The post-modernists who followed did not bother to argue any longer. The debate was over and God had been revealed as an embarrassing flight of fancy for ignorant dunderheads who refused to cope with the real world.

To argue for a personal, all-knowing God is as relevant as the argument that the sun is made of bubble gum. We may as well ask our elites, who are fully versed in post-modernist beliefs, to include leprechauns and unicorns in their projects as to allow for the possibility of one sovereign Almighty who desires relationship with mankind.

The lie of post-modernist thought invades deeper into our lives when we, the audience, blur the unrealities of their on-screen philosophy with the realities of our daily lives. The continual flow of the godless worlds of film and television meld into our casual thinking. Before long we see the world through secular, godless eyes, and incidents which many Faithful should understand as the obvious providence of God in daily life are completely overlooked.

When our population began to filter their world though a post-modern worldview, our reliance upon inherent, natural truth broke down. The average person was taught that no reliable truth exists other than one's own perceptions. What then becomes true? What is false? The answer is, logically, nothing. Then again, logic itself becomes questionable.

The average person is left without a foundation on which to build their view of the world. Onto this blank slate, new truths are written—truths devised by men. The wisdom of the ages is deemed faulty and then the divine *we,* your illuminated leaders, will decide what is right and wrong for you. Morality, even social norms, become pliable, molded by the loudest voices of the moment.

In an amoral universe, the only consistent wrong is to insist there is a moral code to be followed. Acknowledgment of a standard for right and wrong is one of the primary reasons Christians are easily portrayed as evil in films, and it explains how we have moved from a society which held Christian faith securely within the public square to one in which we now hesitate to even wish each other Merry Christmas.

An artist is a creator. His works reflect the efforts of God, Himself. When the artist denies his role under God, when he denies God's laws, he finds the very world he desired his work to celebrate is without reason or purpose. To employ the Arts and Sciences and ignore the governing hand of God is to complete a jigsaw puzzle with the cardboard side up. You may figure out how the pieces fit together, but you will miss the beauty, function, and purpose of the design.

Storytelling is no different. God is at the heart of all stories; to deny His influence is to remove the purpose of the work. Yes, the story may still be functional, but Art without purpose is simply design and mere design will never sustain a civilization. It is not accidental that as our culture accepts the doughy arguments of secularism, we have pawned high Art for low entertainment.

When Fredrick Nietzsche said "God is dead,"[3] his point was not that God is actually dead but that He is irrelevant. Our lack of need for God makes Him a non-entity since, in Nietzsche's way of thinking, God fails to exist the moment we stop believing in Him.

---

3. Friedrich Nietzsche. *The Gay Science: With a Prelude in Rhymes and an Appendix of Songs.* Translated with commentary by Walter Kaufmann. Vintage Books. 1974. Sec 108.

7

The Disposable Paradise

"We always keep God waiting while we admit
more importunate[1] [burdensome] suitors."[2]
— Malcolm de Chazal

AMERICANS RETAIN THE MOST PRODUCTIVE, WIDE-RANGING CULTURE ever seen on the face of the earth. We also have the only culture that comes with an expiration date.

American movies, books, and television should be sold in Styrofoam along with fries and a drink. We have taken culture—the enlightenment and excellence of intellect and esthetic, the fruits of a people's disciplines and creativities—and turned it into a scrap pile of disposable, happy-thought fluff.

Our greatest actors spend years in training to hone their craft. When they achieve success, do they perform Shakespeare, Molière, Sam Shepard, or Tennessee Williams? No.

Do they introduce the masses to new characters and explore the next great scripts of the century? No.

After all their effort and training, our best and brightest performers use their careers to portray superheroes like the X-Men, Batman, and the

---

1. *Importunate* = burdensome, troublesome : overly persistent in request or demand.
2. Malcolm de Chazal. http://www.brainyquote.com/quotes/quotes/m/malcolmdec383651.html
   Last accessed December, 2009. Used by permission. DeChazal was a French-African painter and engineer.

Incredible Hulk. When future generations look at us, they will find grown adults fascinated more with Marvel Comics than literary classics.

Most American film is no longer an art made to express an artistic vision. A majority of films are made for two reasons. The first and biggest reason is to turn a buck. The second reason is for social engineering. Filmmakers have a political or social axe to grind and they grind it on their audiences. While neither of these motivations are unique to our generation, both tend to feed short-term goals and offer short-term products.

McMovies—To Turn a Buck

One type of film that is the fruit of our generation is the corporate movie, also known as the blockbuster. We all know these movies—*Armageddon, Independence Day, Iron Man.* These bloated chunks of cinematic nonsense have more boom than brains and offer nothing to the audience except immediate thrill of spectacle. They are amusement park rides put to film.

The blockbuster is intended as sheer entertainment. And they are entertaining—much in the same way we can watch a screen saver to be momentarily amused. Since they offer the audience nothing meaningful, they are quickly forgotten. Audiences pay attention then discard the movies like children bored with a new toy.

I call these productions McMovies—Hollywood's fast food. They crank out a filling McMovie in no time flat, grease it with a slick marketing campaign, and launch the product in dozens of countries simultaneously. Like fast food, most Hollywood products are empty, tasteless experiences geared to please the masses long enough to keep them coming back for more. And, like fast food, these films will not sustain anyone for long.

It is pleasant to watch big, stupid Hollywood movies, just as it is fun to eat a greasy burger or some thawed-out, breaded chicken chunks in a paper box. Where things run afoul are when the fast foods of Hollywood become the only foods on which our souls feed. Consumption of nothing but greasy, processed hamburgers has a negative impact on the body. We bloat and begin to starve for real nutrition.

Our reaction to the McMovie is the same. Someone who consumes nothing but the culture doled out by corporations will have a brain that is mush. The greater the number of mainstream movies one consumes, the weaker the mind becomes because it is not being fed anything it can use. Think of Hollywood movies as empty calories dumped into our heads—but these empty calories have the ability to alter our perception of the world.

Smart Movies—Social Engineering

Either from an attempt to market to a broader audience or perhaps to satisfy their fondness for irony, there have been times when fast food corporations released products promoted as healthy. The menu is extended to include salads and soups designed to appear as healthy alternatives. Often these alternatives are littered with the same chemicals, saturated fats, and other dietary nasties found in the regular fodder.

Hollywood, likewise, offers products which seem to be healthy alternatives. This type of film is the Smart Movie. It claims to offer examinations into the human experience and is promoted as being important (*Revolutionary Road, Children of Men, Mystic River*), the "message movie"—socially conscious productions which cram agendas down your throat (*Che, Milk, North Country*). They give the illusion of being heady but are simply wordier versions of their less intellectually adventurous counterparts. The acting and scripting may be more advanced, but the product itself is just as temporary and needless. They offer pontification but are low on meaning and will often be released during off-season, autumn and winter, so they can be cherished during the awards season in the spring.

Because they fuel the political machinations of their time, these politically-fueled movies feed the short-term aspirations of our culture. They serve to drop off some bit of propaganda then fade into the massive noise that is our modern culture. Think of them as intentional sniper shots during a rain of machine gun fire coming out of corporate Hollywood. They have an impact, but it is localized. They make news for a few weeks, long enough to get some "discussion" going, then recede into the oblivion of the Netflix queue. They were never intended to be long-lasting or great works of art but, rather, dramatic blows to forward some ideal.

Cinematic Art or Toys?

Both of these types of film—the McMovie and Smart Movies—have given us a useless, cluttered culture, particularly when they combine forces (*The Day After Tomorrow*).

The continual flow of these movies has turned a once vibrant film community into a corporate, politically-hypersensitive beast which churns out cinematic toys on a conveyor belt.

Two generations have grown up with this disposable culture. We were raised to constantly look for the next thing coming because what came yesterday did not satisfy. This led to our forgetting history, disregarding old things, and never expecting much from today.

A look back at the 1930s and '40s shows us meaningful films; productions that supported a healthy society—or at least did not intend to tear it down: *On the Waterfront, Sunset Blvd., All About Eve, The African Queen, Harvey, The Killing, High Noon, Singin' in the Rain, Some Like it Hot, Rear Window, Strangers on a Train, To Catch a Thief, The Asphalt Jungle,* and *Marty.* Sure, there were politically and socially-charged films like *Rebel Without a Cause, Paths of Glory, The Day the Earth Stood Still,* and *The Grapes of Wrath,* but they tended to be more commentary than blatant propaganda (although, to be fair, *The Day the Earth Stood Still* is heavy-handed in spots).

A look at the films created prior to the late 1960s shows us a rich history of cinematic art, brilliant, intelligent works that still have the ability to move and enlighten audiences. Compare them to what is being pushed today and it is clear something has drastically changed.

To make this point, let us put it to the audience. Here are the top ten grossing movies of 1957 versus the top ten from 2007:

1957[3]

1. *The Bridge on the River Kwai*

2. *Peyton Place*

3. *Sayonara*

4. *Old Yeller*

5. *Raintree County*

6. *A Farewell to Arms*

7. *Island in the Sun*

8. *Gunfight at the O.K. Corral*

9. *Pal Joey*

10. *Don't Go Near the Water*

We had an adaptation of Ernest Hemmingway, a classic children's tale, and a large number of films about the complexities of love and war; films starred Marlon Brando, Frank Sinatra, Rita Hayworth, Elizabeth Taylor, Alec Guinness, Rock Hudson, Montgomery Clift, and William Holden.

2007[4]

1. *Pirates of the Caribbean: At World's End*

2. *Harry Potter and the Order of the Phoenix*

3. *Spider-Man 3*

---

3. http://en.wikipedia.org/wiki/1957_in_film. Accessed February 2010.
4. http://en.wikipedia.org/wiki/2007_in_film. Accessed February 2010..

4. *Shrek the Third*

5. *Transformers*

6. *Ratatouille*

7. *I Am Legend*

8. *The Simpson's Movie*

9. *National Treasure: Book of Secrets*

10. *300*

Now we get superheroes; cartoons; toys; half-naked, sword-wielding Greeks; and the Fresh Prince of Bel Air with zombies.

To be fair, not all films prior to 1960 were stellar works of art, nor were they all morally honorable. Many silly monster movies like *Creature from the Black Lagoon* (1954) or *The Giant Gila Monster* (1959) are evidence of this. *Freaks* (1932) and *Baby Doll* (1956) demonstrate that deviancy is an issue that knows no generational bounds, but recent decades have shown an inordinately steep increase in the numbers and prominence of films intended as neither Art nor as contribution to the improvement of the human condition.

Wrecking the Culture for Fun and Profit

In my estimation, the loss of our culture occurred when the political left snapped up the movie industry during the 1960s. The Baby Boomers have done their damage. The elites of the '60s deconstructed the mechanics of our society and rebuilt it in their own likeness. Charlton Heston went from portraying Moses and Ben-Hur to battling talking monkeys (*Planet of the Apes*) and groovy zombies (*Omega Man*).

Storylines changed, as well, and went from tales with a moral foundation (*The Magnificent Seven, Lawrence of Arabia, Angels with Dirty Faces*) to stories proposing amorality (*Chinatown, Taxi Driver, Manhattan*). Films that celebrated the goodness of mankind or showed our sense of justice (*The Miracle Worker, To Kill a Mockingbird, The Man Who Shot Liberty Valance*) became outmoded. Films mired in darkness investigated our corrupt natures (*The Godfather, Apocalypse Now, Harold & Maude, Straw Dogs*).

Yes, we have always had anti-heroes, those men and women who donned the mantle of the heroic role only to display evil. Macbeth is one of the most striking examples. *Psycho, The Maltese Falcon, Casablanca, The Searchers,* and *The Killers* all fronted low men in the heroic role—not the kind of men you wanted to have over for polite dinner conversation.

Throughout the '40s and '50s a change in tone brewed. In the late 1960s, the anti-hero went from being an uncommon figure used to show how *not* to live, to being a mainstay who glorified the corruption of the world at large. Since the 1960s, generations have grown up with no understanding of what it was like to go to the cinema and unreservedly expect an uplifting experience.

When you review the sharp change in tone and content that occurred in the film industry in the late 1960s and '70s, it may seem reasonable to push the decay of our society onto the shoulders of hippies then call it day. I enjoy deriding hippies as much as the next guy, but they are only a part of the problem. The political and social leftists are to be blamed for the initial chipping away at the foundations of American society, but it is the corporate masters whom the hippies so despised that have done the real damage.

A Cinematic Simulacrum: The Disposable Paradise

In *The Matrix,* Neo learns that the overlord computers lulled humanity into a trance where they live in a false reality—a concept eerily close to what we live in today. Corporations create alternate realities—a *simulacrum:* an image, an effigy, a falsehood meticulously built to appear to be as perfect as the real thing but with no actual substance.

In our society, the simulacrum is a disposable paradise—a super-reality fashioned by corporations. Airbrushed models smile at us from magazine covers, and market-tested advertisements promise us happiness, while PR-controlled celebrities are presented as god-like, living wonderful lives in their sun-drenched, palm-tree-lined paradise. The most mundane facts of their lives are promoted as special events far more impressive and vital than our boring, useless existence.

Unlike *The Matrix,* the average person in the United States does not actually live inside this false reality but, instead, is always left on the outside looking in. Billboards, commercials, radio, Internet, cell phones, and digital television show us a fake world and offer us a ticket to the Promised Land if we only buy the right thing and think the right thoughts.

Celebrity images are like the Sirens of Greek mythology—deceptive creatures who sang beautiful songs to passing ships and entranced sailors to their doom. Hollywood's deceptive, disposable paradise draws people in with promises of happiness and allows us to chase the ideas wafted to us by their images— illusions which lead us away from God.

The false and disposable paradise is so engrained into our lives that most people will not recognize its existence, they simply react to it. To them it is like oxygen, just something that is there. They live their lives numb to the increasing barrage of noise which flows from corporate marketing machines.

This false paradise is a trap. It offers all manner of pleasure without any possibility of ultimate redemption or satisfaction. It implies we are part of something important, something bigger than ourselves, but we are dupes in a sad Pavlovian exchange where they ring the media bell and we salivate.

Advertising has been around for a long time and is a necessary part of business. But today's advertising world has metastasized into a marketing culture, has become a massive machine under which we live. It engulfs our daily lives and directly impacts how we literally and figuratively see our world. It requires great strength and intentionality to avoid today's marketing.

This marketing culture is tied to the rise of the secular movement of the late 1960s (thank you, soapless hippies). A combination of commercialism and democratic socialism gives the average person a terrible burden to overcome. The combination seeks to remold us into useful cogs for its own ends. Corporate domination of almost all aspects of modern culture leads to marketing of products that speak to the lowest socio-strata. Achievement in life moves from personal excellence and helping your fellow man under the guidance of a loving Almighty, to the accumulation of goods and services. We are trained from childhood to be consumers not producers. Life becomes all about what I can do for me, not what I should do for you.

> It will not be long before we see their attempt to replace God with man's ultimate product, the State.

In tandem with this, secularists push their socio-political agenda onto an already overburdened populace. The goal of the secularist is to replace God with man. The corporations, left to their own devices, will replace God with products. When those forces combine, it will not be long before we see their attempt to replace God with man's ultimate product, the State.

What does this have to do with movies? The entertainment industry at large, and Hollywood in particular, is the place where the forces of secularism and corporate domination combine with the greatest effects. Films are fundamental to their machine.

What is "Hollywood"?

Ask *What is Hollywood?* and some answers may cite a favorite actor or film, maybe an icon such as Chaplin, Bogart, or Marilyn Monroe. Some people may think of seedy filmmakers with their corrupting productions who want nothing but to grab a fast buck. The real Hollywood is something more. True, the personalities and perverts are there, but Hollywood is first and foremost a business—a big business.

When the term *Hollywood* is used, it normally describes the workings of the big six movie studios:

> » NBC Universal
>
> » Paramount Pictures
>
> » Warner Brothers Pictures
>
> » Walt Disney Pictures
>
> » 20th Century Fox
>
> » Columbia Pictures

Along with those big ticket guys are a collection of "mini-majors," smaller but still influential studios such as the Weinsteins' company, Lionsgate. From these sources we get the movies at the multiplex and on DVD.

These organizations wield massive power in our culture and have a direct impact on your life. If you never watched one movie or television show and were able to personally avoid their influences, your next-door neighbor, co-worker, and the buyer for your favorite store are still caught in the deluge.

Movie studios are not simply production houses that make movies on a conveyor belt. They are arms of large corporate structures. When we see a film or a piece of marketing, we must realize that we are being approached by not only the film studio but by the corporate entity that owns it. None of the major film studios are an independent corporation. As of the writing of this book, the breakdown is as follows:

> » Viacom owns Paramount Pictures and Dreamworks SKG
>
> » General Electric owns NBC Universal and Focus Features
>
> » The Walt Disney Company owns Walt Disney Pictures and Pixar
>
> » News Corp. owns 20th Century Fox, Universal Artists, and MGM
>
> » Sony owns Columbia Pictures
>
> » Time Warner owns Warner Brothers Pictures and HBO Films

Now take into account the other companies owned by these top level corporations. For example,

> » Viacom not only owns Paramount (home of such films as *Titanic*, *Forrest Gump*, and the *Mission Impossible* and *Shrek* franchises) but is a sister company to the CBS Corporation which controls the CBS Broadcasting Inc., Simon & Schuster Publishing, Showtime, MTV, BET, and Comedy Central along with a cornucopia of CBS affiliate companies.

» Until they split in 2004, Paramount and CBS where one large company known as Viacom. The two companies are both still controlled by another privately held company, National Amusements, which also operates 1,500 movie theatres worldwide plus IMAX theatres in the United States and Argentina. This privately owned company is completely controlled by one family, headed by a man named Sumner Redstone.

> Through his business holdings, one man—
> Sumner Redstone—controls
> what is seen in over 508 million homes worldwide,
> and most people do not even know he exists.

According to Viacom's website, the corporation's brands are worldwide and powerful:

> Viacom connects with audiences around the world through our brands represented in more than 562 million households in 161 countries and territories. We entertain, engage and educate in 33 languages via our 160 locally programmed and operated TV channels and more than 400 online properties. And our global presence grows every day.[5]

This kind of centralized control is not unique since each film studio falls under similar corporate structure. Their tentacles can envelop every aspect of public life.

The entertainment industry is just that, an industry. Warner Brothers, MGM, and Universal are companies no different than McDonalds, Burger King, or Coca-Cola—which indicates that those who own the studios are no longer in the business of making movies.

The marketing campaign for one product line bleeds into the campaign for another. Cross-marketing, corporate partnerships, and mergers combine to influence movie release schedules and production lineups. This conflation of interests results in film products that look more like advertisements than stories.

Production studios and their ruling corporations are not some sly Big Brother that calculates its continued influence over our populace. They can make us neither stupid nor immoral. They can, however, tempt us with sexual imagery

---

5. Reaching Our Global Audience. http://www.viacom.com/ourbrands/globalreach/Pages/default. aspx Last accessed October 2009.

and show stupid heroes rewarded for imbecilic behavior. The issue for us little folk is that production studios create our modern myths—our folktales which explain to us our world.

Decisions over which films to release, what type stories to tell, and what messages to impart are decisions generally not made by either artists or the people concerned with society as a whole. Those decisions too often reside with individuals whose only responsibility is to turn a profit. That fact, alone, reveals one of the major reasons why today's films cater less to Main Street and more to boosting ledger sheets. Trumped, of course, only by agenda-drivers; then the ledger sheets can take a close second place.

What happens when those corporations decide a society mired in conflict or populated with under-educated lemmings will provide them with a more docile consumer base?

THE JERK AND THE FILMMAKER'S WORLDVIEW

When I discuss worldview in films, it is common to hear someone list films that appear to have no philosophical bent to them at all, such as *Deuce Bigelow: Male Gigolo, Pretty Woman,* or *The Care Bears Movie.* But every film, no matter how vacant or silly it seems, does promote a worldview.

Just as every oil painting has brush strokes, every film promotes a philosophy. Even a movie as crass and seemingly hollow as Steve Martin's comedy *The Jerk* delivers specific morality and the filmmaker's worldview to its audience.

The Jerk is a cleverly written comedy about Navin Johnson (Martin), an irredeemably stupid character who goes from the poor house to a mansion thanks to his invention of a fancy handle for eyeglasses, then he loses everything when his invention draws a massive lawsuit. The film is loaded with Martin's signature smart-man's stupid humor.

The beginning of the film presents Navin as a hard-working man who is proud of his efforts. He is kind, trusting, and always helpful. These traits are keys to his quick success in life, both in his business and in winning his love interest (Bernadette Peters). When Navin becomes rich, though, he turns arrogant, materialistic, and belligerent. As his empire crumbles, his arrogant materialism leaves Navin utterly destroyed; he wanders the streets, drunk, with his pants around his ankles. One set of characteristics is shown as useful and desirable, the other destructive and empty.

The film also touches on the subjects of race, racism, sexual relations, mental disorders, and the general coarseness of society. Throughout the film, screenwriters Steve Martin, Carl Gottlieb, and Michael Elias make choices on how these issues are presented. While they attempt to squeeze out as many jokes as they can from their topics, they also make some striking statements that are unknowingly ingested by the audience. A perfect example of this Navin's "special purpose."

Navin begins a sexual relationship with a carnival daredevil by the name of Patty Bernstein. During their first encounter, Navin explains that he was told about his "special purpose" which is clearly meant to describe his manhood. After he has sex with Patty, he writes home to tell his mother about the experience. He has reduced his "special purpose" to participation in pre-marital sex.

Navin's "special purpose" may be considered harmless by some people and offensive to others, but it is usually not immediately seen as influential. But the ultimate impact of that moral statement has, for thirty years, given approval to loose sex, sodomy, and unprotected sexual intercourse.

All of this from a goofy comedy that shows cat juggling and in which the lead character serenades his love with a song about a Thermos®.

8

Have I Ever Told You How Awesome I Am?

"When the people saw that Moses was so long in coming down from the mountain, they gathered around Aaron and said, "Come, make us gods who will go before us. As for this fellow Moses who brought us up out of Egypt, we don't know what has happened to him."[1]

WHAT BECOMES OF THE LONGING FOR GOD WITHIN MEN'S HEARTS when we supplant heaven with our own version of paradise? Though most atheists adamantly disagree that any such longing exists, every human being has a natural need for relationship with God. When the Lord is excluded from life, we will find a replacement—a cheap replacement for our Heavenly Father.

Many people turn to sex, drugs, or rock 'n' roll. As Bruce Marshall says in *The World, the Flesh, and Father Smith*, "the young man who rings the bell at the brothel is unconsciously looking for God."[2] The exchange of life under God for material comforts occurs on an ever-widening scale.

Technology and society offer an endless supply of information, opinion, and history. Each of us have the ability to improve ourselves or destroy

---

1. Exodus 32:1
2. Bruce Marshall. *The World, the Flesh, and Father Smith.* Houghton Mifflin. Boston. 1945 and renewed 1972 by Bruce Marshall. 108. Reprinted by permission of Houghton Mifflin Harcourt Publishing Company. All rights reserved.

everything we know. Hourly, our generation has the expanse of human invention at our fingertips, yet it is not enough. In this technologically advanced age, we abandon our Christian home for the promise of secular freedom. We tell ourselves the grass is greener on the other side of the theological fence and never once acknowledge it is the grazing ground for golden calves.

When God is removed from the public square, other entities move in to fill the void. Men look for God even when they do not know His name, witnessed by the inclination towards the spiritual even in today's primitive societies. We instinctually understand there is a metaphysical aspect to existence—something or someone is at work in our lives beyond our own understanding.

The Gods of Celebrity

As cultures grow, mythologies are developed around an instinctual understanding that there is someone or something bigger than ourselves. Tales are told of great heroes who perform fantastic tasks. Heroes become exaggerated characters, are given immortal qualities, and eventually are seen as gods.

Mankind's innate desire for order and safety expressed itself through the eons in societies' worship of these mythological gods. There was a hunger for the Lord, but ancient cultures, not knowing Him, devised lesser gods as substitutes.

Ancient civilizations developed arrays of gods to explain the universe. The Greeks included figures such as Ares, Apollo, Hera, Poseidon, and the granddaddy of them all, Zeus. Tales of these gods informed the population and gave critical lessons on behavior and history. Their stories covered every aspect of life from the birth of the universe to the consequences of adultery and murder.

Yet these gods, for all of their power and knowledge, were not God, merely god-like. Unlike the God of the Bible, these figures were flawed, prone to lust and hatred—they made mistakes. Still, they were considered supermen like the heroes in today's films. But Zeus has more in common with Superman than he does with Yahweh.[3]

This may seem primitive and silly to our modern minds, but the uncomfortable truth is that we busily do the same. Like our Greek, Roman, Indian, Chinese, and Scandinavian ancestors, we have developed our own pantheon of gods as replacements for the one and true God known in Scripture. We call this pantheon of gods *celebrity*.

---

3. Yahweh (from Hebrew) or Jehovah (Latin) comes from the Hebrew tetragrammaton "יהוה" and is the personal name of the God of the Bible.

No, we do not worship Zeus or Athena. We are asked, instead, to honor George Clooney and Halle Berry—or, more accurately, to worship their images. The Harrison Ford we see on screen or in interviews is not the same man who failed college in Ripon, Wisconsin, and who spends his spare time woodworking or flying a helicopter. The actor and his image are separate entities. We follow the illusion.

Celebrity culture provides a surrogate connection between man and deity. Corporate images of the rich and famous show people who possess no miraculous powers nor offer any real answers to life's problems, but they are treated as though they possess far greater value than us plebs.

Heath Ledger dies of complications from drug interactions and devastated crowds surround his New York apartment for a month. O. J. Simpson is arrested and it becomes a national crisis. Angelina Jolie adopts a child or Michael Jackson dies and the news rushes around the globe.

Like the Greek or Mayan gods before them, our celebrities' lives become dramatic stories we can follow. They appear in our films and on our televisions to demonstrate how we should talk, dress, and think. This god-like quality is why they are known as *stars*—brilliant, other-worldly creations.

> Men look for God even when they do not know His name.

Our inclination to turn to man-made gods as replacements for the real One is common and extends beyond mere storytelling. In communist or fascist countries, the State replaces God. Churches under these regimes are neutered or destroyed and the population is re-educated to accept that God never existed.[4] Rather than submit oneself to God and find purpose under His guidance, commoners are to bend their knees to the needs of the State and serve the oligarchy.

When truth is removed, the best lie will be believed. Those who snatch away freedom must disguise humanity's dreams of God.

Examine the political propaganda of Nazi Germany, Stalinist Russia, or any number of communist movements in Africa or South America and you will see a deified political leader shown in grand postures and referred to in pseudo-religious terms. This god-like leader offers hope, redemption, and salvation to the masses.

Personality cults have led nations to adopt political ideologies directly opposed to their own long-term good, and that espousal was a pursuit of anything to quell their thirst for the Living Water of God's presence.

A casual reading of the Bible shows numerous occasions when mankind has been misled. Left to our own devices, we turn our hunger for God into self-

---

4. For further information on this and other philosophical and social aspects of man's relationship to God, check out www.rzim.org.

serving disaster. Our desire for God underscores most of life's motivations. Each of us possesses the drive to know God, even those in charge of our media outlets.

Though many filmmakers may not recognize this desire for God, they know how to take advantage of it. The creation of figureheads, heroes, and celebrities is central to everything they produce. These products, in turn, attempt to fill our need for the Lord's guidance.

Material things can never satisfy a hungry soul. Notoriety provides no ultimate fulfillment. Not convinced? Study the fall of Tiger Woods, the experimentation of Michael Phelps, the restlessness of Elvis Presley, or the chaotic lives of Britney Spears, Robert Downey, Jr., Winona Ryder, Ryan O'Neill, Carrie Fisher, Michael Vick, and countless other floundering celebrities. Status offers no salvation; riches offer no peace. To have everything except Jesus Christ is to have nothing at all. Or as Cynthia Heimel states it in *The Village Voice*:

> I pity celebrities. No, I do. … Sylvester Stallone, Bruce Willis, and Barbra Streisand fervently … wanted fame …. The night each of them became famous they wanted to shriek with relief. Finally! … All their fantasies had been realized, yet the reality was still the same. If they were miserable before, they were twice as miserable now because that giant thing they were striving for, that fame-thing that was going to make everything okay, that was going to make their lives bearable, that was going to provide them with personal fulfillment and (ha, ha) happiness, had happened. And nothing changed. They were still them. The disillusionment turned them howling and insufferable.[5]

When people remove God from their lives, they must replace Him with something. Just as generations have done for eons, we replaced Him with ourselves. It is not too late for us to learn from those previous generations that this is a bad idea.

We may try to remove God from our lives, but that does not mean we will not miss Him.

What distracts us from God
can never replace Him.

---

5. Cynthia Heimel. Tongue in Chic. *The Village Voice*. Jan 2, 1990. 38-40.

9

The Hays Code: Back in the Days When Hollywood Cared What We Thought

"The very aim and end of our institutions is just this: that we may think what we like and say what we think."[1]
— Oliver Wendell Holmes

CHRISTIANS HAVE STRUGGLED TO CONTROL THE IMPULSES OF THE FILM industry since the end of the nineteenth century. Groups such as The Catholic Legion of Decency (no, they were not superheroes) along with a collection of state and local censorship boards held a tight grip on the industry for decades.

These theologically-based censors did their best to restrict access to the content they felt was harmful to the public. Many of these boards maintained control with the argument that restriction of film content was under the realm of public health, not free speech. This was supported by the U. S. Supreme Court when, in 1915, they ruled unanimously that films were not covered under the First Amendment (free speech) since they were not a part of the press.

---

1. Oliver Wendell Holmes. *The Professor at the Breakfast-Table*. 1916. Houghton Mifflin. 168. — Oliver Wendell Holmes (Aug 1809—Oct 1894) was an American physician, professor, lecturer, and author. He was regarded by his peers as one of the best writers of the 19th century, was a member of the Fireside Poets and recognized as an important medical reformer.

There were as many reasons during those years to worry about the corrosive effects of Hollywood as there are today. Despite wanting to believe otherwise, there are no good ol' days when it comes to morality. Our grandparents and great-grandparents' generations were as devious and shameful as ours. Films have always been used for both good and evil and will continue to be as long as there is sin.

The Early Years

Cinematic pornography has a long history dating back to the 1890s (Eugene Pirou's stag film *Le Coucher de la Marie*). Censorship of sexual content has been around for just as long. It is widely held that the first instances of cinematic censorship came in 1896 with Fatima's *Coochee-Coochee Dance,* which displayed a belly dancer and *The May Irwin Kiss* which showed a man and woman kissing.

More sin was on the way with numerous films showing the evils of white slavery in productions such as *The Downward Path* (1900) and *Traffic in Souls* (1913). Crime also was on the menu in films like *The James Boys in Missouri* (1908).

By the 1920s, the rambunctious nature of the film industry had become a blight on the American scene. Tales of lurid behavior became commonplace and were in stark contrast to how people were expected to conduct themselves in public. The private lives of the stars and producers became public embarrassments. The content of film became more lewd, even by today's standards.

Crisis point was reached in a series of infamous scandals that plagued Hollywood, including the trial of Roscoe "Fatty" Arbuckle for murder. The popular actor was entangled in a scandal involving sexual deviancy, drug use, and the rape and murder of young starlet Virginia Rappe. This was the O. J. Simpson case of 1921. The murder of director William Desmond Taylor (Feb. 1922), the drug-related death of actor Wallace Reid (Jan. 1923), and the probable murder of film producer Thomas Ince (his Nov. 1924 death remains a mystery), as well as other scandals, put an unwanted spotlight on the film industry.

With the rise of more conservative post-WWI attitudes, Hollywood's scandals sounded a call to end the freewheeling days of the film industry.

In 1922, the industry moved to spare itself from further public control and government intervention and began development of the Motion Picture Producers and Distributors of America (MPPDA). This organization (which later evolved into the Motion Picture Association of America, discussed in the next chapter) was constructed to further the political and business interests of the film industry—which included fending off those pesky religious groups who pushed for cleaner content in the cinema.

The MPPDA hired William Hays, former campaign manager and Postmaster General to President Warren G. Harding. The hiring of Hays was a public relations move intended to quell Protestant groups since Hays was a Presbyterian deacon. Hays worked diligently on the film industry's behalf but was sympathetic to the social groups which called for decency in film. He promoted the idea of self-control rather than government-control of film content.

As a public relations effort, Hays developed what he called "The Formula"—a list of "Don'ts and Be Carefuls" for film producers. These Dos and Don'ts included prescriptions against frivolous nudity, support of criminal behavior, and drug use. The list was not law but a voluntary guideline so it did not carry much weight when placed against the power of the dollar. The truth is simple: sex and violence sells.

The moguls of Hollywood quickly strayed from the straight and narrow and distributed more lurid content about easy women who made money off their bodies and corrupt gangsters who lurked in the underground. Despite Hays' attempt to bring some guidance to the industry, the media continued to produce what church groups considered unfit. While church groups stuck up their noses, the general public flocked to violent gangster films such as *Little Caesar* (1931) and *Scarface* (1932) along with the works of film personalities like Mae West and W. C. Fields.

The Production Code

With continued pressure from public groups, the list of Dos and Don'ts simply changed into a list of Don'ts. The Production Code (a.k.a. the Hays Code) became a standard of behavior installed by the MPPDA in 1930. Enforcement began in 1934.[2]

The Hays Code was a set of industry standards that laid out what was and was not acceptable in a film released for public viewing. Much of the previous items from "The Formula" remained, but this code was enforceable.

In 1934, the Production Code Administration (PCA) was created and reviewed all motion pictures released in the United States. With approval from the PCA, a film would obtain a certificate effectively clearing it for distribution. This path to film release was in place for over thirty years.

---

2. The original version of The Production Code was penned by Father Daniel A. Lord, S.J. who was consulted by Cecil B. DeMille for the film *King of Kings*. Father Lord gave the Code to Hayes who modified it and put it into practice. For a detailed presentation of the complete Hays Code, its history, alterations, amendments and editings, see http://productioncode.dhwritings.com/multipleframes_productioncode.php.

The Code itself contained what most conservative individuals would see as reasonable standards. Its General Principles were:

- » No picture shall be produced that will lower the moral standards of those who see it. Hence, the sympathy of the audience should never be thrown to the side of crime, wrongdoing, evil, or sin.

- » Correct standards of life, subject only to the requirements of drama and entertainment, shall be presented.

- » Law, natural or human, shall not be ridiculed, nor shall sympathy be created for its violation.[3]

These are vague statements which a clever film producer could drive a truck through. Imagine arguing what is and is not a "correct standard of life, subject only to the requirements of drama and entertainment." It would not be long before the participants fell into useless "I know pornography when I see it"-type arguments.

It is important to remember as we discuss this Code that it was, at its core, a public relations tool. That said, the Hays Code did have some teeth and films were eventually held to a recognizable standard.

These general principles were just that, general, but the Code also provided more detailed rules which tended to be harder to avoid. Many Christians will look on these items and nod in agreement.

For example, in the area of crime, the act of criminality should "never be presented in such a way as to throw sympathy with the crime as against law and justice or to inspire others with a desire for imitation."[4] It would seem logical that someone who displays art in public should be held responsible for their art not inspiring viewers to harm others. Why would such a rule need to be in place? A film such as *The Poughkeepsie Tapes* (2007) demonstrates why this type of regulation is relevant. In that film, the audience is shown actual videotapes of brutal murders recorded by a serial killer from his point-of-view.

To show murder, the Code demanded the following restrictions:

- » The technique of murder must be presented in a way that will not inspire imitation.

- » Brutal killings are not to be presented in detail.

- » Revenge in modern times shall not be justified.[5]

---

3. *General Principles, A Code to Govern the Making of Motion and Talking Pictures, the Reasons Supporting It and the Resolutions for Uniform Interpretation.* Motion Picture Producers and Distributors of America, Inc. June 13, 1934.
4. Particular Applications: I. Crimes Against the Law. *A Code to Govern the Making of Motion and Talking Pictures, the Reasons Supporting It and the Resolutions for Uniform Interpretation.* Motion Picture Producers and Distributors of America, Inc. June 13, 1934.
5. Ibid.

The Godfather series just got pushed to the curb—as did *The Passion of the Christ, Raiders of the Lost Ark, Downfall,* and *Band of Brothers,* which all show killings in detail.

On the topic of sex, "The sanctity of the institution of marriage and the home shall be upheld. Pictures shall not infer that low forms of sexual relationships are the accepted or common thing."[6] The Code also condemned the use of seduction and rape as a means of comedy, and stated that passion in general should not be used to "stimulate the lower and baser element." We just lost *Body Heat, Do the Right Thing,* and *Titanic*.

How about vulgarity? "Pointed profanity [includes the words God, Lord, Jesus, Christ—unless used reverently—hell, S.O.B., damn, Gawd] or every other profane or vulgar expression however used, is forbidden."[7] Most of the films of the last half of the twentieth century would have been banned.

The Hays Code also covered how religion should be shown in film:

>   » No film or episode may throw ridicule on any religious faith.

>   » Ministers of religion in their character as ministers of religion should not be used as comic characters or as villains.

>   » Ceremonies of any definite religion should be carefully and respectfully handled.[8]

Wallace & Gromit in the Curse of the Were-Rabbit and *Doubt* would have arguably been denied release under these rules.

It is commendable that the Code attempted to protect the clergy from attack. It is not a mistake that the Code says "ministers of religion *in their characters as ministers of religion* should not be used…"[9] (emphasis added). It is fine to mock a fool when he's just a fool doing foolish things. It is a whole different kettle of fish when it is done while he wears a frock. When performing pastoral duties, he is acting as a conduit to God. Insulting a priest or rabbi who performs this role serves to move beyond criticizing the human and moves to insulting God, Himself. It is a shortcut to blasphemy and insults a whole religion.

This kind of thoughtful wording and careful application of restriction was seen throughout the Code. Hays judiciously approached his task, but his task was still to force compliance on an artistic format. This is why, along with the clear rules of right and wrong, Hays included so many exceptions that the Code was more a regulatory sieve. For example, "Brutal killings are not to be presented in detail."[10] This may seem to say you cannot show brutal

---

6. Ibid, Particular Applications: II. Sex
7. Ibid, Particular Applications: V. Profanity
8. Ibid. Particular Applications: VIII. Religion
9. Ibid.
10. Ibid. Particular Applications: I. Crimes Against the Law

killings. A film producer would only see the final two words "in detail." They were still able to include much of the lurid content; they just could not be pornographic about it.

Previous generations sinned and, in many cases, their sins were as great as our own. The Code may have been informed by Biblical teaching but it was shaped by the hand of men, not by the Word of God. In whatever man builds, flaws will be found.

It would be nearly criminal of me to discuss the Hays Code without mentioning Section II, Article 6. Under the section of the Code dealing with sex, Hays rules that "Miscegenation [sexual relationships between the white and black races] is forbidden." The offensive nature of this rule is obvious to today's reader. I mention it because I believe this racist holdover from a bygone era reminds us that this document, regardless of its intent, was written by men who were just as fallen as we are.

The ABCs: Argument, Breathing Room, and Creative Expression

The Hays Code was in place from the 1930s to the late 1960s. During that time it helped instill a sense of respect into the works that were released under its control. The Golden Age of Hollywood would have looked entirely different if this Code had not been in place.[11] Again, our grandparents and great-grandparents were as sinful as we are today. One reason we look back on previous generations and consider them quaint and simple is partially due to the neutering effects of the Hayes Code on the entertainment of that era.

While the Code did curtail the coarsening of Hollywood productions, not everyone applauded its regulatory might. Many, if not all, people within the creative side of the film industry saw the Code as blatant censorship and a violation of human expression. From the very inception of the Code as a means for the industry to watch itself there were internal forces working against it to counter its restrictive reach.

Throughout the 1930s, 1940s, and early 1950s, the Hays Code was a dominant force in the industry even though its influence began to wane even from its inception as filmmakers continued to produce works that flaunted and pushed the boundaries. By the 1960s the Code was a laughable relic of what seemed a more ignorant past. In 1967, it collapsed under the weight of its own irrelevance and was replaced by the Ratings Code we know today.

---

11.   Artists today are quick to fight even the most benign forms of control on public speech. An aspect of the Code rarely considered today is the restrictions it placed on the creative process. While I am not an advocate for censorship, it stands to reason that directors who faced such rules were forced to be more creative than they otherwise might have been—much like a poet who must adhere to predetermined meter and rhyme. Often restraints and discipline produce higher, more meaningful Art than would have otherwise occurred.

It is probable that most of today's film releases would not exist if this Code had survived. That actually sounds like a good thing now that I write it.

It is likely there are some who would consider the loss of such movies as *Lethal Weapon* or *The Terminator* to be a net gain for our culture, and there are those who believe the Code is something we should revive. While we may disagree on the value of some of these movies, I do agree that the restrictions in the Code provided a worthy goal. My personal concern is that they were mandatory and tried to force one size to fit all.

Admittedly, the original Code allowed breathing room for context, but it still constrained God-given creativity. Human creativity is intended to reflect the beauty and skill of the Divine Creator, so strict rules which attempt to restrain artistic expression are like trying to shape a puddle of water with your hands. Like the Sciences, the Arts are effective and worthy pursuits only when allowed to develop and grow within an environment which offers both freedom and discipline—the physical, spiritual, and emotional surroundings that inspire imagination and harness creative energy. The Arts are not trivial baubles to be casually tossed into a drawer but are central to and essential for a healthy, thriving civilization.

Too often, when confronted by artistic expression that is offensive, be it film, book, song, sculpture, or painting, Christians tend to rely too heavily on censorship as the proper reaction. If an artist uses the power of their voice to insult us, we should not simply react to silence it. Rather, we should look to oppose their free speech with our own free speech.

Argument can be a beautiful thing, a foundation to human advancement, and a product of working minds. Jesus did not simply dwell among us to make proclamations all day long. He argued His case. He used examples, provided demonstrations, told stories, and countered evil thoughts with godly reality. When confronted by the Pharisees—whom Christ knew would lead Him to His painful death—He did not censor them. Rather, Jesus Christ mocked them, debated them in public, and showed them to be the pathetic legalists they were. That should be our tactic as we battle our media opponents.

When a film such as *The Last Temptation of Christ* is released, we find it offensive and agree it should be roundly denounced. We should not, however, move to have it banned. Instead, we should seize the opportunity to educate the public, work to counter its message. We should look forward to talking about why it is wrong, why it is offensive, why it is dangerous.

How else will souls around us hear God's
truth and find hope?

The Christian faith is strong enough to withstand the ponderous works of Martin Scorsese. *The Last Temptation of Christ* is indeed blasphemous and we should react with that in mind. However, when we begin to take a stand that the film should not be allowed to be viewed by anyone, we begin to trip through the minefield of our own intolerance.

If we suppress speech, even blasphemy, we set ourselves to the same standard—we establish that we, too, should have our speech suppressed. This is the natural result of working against God's Word:

> So in everything, do to others what you would have them do to you, for this sums up the Law and the Prophets.[12]

> And do not be conformed to this world, but be transformed by the renewing of your mind, so that you may prove what the will of God is, that which is good and acceptable and perfect.[13]

How can we, on one hand, demand that something which does not fit our standards be demolished while, on the other hand, we complain our voice does not get heard? We set up the very condition of "might makes right," for whomever has the strongest arms will have the strongest voice.

If I were to say or do something deemed wrong, even blasphemous, to another group, I would rather they counter me in like manner than deny me my voice. A society ruled by religious fiat is populated with slaves. Freedom of choice, freedom of speech is paramount when it comes to what is and is not available within our culture.

---

12. Matthew 7:12
13. Romans 12:2 (NASB)

10

The Ratings System: Making the Irresponsible Seem Responsible Since 1968

"Good people do not need laws to tell them to act responsibly,
while bad people will find a way around the laws."

———Plato[1]

I HAVE TAUGHT FILM CLASSES, DISCUSSED FILMS WITH COUNTLESS CHRISTIANS, and reviewed films online for years. If you ever meet me and are at a loss for what to say, simply ask my opinion of a movie. Your conversation worries will be long gone. I love talking about movies and, in particular, I enjoy talking about them with other Christians.

Christians bring a wonderful backdrop of faith and history to film viewing and have a perspective that can open new avenues of interpretation. A Christ-follower who gets it, who understands how films work, is a delight.

There also are G-Rated Christians who use the subject of film as a means to express their righteousness. Smart, educated, successful, grown men have looked me square in the eye and proudly claimed, "I do not watch any movie above G." Others have made the same claim but have not seen anything but

---

1. Widely attributed to Plato though no specific citation reference could be located. The quotation does correlate to Plato's doctrines as cited here: http://plato.stanford.edu/entries/plato/. Accessed May 2010. Quotation can be found at http://www.brainyquote.com/quotes/quotes/p/plato161536.html and www.wisdomquotes.com/000341.html.

PG-Rated films. When I hear this, I pause to see if the person is joking. They never are.

I retort with the natural question, "Why would you do that?" I get the response that Hollywood makes junk, or the individual does not want to be tempted, or they are all just sex and violence. At that point I am tempted to ask, "If you've not seen any movies, how do you know they're so corrupting?"

Then there are the permissive Christians who put little or no thought to their movie selections. Perhaps they have some restraint when it comes to their children, but otherwise they just go with the flow.

One of the biggest problems of both the G-Rated Christian and the gluttonous Christian is they place faith in the ratings system bureaucracy. The G-Rated Christian holds the ratings as the determiner of whether they see a film. The gluttonous Christian consumes everything, with a nod to the ratings if they check them at all.

The MPAA

The Motion Picture Association of America (MPAA) is the organization which places ratings on movies based upon the decisions of their rating board, the Classification and Rating Administration (CARA). CARA consists of ten to thirteen board members appointed by the MPAA. Some portion of the board will view each submitted film. The panel will then judge the film and, based on items such as cursing, violence, sexual imagery, and suggestiveness, will apply a rating to the production. Current ratings are G (general audience), PG (parental guidance), PG-13 (parental guidance for viewers under 13), R (restricted), and NC-17 (no one under 17 admitted—formerly X-Rated).

A rating can be contested by the film's producer. Often films which receive an NC-17 or R Rating will argue for a lower score. If the producer disagrees with the rating received, they have the option to re-cut their film and resubmit it to the panel. In other words, they can eliminate offending material to get a lower rating.

We must understand that the MPAA's primary goal is the protection of the movie industry. Issues concerning the general public are secondary and always viewed through the lens of the organization's main purpose.

The ratings system, itself, originated following the dismantling of the Production Code. As films slowly crept around the restrictions of the Code and public and professional opinion turned away from self-censorship, the MPAA built the ratings system. Instead of telling film producers what content restrictions they had to meet, the industry removed all barriers to creativity and placed viewing responsibility upon the audience. When the film industry's central public policy became "buyer beware," directors were free to do as they pleased. The ratings were a formality to keep conservative busybodies and politicians at bay.

After adoption of the ratings system, American cinema was revitalized; new voices and forms emerged. Film's standards of morality lowered and more violence filled the screen. Frank talk about sex and lingering shots of nudity became normalized. Liberated filmmakers could express themselves in ways previously unavailable and could explore myriad topics previously untouched. The changes occurred in 1968. In 1970, the X-Rated film *Midnight Cowboy* won the Oscar for Best Picture.

In his brief history of the code, *The Birth of the Ratings,* the system's architect, Jack Valenti, offered this recollection of the development of the X-Rating:

> Our original plan had been to use only three rating categories, ending with R. It was my view that parents ought to be able to accompany their children to any movie the parents choose, without the movie industry or the government or self-appointed groups interfering with their rights. But NATO [National Association of Theatre Owners] urged the creation of an adults only category, fearful of possible legal redress under state or local law, I acquiesced in NATO's reasoning and the four category system, including the X-Rating, was installed.[2]

Hence, the only reason any distinction was made between adult content (*Body Heat*) and flat-out pornography (*Debbie Does Dallas*) was because of external pressures from representatives of local theatre owners concerned about real-life fallout back home.

Valenti openly admits he sees nothing wrong with, and actually cites a right for, a parent to take their child to see hardcore sexual imagery. With Valenti's mindset, you should see that the ratings system has nothing to do with protecting anyone other than film executives.

What Do the Ratings Really Mean?

A G-Rating should tell everyone they can watch the movie and not be offended—you can take a three-year-old and your elderly Aunt Ginny. But hold on. Ratings are helpful only to a certain degree when making decisions regarding the content of film.

As a parent, I use them as a tool to decide if I should let my kids see a film. If a film gets an R-Rating, I understand it is not for my eight-year-old to see.

---

2. Jack Valenti. How it All Began, The Birth of the Ratings. http://www.filmratings.com/about/content2.htm. Last accessed July 2009.

But what about the lower ratings? Can he watch PG-13 movies like *Iron Man 2* or *Star Trek*?

It is not wise to rely on the ratings system when making these kinds of decisions. Parents and others concerned with a film's content should understand that the ratings themselves actually tell very little about a movie's content, and just because a film is devoid of offensive material does *not* make it a movie worth seeing. It may not be a matter of quality but of message.

A G-Rated film can still contain messages some parents find offensive— the promotion of blatant disobedience of parents (*The Little Mermaid, Aladdin, Finding Nemo*), paganism (*Hercules, The Lion King*), or animal worship and eco-spirituality (*Brother Bear*). These types of messages should be a real concern for Christian parents. The ratings system is also *not* a proper judge of the spiritual value of a film (*Pocahontas*), so before you let the young ones view a film, look beyond the ratings and consider what a film is saying.

Context Counts

If a Christian is only interested in avoiding content such as nudity, sensual scenes, harsh language, and violence, then yes, the ratings will work to a certain degree. The problem is what the ratings do not cover: context—the area of greatest concern for Christians.

In his scathing denunciation of the ratings system written for *Variety* Magazine, "'A' for Adult Opens Up New Possibilities," famed film critic Roger Ebert took Valenti to the woodshed over the nebulous system, in particular the use of the R and NC-17 Ratings:

> In the name of providing guidance for parents, Valenti has presided over an explosion of smutty material that should be 'A' but is being retailed as 'R.' This is the Summer of Raunch, and Valenti and his hypocritical rating system are its authors.[3]

In his article, Ebert suggested the ratings system stifles artistic freedom for the sake of sparing studios' potential box office revenues. Ebert also proposed that if the MPAA was serious about rating the content of films, it would develop an "A-Rating" which would cover films with content too explicit for children but not lurid enough to be consider pornographic.

While we can argue over the actual value of sparing films' extreme content from the rigors of the ratings system, Ebert's proposal reveals a basic flaw in the MPAA's processes. The ratings are a one-size-fits-all system that cannot explain itself. It defines content but not context. If the ratings system cannot parse the difference between hardcore porn and legitimate artistic

---

3. Roger Ebert. 'A' for Adult opens up new possibilities. *Variety.* Jul. 22, 1999. http://www.variety.com/article/VR1117744086.html?categoryid=9&cs=1&query=roger+ebert+valenti Last accessed October 2009.

expression, how can it handle more delicate contrasts, such as the difference between the violence in *No Country for Old Men* and that in *Scarface*?

We, the audience, should be asking, Is there nudity? Is there violence and strong language? But we should also be asking, *Why* is there nudity? What *causes* the violence? Is the language *necessary*?[4] These questions are the difference between a passive audience who accepts what the industry places before them, the fearful populace who buries its head in the sand, and thoughtful movie-goers able to make intelligent decisions in how they spend their time. This deeper level of consideration is what we must strive to achieve and what will be discussed in the chapters to come.

---

4. See Chapter 26 for a more detailed presentation of this important topic.

11

Christians and the Culture: Backseat Driving on the Road to Hell

"Turning the other cheek doesn't mean
accepting the arguments
of evil men."[1]
——K., regarding an online commentary

ONE OF THE MAIN FUNCTIONS OF ARTISTIC EXPRESSION IS TO HOLD A mirror up to society and reflect what truths may hide from normal view. Our entertainment industry, with its opinion of Christianity, has held up a fun-house mirror then complained we look funny.

Through the past fifty years American Christians have been asked to turn every cheek they have as they are pounded with the constant drumbeat that followers of Christ's teachings are intolerant fools. Christian theology has been openly maligned in films and television, and this misrepresentation is marketed to a worldwide audience.[2]

Christ-followers endure a parade of slights and insults to Christ while secular humanism marches brazenly into every aspect of our lives. Some advise us

---

1. Comment of the Day: Stop Being Christian, It Makes Me Feel Funny. Good News Film Reviews. http://www.goodnewsfilmreviews.com/2009/03/comment-of-day-stop-being-christian-it.html#comments. Last accessed March, 2010. Used by permission.
2. An ironic twist is that most Americans profess to be active Christians; so the entertainment industry has loudly proclaimed a majority of their American audience is inherently wrong and dangerous. [In 2008, over seventy-five percent of American adults identified themselves as "Christian." It should be noted that the term "Christian" can be broadly defined within the context of the survey. (Barry A. Kosmin and Ariela Keysar. *American Religious Identification Survey, 2008*. Trinity College. Hartford, Connecticut.)]

to forget the barbs, to take the mockery—it is all part of being a Christian. Peter told us to expect to get hammered for our beliefs: "However, if you suffer as a Christian, do not be ashamed, but praise God that you bear that name" (1 Pet. 4:16).

Acceptance of the mockery and criticism of the secular culture may appear to be the Christian thing to do. It gives, however, the illusion of a moral superiority over those who do the insulting: *They're lost sinners so of course they're going to attack us.* We can rationalize away the feelings: *The truth's a hard thing to bear*, and *Sinners react as sinners will.*

It is Christ-like to forgive (Lk. 23:34), it is Christian to be patient (Ps. 37:7–9, Pv. 19:11), but it is *not* Scriptural to be a doormat for those who are wrong:

> When Peter came to Antioch, I opposed him to his face, because he was clearly in the wrong. — Paul (Gal. 2:11)

> You stiff-necked people, with uncircumcised hearts and ears! You are just like your fathers: You always resist the Holy Spirit! Was there ever a prophet your fathers did not persecute? They even killed those who predicted the coming of the Righteous One. And now you have betrayed and murdered him—you who have received the law that was put into effect through angels but have not obeyed it. —Stephen (Acts 7:51–53)

When we take the insults of the ungodly lying down and let those who abuse us do as they please, we can grow accustomed to the humiliation. Let yourself be a victim too long and eventually you will be defined by your victimization.

It is a grave mistake to define ourselves by the perceptions of today's cultural leaders. We must return to defining ourselves by our service to Christ:

> But even if you should suffer for what is right, you are blessed. "Do not fear what they fear; do not be frightened." But in your hearts set apart Christ as Lord. Always be prepared to give an answer to everyone who asks you to give the reason for the hope that you have. But do this with gentleness and respect, keeping a clear conscience, so that those who speak maliciously against your good behavior in Christ may be ashamed of their slander. It is better, if it is God's will, to suffer for doing good than for doing evil. — Peter (1 Pet. 3:14–17)

The conflict between church-goers and the Arts is a long, ongoing scuffle of ideas and ideals. Traditional religionists favor a more rigid and lawful society. Conversely, artists' natural inclinations toward feelings and emotional examination often sets them against the rigors of faith. Yet despite their natures, the influence of Christ's presence imposes itself upon an artist's work.

A culture fueled by Christ breeds the best of human endeavor. Regardless of Shakespeare's, Mozart's, or Da Vinci's confrontations with authority, they were still held to a high standard because of the overriding Christian influence on their thinking and culture. These standards, bolstered by the Christian worldview, allowed their talents to flourish.

Today, the Christian mold has been broken and replaced with something far less constructive. Our civilization once produced foundational works that fed the minds of generations. Now it churns out swill that cannot sustain us for a full news cycle. Where we once had the Sistine Chapel and Beethoven's Fifth Symphony, we now have "Piss Christ" and *Borat*.

Christians are notorious complainers about the trash-culture we live with, but there is one thing most Christians refuse to see: We only have ourselves to blame.

The entertainment industry insidiously portrays Christians as dangerous throwbacks to the Spanish Inquisition or the Salem Witch Trials, so Christians have turned up their collective noses in disgust at the entire industry. This has led much of the church in the United States to refuse to deal with the broader society and, thereby, has abandoned it to the millions who consume whatever Hollywood chooses to sell.

Rather than remain relevant, Christians retreated into the development of our own separate subculture. We armed ourselves with Bibles, boxed sets of the *Left Behind* series, and autographed John the Baptist commemorative plates and now stand firm against the dung brokers of Hollywood. We produce irritating pop music and pride ourselves on a straight-to-video film industry that has claimed for decades it was about to break into the mainstream.

In actuality, we have disengaged from the mainstream and settled for being an eddy, a cultural pond known as Christian Media.

Examining Our Reflection

By definition, a pond is a shallow, often stagnant body that does little beyond feed the plants within its reach. Like today's Christian media, it has no directional flow and ultimately serves no purpose beyond its own boundaries.

This disengagement from the world is a mistake and, I believe, one of the major reasons our culture is withering.

Innumerable Christians have told me they have not seen a film in years or, in some cases, have never seen one. These Christians have checked out of the culture—in direct disobedience to Jesus:

> You are the salt of the earth, but if salt has lost its taste, how shall its saltiness be restored? It is no longer good for anything except to be thrown out and trampled under people's feet.
>
> You are the light of the world. A city set on a hill cannot be hidden. Nor do people light a lamp and put it under a basket, but on a stand, and it gives light to all in the house. In the same way, let your light shine before others, so that they may see your good works and give glory to your Father who is in heaven
> — Jesus (Matt. 5:14–15).

What good is salt if it has lost its savor and its ability to permeate and preserve? What good is a light if it is hidden?

While Christian media is not inherently a bad thing, a media that leads people into theological isolation is troublesome. It is now too common, too acceptable for Christians to hide in their media echo-chambers and chant, "Be saved, and then keep to yourself." That is not enough.

God has delivered you despite your sinful nature, despite the fact you did nothing to deserve it. His grace is greater than your depravity. He died for your sins. He paid your price. You are to spread His word and share in His glory, not just with other Christians but with people who have not yet experienced His love.

Films are a mode of communication. They are a tool. It is time we used that tool to influence the world. For too long we have blamed the medium of film for how secularists have used it; we have cast all film aside or relied only on the most simplistic products because of a belief that films are corrupting. Would you refuse to ever again use a hammer because a sinner used one to build a whorehouse?

The entertainment industry is made up of people; flesh and blood human beings like us, with all the same faults, fears, and positive qualities you and I possess—people who, like us, are lost until they find The Way. With prayer, the Lord's guidance, and inventive, hard-working artists we can help culture find its way home.

It is God's people who are uniquely equipped to step into leadership positions. There are Christian filmmakers and production studios, even film departments on Christian college campuses. The foundations are in place. Why then have we failed to have an impact? Failed to counter the destructive voices in the mainstream? We have attempted to offer a healthy alternative to the poison currently offered by the film industry, but why do general audiences turn up their noses at what we produce?

Any discussion on how we define ourselves must begin with a frank look at who we are today. If we hope to produce change, we must first examine our own reflection and be honest about what is there.

12

Since We're Lost, You May as Well Let Me Drive

"There is no street for the music to rise up from. There is no time for the music to develop in a natural way that we can all embrace when it ripens and matures. That's why the general public doesn't really care. It's not that the people don't still love music; of course they do. It's just the way it is presented to them that ignores their humanity."[1]

—— John Mellencamp

LISTEN TO THE NEWS OR ANY ONE OF A NUMBER OF TODAY'S PUNDITS and you will hear that our generation may witness the fall of Western Civilization. It appears all signs indicate a societal collapse. We have abandoned all sense of morality in favor of unfettered access to pleasure. Pornography has been mainstreamed. Popular culture is strewn with references to the most debasing sexual practices. Self-abuse through drugs and alcohol are celebrated in films and television. No human flaw remains that has not been excused and promoted by our popular culture. Society believes the only sin they can be guilty of today is to judge the behavior of another person.

When future generations look back on us they will see a culture of petulant brats who held the reins to the most advanced society in human history and were still dissatisfied. For all of our advancements we have the moral

---

1. John Mellencamp. On My Mind: The State of the Music Business. *The Huffington Post*. March 22, 2009. Used by permission. http://www.huffingtonpost.com/john-mellencamp/on-my-mind-the-state-of-t_b_177836.html. Last accessed January 2010. His views on the music industry are appropriate for the film industry as well.

instincts of an abused twelve-year-old boy left alone with a bucket of frogs and a box of firecrackers.

The quickest cure for hope and happiness is to watch movies—our entertainment actively tries to depress us. We are shown American history as a sordid trail of victimization and cruelty (*1492: Conquest of Paradise, Mississippi Burning, Far from Heaven*). Modern life is displayed as being without value (*Office Space, Visioneers, Brazil*). It is as if they want us to loathe ourselves and our society.

The typical characterization of an average American is seen in films such as *Fight Club* or *Wanted*. The hero is a pathetic, office pack mule who sleepwalks through life, smart enough to know his life is meaningless but too stupid to do anything about it. Only when he is pulled into a fantastic world of violence and self-aggrandizement does he find purpose.

That message is passed to us again and again: Your life is meaningless; you are small; there is something better out there but it is beyond your grasp. Infused in this message is the claim that morality and truth are unstable. Any wonder we are a population of joyless lunks?

The Arts should enliven the spirit and celebrate the beauty of the world. Even darker works of art, such as the paintings "The Death of Marat" by Jacques-Louis David (1793) or "The Raft of the Medusa" by Théodore Géricault (1819), can inspire us with their somber beauty. They dealt with horrific subjects, but their quality and artistry are breathtaking. The cruel subject matter had a purpose, gave depth to the bleak depictions of death and misery.

Today's works are darker and their reasoning has been removed. Only the shadowy, senseless evil in men's hearts is left to splash across the screen.

When we, as Christians, examine the culture in which we live, it could be easy to turn away and leave it for dead. All of this ugliness and negativity, who needs it? The entertainment industry hails the pervert, scorns the priest, and often claims they are one in the same. Godliness is constantly insulted by artists who no longer pursue Art for its beauty but rather obsess over the hideousness in the world. Critics and awards shows offer accolades to those portraying serial killers (*The Silence of the Lambs, Monster*) and pornographers (*The People vs. Larry Flint*) while promoting intentionally offensive rants against Christendom (*The Last Temptation of Christ, The Da Vinci Code, The Golden Compass*). At times, it seems the whole entertainment industry is determined to tear down all vestiges of a solid, Christian foundation and replace it with their tenuous, secular whims.

While the lack of clear morality in modern culture has Christians reeling, the Faithful must also contend with the stupidity that defines our public discourse. The term "artist" has been dumbed-down to include the slack-jawed propagators of music videos on MTV. Literary novels must compete for bookstore shelf space with graphic novels (comic books with spines).

Much of the intellectual class has been replaced by learned loudmouths who mistake education for wisdom.

Our civilization has suffered greatly under the past few degenerate generations and the Arts reflect our shameful fall. Across the board, we have lowered our expectations to fit the abilities of an Art community that has dropped all standards save one: there are no standards. They desire a world where the rules of morality, sexuality, even gender itself, are fluid. This has led the Arts into a downward spiral. The public is so starved for creativity that we often forgo quality to satisfy ourselves with quantity. And film producers are all too happy to oblige.

We have asked little of our culture, and it has asked little of us in return, so now we live in a world where grown men still collect action figures and baseball cards and play video games while their children grow up not knowing their dad. Previous generations of adults passed time reading Dickens, Hemingway, and Steinbeck. This generation has traded in Shakespeare for Spider-Man and debates whether or not Han Solo shot first.

We are the self-esteem generation. We have been taught that we are important no matter what we do. To us, history is forgotten because it is something that did not happen to us. Our deplorable lack of knowledge of history plus our abundance of distractions has led us away from reading and learning. Our culture stopped growing because we no longer expected to build on the foundations of the past.

Today's filmmaker cannot refer to a historical event or work of art because audience members will never understand the reference. The culture-makers must, therefore, only use references to the past couple of decades. We are stuck in a cultural loop which began in the 1960s. Why else do classic rock stations that play music from 1975 still proliferate, or why are

> The public is so starved for creativity that we often forgo quality to satisfy ourselves with quantity. And film producers are all too happy to oblige.

we remaking every movie since 1968? The Gen-Xers have gotten older but have no sense of who came before them. They are left to refer to their own childhoods for wisdom—childhoods consumed by Saturday morning cartoons and primetime sitcoms. Instead of being able to recall Anthony Mann, Krzysztof Kieslowski or Akira Kurosawa, we prattle on about *Batman, G. I. Joe,* and *Transformers.* As a generation, we are desperately lost, and we do not even realize we have fallen off the track.

Christians must understand this is not our culture. I argue that what we live in today is not even traditional American culture. What is dying is modern secular culture—the product of the 1960s revolution.

Most Americans do not see themselves reflected in current culture—it has become a separate entity from the masses. Fed by corporate and governmental interests instead of stemming from a definable and organic movement of artists, it cannot sustain itself. The desperate attempts of the past twenty years—the remakes, the films based on comic books, sitcoms, and board games—are the result of a culture with nothing new or relevant to say.

Secularists and corporate controllers do not work for God, they work for themselves. Their goals are material. Their philosophies are geared toward the material. But the material decays and eventually dies. Their movement does not inspire because it offers nothing lasting, nothing that feeds an audience's soul.

True artistic movements inform and inspire. They are birthed from individuals who create great works expressing their views on the beauty, tragedy, or reality of the living world. This natural progression of the Arts has been shortchanged by the '60s generation and their agenda-driven attack on the public square.

Corporations commercialized the Arts while secularists drained away any useful philosophy or theology that undergirded the works. We removed the need for quality and intelligence, then replaced it with meaningless stylization. Artists no longer create to express truth but to make money, get political points, or incite shock from the audience. Actors and musicians no longer perform to entertain, they get on stage to become famous and cash in. This is how a society goes from Tony Bennett and Rosemary Clooney to Marilyn Manson and Brittany Spears in a single lifetime.

We have a huge void in the center of our civilization. Where are our generation's Spielberg, Hitchcock, Kubrick, Lean, or Ford? These men, in their twenties, already produced notable works foundational to their later classic films. Today's generation seems to be without great artists. There are moments of possibility— David Fincher, Darren Aronofsky, and Christopher Nolan—but they do not add up to a definable movement of any value. Corporate takeover of the Arts has sapped the ability for growth and left no crew of vibrant young artists to take the helm. What we have are corporate posers who do as they are told.

Cultural movements are born out of necessity, not preference. That is the difference between a movement and a trend. A trend is an alteration of taste. A movement is a sea of change in the way mankind thinks.

Civilizations can be defined as a continual string of experiments in how we choose to live with our fellow man. A way of life is developed, tried, then cycles its way into irrelevancy. Western culture in the hands of secularists and existentialists has begun the downward end of that cycle. The way we have chosen to conduct our lives no longer works. Our culture is failing.

Christians should prepare themselves to rush in to fill the void. We are the carriers of truth in a land of lies. This is not a call for a new oligarchy bent on theocratic rule, but for the rebirth of common standards of decency and intellectual vigor. Christians have been whining in the backseat of the cultural car for too long. The path of self-worship has led us astray. We must turn from our low natures and strive for the higher esthetic found only in the Master Creator.

Western culture is desperate for a vibrant, meaningful artistic movement. God has provided us with the tools necessary to direct this culture back to the right path. I propose this movement come from our ranks, our artists. It is time for Christians to stand up, grab the wheel of this society, and steer us in a godly direction.

The Structure of Film: Seeing What's Right in Front of You

13

What Are Films?

"You do ill if you praise, and still worse if you reprove
in a matter you do not understand."[1]
—— Leonardo da Vinci

IT IS TIME TO CHOOSE THE BLUE PILL TO CONTINUE THE ILLUSION OR THE red pill to plunge into the knowledge of reality. The information which follows will change the way you view movies. If you have any inclination toward continuing mindless viewing habits, stop reading now. Put the book down and walk away, for if you continue things will change. You will know how the rabbit got into the magician's hat.

Am I being overly dramatic? Many people, even weeks after hearing my lecture, comment that they will never see film the same way—they have a new appreciation, see elements never before noticed. Some people do not appreciate knowing how things work, so you have been warned. Now swallow your pill. If it was the red one, read on.

What is the big revelation, the brilliant epiphany that descended upon my simple mind while sitting in that Bible class? What will forever change the way you see film?

All films are stories.

---

1. *The Notebooks of Leonardo Da Vinci, Volume I.* Jean Paul Richter, translator. Plain Label Books. 1970. 896. Used by permission of Dover Book.

That was it. If we were sitting across the table from each other, you would be slowly blinking your eyes and eventually stutter, " . . . aaaand?"

To understand film you must understand one simple fact: all films are stories. *Dr. No., Blazing Saddles,* and *King Kong* work in the same way as "Little Red Riding Hood," *Don Quixote,* and *For Whom the Bell Tolls.* With few exceptions, every film ever released was written before it was produced. Screenplays (the script) create the story. Movies are, in essence, stories brought to life and flashed upon a wall. This fact explains why recent generations use films in the same way previous generations utilized books. At their core, they both serve the same function: to tell stories.

Story is an amazing device when you see it as a form of communication. Stories are forms of conversation used to frame an argument, to explain how the world works. Each story we are told, whether in book form, a film, or the big fish tale Uncle Bud guffaws over every Thanksgiving, communicates insight into this world we inhabit.

Imagine I catch my daughter lying to me. I can tell my daughter in a straightforward fashion that lying is wrong. She may or may not get the point, and if she does not I will never know because she will probably lie about it. Another option is to provide her an example of why lying is wrong, to give her young mind a cause-and-effect to ponder. I tell her the story of "The Boy Who Cried Wolf" and through this brief tale I have shown her how lies only lead to mistrust and trouble. Now she understands the message and it has been reinforced with vivid consequences. She is far more likely to remember this example than a common warning.

All stories have this affect whether we acknowledge it or not. From cautionary fairytales ("The Boy Who Cried Wolf," "Hansel and Gretel") to broader works (*Moby Dick, Macbeth, The Great Gatsby*), stories provide explanations of how the world works and offer advice on how we should live our lives. This is why we end tales with, "and the moral of the story is. . . ."

The moral of a story reveals its worldview—"one woman can change the world" (*Erin Brockovich*), "freedom is worth sacrifice" (*Braveheart*), "believe in an impersonal, amoral, spiritual entity that divines special gifts on hippies in bathrobes" (*Star Wars*).[2]

---

2. "The Force" promoted by *Star Wars* results from a person's midichloreans count, meaning a person's blood determines their abilities and worth, demonstrated by the Jedi's rescue of Anakin Skywalker from slavery following his identification as being one of their kind. So, when taken in context of the whole slew of films, *Star Wars* asks us to support a gang of rebellious, Buddhist-esque elitists who operate within the realm of a race-based, secret society.

Uncle Bud's Fish Tale

The use of Story to make a point goes back to the time of cave paintings. Plainly telling facts has never been enough for us; we are compelled to flesh out our facts with drama. Uncle Bud cannot simply tell you he caught a fish, he has to develop a narrative, a story around the event.

> I was out on the lake with your Aunt Missy. Well, you know her, she'd rather pick up needles with her eyelids than be fishin.' So she's whining back there at the back of the boat and eventually I'd had it. I started readyin' to head on home when, whadda ya know, I got a bite—and it were a big one. My line zipped out and I started reelin'. That fish was a fightin' me and fightin' me. I dug in my heels, then I slipped on some bait and went down—wham—flat on my back. The pole flew outta my hands and shot across the boat.
>
> I thought sure all's lost when, lo and behold, I jumped up and saw my pole's wedged between the engine and the hull. I scrambled back, yanked out my pole, and pulled for all I's worth. That fish fought me for every inch, but I got that sucker right outta the water. Biggest fish caught in that lake in a decade.
>
> Well, I get the fish and turned 'round to show Missy and she ain't there. I looked 'round and she ain't in the water, either. I's startin' to consider something might be wrong—then I see her on the shore givin' me a gesture. Turns out when I fell back against the boat, it knocked her plumb out into the water. She couldn't get back in the boat and, naturally, well, I obviously couldn't hear her while fightin' with such an enormous fish, so she'd just swum to shore. Yep, that was the day I got the biggest fish in a decade and your Aunt Missy left me.

The fact Uncle Bud caught a big fish is transformed into a story of his broken marriage. He battled the fish and his wife and eventually outlasted both. His fact, "I caught a big fish," turns into a tale about perseverance. It reaffirms that, indeed, there are fish to catch and shows how one goes about getting them. Deeper, however, Uncle Bud's fish tale offers a worldview where hard work and patience pay off; there is a cause-and-effect in our universe between effort and reward, indeed, work is deserving of reward and promotes the idea that being a complaining, unpleasant spouse is a bad thing. It also shows that being a dismissive spouse can lead to divorce. All of this from a fish story.

We are not simply compelled to tell stories, we long to hear them told. For Christ-followers this should be particularity apparent since our faith is taught to us in story form. Narratives of Adam and Eve, Noah, Jonah, even Jesus Christ are told in the pages of Scripture. We read these stories and react to them in the same way we react to other stories, whether fiction or non-fiction.

As we will discuss later, it is not accidental that Jesus expressed truth by telling stories called parables. If for no other reason than this, it is vital for Christians to understand what stories are and how they impact our lives. It is also critical for Christians to understand that, just as Jesus taught through storytelling, so does our enemy. We must learn to discern when the stories we hear lead us astray from our walk with God.

14

The Story We Tell Ourselves

"What has been will be again, what has been done will be done again;
there is nothing new under the sun."[1]

WHEN YOU READ A BOOK, WATCH A MOVIE, OR LISTEN TO SOMEONE drone on about their vacation, you are an audience to a story. The hope of all audiences is that the time invested will be well spent. This hope stems from more than a desire to be entertained, though entertainment is certainly part of the equation.

People like to be preached at during a movie the same way they want to have an animal rights activist give them a tour at the zoo. The last thing most people want when they watch a movie is to be told what or how to think. We do not crack open a Dickens novel or toss in a Francis Ford Coppola movie and think, "Good. I'm gonna learn something," but learn something we will. While we sit back and enjoy that movie, book, or television show we are also delivered a moral message. Ever heard of 'the moral of the story'?

How can we be preached at and not even know it? In this case it is because we are being entertained. The entertainment aspect of movies sweetens the moral message, but the lesson is there and it is delivered in a surprisingly systematic way.

Each story begins with a Central Question—Will the boy get the girl? Can the hero learn to forgive? Can you fight city hall? The hero struggles through

---

1. Ecclesiastes 1:9–14 (NIV)

various trials on his way to learning the moral of the story—and in that ending we see the Answer to the Central Question.

We inherently recognize this structure and unconsciously expect to hear it when we hear a story. When the structure is broken, we lose interest and begin to grumble. If the middle of the story is too long, we become bored. If the Central Question is not posed clearly enough, we are confused. When the final Act does not answer the Central Question or does not show the Central Answer in practice, we feel the ending was a letdown. As naturally as we expect food to taste good and sleep to revitalize us, we expect stories to be delivered in this systematic, fulfilling way.

All cultures tell stories. Ancient Mayans, Chinese, Chaldeans, and Inuit made storytelling central to their cultures—transmitted one generation's wisdom to the next, all infused with valuable lessons. Even in many of today's tribal societies the office of storyteller is sacred and holds religious weight. In both Middle-Eastern and modern Western society this is seen, to a certain degree, through Biblical stories—stories accurately passed from one generation to the next until recorded by Moses or Samuel or John. Through storytelling, people consolidated their beliefs and an identity was created.

Why do we tell tales of great heroes and terrible villains? Our answer may lie within the astounding fact that across all times and cultures, people not only told stories, they told the same story.

From Gilgamesh to Cinderella to Harry Potter, all stories follow the same path. In effect, they are the same story. Yes, I am saying that *The Count of Monte Cristo* follows the same narrative path found in *Fletch*. From Native American myths, to centuries-old Sub-Saharan African folktales, to Norse legends, our stories have the same foundational structure and characters. No matter the place or the time, in its essence Story remains the same and, collectively, tells the same narrative. Its repetition connects all of mankind. We are compelled by a strange urge to repeat this identical story, in one form or another, to all who will listen. This is what I call The Great Story.

The Great Story

Ultimately, the only differences between one story and another are ornamental. Each is nearly identical in structure. [2]

Great minds have spent decades of research in attempts to define the structure of Story. Luminaries such as Joseph Campbell, Otto Rank, Lord Raglan, Phil

---

2. While I call this structure The Great Story, much of this material is not original to me. The classic three-act structure can be traced back to Aristotle. It has been fleshed out by numerous intellectuals such as Joseph Campbell, who lifted the term *monomyth* from James Joyce to describe the structure.

Cousineau, Georges Polti, Christopher Vogler[3], and Alan Dundes have all written books and essays on the subject, explored the subject with academic poise. Despite all the relentless, dry writing and stuffy talk, the work of these men produced fascinating results.

The Great Story is a simple story we react to positively whenever we encounter it. Like a house, this story has a framework that keeps it stable. The common way this structure is expressed is that it has three parts: a beginning, middle, and an ending. In practice, it looks like this:

> Having reached the end of my rope, I decided to make a change.
> I went to the store and bought a flamethrower. I came home to
> get rid of those pesky squirrels once and for all.

As clumsy as this is, it replicates The Great Story. Following the three-part structure, it provides a beginning ("Having reached the end of my rope, I decided to make a change."), follows with the middle ("I went to the store and bought a flamethrower."), and then seals the deal with an ending ("I came home to get rid of those pesky squirrels once and for all.").

Every story deemed worthwhile follows this basic structure. Not to say that this particular story is worth telling; it is rather abrupt and unpleasant. However, this is the basic structure for all stories, be they from ancient China, the Roman Empire, or by a Canadian in a Toronto bar explaining how he lost his foot to a badger.

If the storyteller follows the traditional story structure, we instinctively understand the gist of the tale. Comprehension breeds a willingness to agree and, by extension, to enjoy what is being said. Now, the tale I have about purchasing a flamethrower to do away with the pests in my backyard may not strike you as a rational tale (and it is not rational, for those of you still on the fence about that), but by following the set structure, I have laid out a story which explains what I am doing and how I plan to do it.

Each part of this story has a purpose and serves the whole. You, as an audience, expect each part of this structure and react negatively if any parts are missing.

> Having reached the end of my rope, I decided to make a change.
> I went to the store and bought a flamethrower.

The story does not satisfy without the last sentence, does it? It goes from being oddly over the top to being downright threatening. We need each part of a story but, in particular, we need the beginning and the ending.

---

3. Vogler's work *The Writer's Journey: Mythic Structure for Writers*, is a standard text for aspiring screenwriters and film students. Vogler takes Joseph Campbell's heroic journey and makes it readily accessible, removing the intellectual musings Campbell was prone to allow. Anyone interested in getting a quick but solid understanding of the basics of story structure is well advised to read this popular book.

Notice the change made here:

> Having reached the end of my rope, I decided to make a change.
> I came home to get rid of those pesky squirrels once and for all.

The beginning and the ending were kept. We still have a story without the middle.

The beginning of a story is simply a question. At the start of a story, an inciting question is asked—it incites or initiates the drama of the story. That question is the foundational problem that will be resolved by the telling of the story. In the illustration above, the question is, "What is the change?"

Within the ending of a story, we are given the answer to the inciting question. In the example above, the answer to "What's changed?" is that I have decided to get rid of all of the critters that infest my yard. We only need a beginning and an ending to make sense of a story.

So, what is the deal with that whole middle part? The beginning and ending of a story are the *what* of that story; the middle of the story is the *how*. The middle contains one or more possible answers to the question, and, within the ending, we discover the correct response and can answer our Central Question. This format is how successful stories are achieved.

But let us look deeper. There is a more detailed structure hidden within our myths, legends, parables, and folktales. Careful examination reveals a pattern, and marked similarities begin to appear within these tales. The story of *Sweeney Todd: The Demon Barber of Fleet Street* is not significantly different than *Robin Hood*; the Chinese folktale "Aniz the Shepherd" is much like the Mayan tale "The Rabbit and the Coyote." Though these stories are different in time, place, and details, their structures are the same.

The Four-Act Structure

I break from the standard three-act structure because, in my opinion, what is normally seen as Act Two should be two separate acts: the Rise of and the Fall of the Hero. So this is the basic structure of all story:

Question	Act 1	Act 2	Act 3	Act 4	Answer
		Reversal			
	Beginning	The Rise	The Fall	Resolution	

Not much to look at, is it? The truth is, that simple graph contains the guts of human culture. Now *that* is saying something.

A traditional story is most easily broken down into four equal parts. Each of these parts represents a specific section of action known as an Act. Each of these Acts has a purpose that serves to move the story forward.

Act One is the beginning. During this time the hero and his friends are introduced, we are often introduced to the villain and his minions, and the Central Question is posed.

Act Two is what I call The Rise of The Hero. In Act Two the hero begins his journey. He collects his allies and tools and heads out. During this Act, the hero is given a special gift or piece of wisdom or knowledge which he will use along the way.

Then everything falls to pieces.

The Reversal occurs at the exact middle of the story. Now the hunter becomes the hunted.

In *Pirates of the Caribbean: The Curse of the Black Pearl,* Elizabeth Swann's blood does not end the curse. Barbossa and his men must stalk Will Turner. In *Raiders of the Lost Ark,* Marian is kidnapped by the Nazis. Indiana Jones loses her and believes she has been killed.

After this reversal, everything goes to pot for our intrepid hero and he experiences the lows of Act Three.

Act Three is The Fall of the Hero. What was once easy is now hard, and nothing goes his way. During this Act, no matter what the hero does, he fails. All of his options are exhausted and, by the end of the Act, it appears all hope is gone. He is as successful as a beer vendor at a Baptist pastoral convention.

Then he dies.

The hero always dies—in a manner of speaking. About three-fourths of the way through Act Three—seventy-five minutes into a two hour film—the hero appears to die. His car explodes, he gets shot, he is seen going over the side of the cliff, he is pulled underwater until the bubbles stop rising to the surface. The other characters, and the audience, believe that he is dead.

Then, against all reason, he is reborn. It was someone else who was in the car, he exposes his bulletproof vest, he grabbed a vine as he went over the cliff and is hanging for dear life, he appears on shore down river.

After his death and rebirth, the hero is renewed and somehow more heroic. His determination is sparked, he has become stronger and smarter through the experience, and he is ready to bring this conflict to a close. He rallies his companions and heads straight for the villain.

Act Four is the conclusion. The hero and the villain compete until only one remains standing. With the final conflict resolved,[4] the hero proves his effectiveness and returns home.

The Dénouement (pronounced dā-nū-mah) is a brief epilogue added to the end of the end of a story to show the results of the hero's efforts. In the dénouement, we see the moral of the story in practice. Everyone is happy, everything is resolved.

That is the Four-Act Structure in a nutshell. That is the story we tell each other every day. It is present in our novels, jokes, commercials, and stage plays.

This Four-Act Structure is the building block of all narrative. Every memorable—and note that word memorable—story follows the path of The Great Story. If a story wanders too far off this narrative path or takes too radical a shortcut, it will fail to fully reach its intended destination. In the same way that a listener is naturally uncomfortable with a sour note in a piece of music, the moviegoer can sense when this natural Act structure is incomplete or uneven. He will find any distortion disturbing or, even worse, boring.

Regardless of culture or time period of creation, this basic structure is how mankind has naturally told his stories, so this is also the structure of all films produced today. When you watch a movie and feel a sense of déjà vu—think to yourself, *Sure seems like I've seen this a thousand times*—you are absolutely right. You have seen it before.

It should not be surprising to learn that since The Great Story presents the identical series of events in most stories, our stories are also populated with the same heroic character. This singular hero is shades of the same person whether his name is James Bond, Will Kane, or Napoleon Dynamite. The hero retains the same traits and performs the same tasks at roughly the same places in each story told. He is surrounded by a set of characters who also retain consistent attributes and roles within a story.

Recognition of The Great Story pattern and identification of the hero are only the first steps toward becoming a more aware audience member. We must cover a great many details before we even begin to reveal the inner workings of Story. Consider the Four-Act Structure of Story to be our recipe. Now we must become acquainted with the fundamental ingredients.

---

4. Assumes the hero is successful—known in classical theatre and literature as a comedy. In tragedies, however, the hero fails and often dies at the end of the story (*Armageddon, Braveheart, Gladiator*). In a majority of these stories, the hero's death is sacrificial and his ultimate gift brings redemption to the world. Following the hero's death, the audience is given a look at the world he has saved. The evil has been undone and the world is balanced once again. Hey, that sounds like Someone else we know.

We will first look at the common cast of characters found in stories then will lay out how these characters work together within The Great Story. Once this recipe and its ingredients are understood, you will likely begin to see the underlying structure of Story in every film, television show, and book you consume.

Slasher Movies, Chick Flicks, and Fairy Tales

It is traditional to have a damsel as the hero of a slasher movie such as *A Nightmare on Elm Street, Friday the 13th,* or *Halloween*—movies in which an ominous psychopath hunts down a gaggle of teens. This damsel is bright, clean, innocent, and morally straight when compared to her friends. To speak plainly, she's a virginal princess. She still represents fertility and youth, but instead of relying on a heroic boy to help her, she is on her own. In many cases, she will have a boyfriend, but he will generally be slaughtered with all the rest and leaves her to fend for herself. The slasher movie employs the damsel archetype as a powerful image to engage teenage audiences.

The damsel archetype is also used in fairy tales intended for little girls. Disney films (*The Little Mermaid, Mulan, Sleeping Beauty*) feature a wide-eyed, peppy damsel character in the hero role. While this teen has an independent streak, her story is only complete when she captures the attention of a handsome suitor.

As girls grow into women, the damsel heroine is further developed in chick flicks. Instead of being hunted down by a murderous killer, the damsel is on the hunt to find an upstanding, eligible bachelor hidden within these morally confused, cynical times.

Chick flicks involve a group of women dealing with relationship issues. It has nothing to do with women being independent or achieving a feminist agenda since the characters spend their time pining after guys while some social rule or tradition stands in the way—he will soon marry her best friend, he is not in her social sphere, they are separated for one of a hundred other reasons.

Chick flicks are the reverse of the "boy meets girl" movies. Even in versions of chick flicks which concentrate on women as empowered individuals (*The Women*, *Fried Green Tomatoes*, *Crimes of the Heart*), their stories are still tied to their interactions within the context of relationships.

In chick flicks, the damsel shows women as an idealized version of femininity. Some feminists may claim this is the corporate image of women sold by Hollywood to the masses, but corporations exploit this image because it works. If women wanted to see tired, stretch-marked, middle-aged women in these roles instead of Julia Roberts, Anne Hathaway, or Isla Fisher, then producers would jump at the chance to meet that demand.

In the same way men find touchstones to identify masculine traits through our stupid, over-the-top action movies, so women take cues from their fairy tales and chick flicks.

15

Many Heroes—One Man

> No, no! I don't want to go! I'm too young to fly! Stop!
> I've got a wife and kids——millions of kids! Help! I don't wanna be a hero![1]
> — Bugs Bunny

NEO FROM *THE MATRIX*, FORREST GUMP, AND THE MYTHOLOGICAL Perseus appear to have little in common. One is a computer geek, the second a slow-witted runner, and the third a Greek warrior—about as different as men can get. But one thing ties each of these characters together: they are all heroes.

Each of these characters is the center of their own story and performs heroic deeds which transform them from a common person into a heroic figure. Through their transformations, their worlds are also changed for the better. Neo grows from grumbling geek with a dead-end job to become the savior of all mankind. Forrest Gump grows from an ostracized, developmentally-disabled child into a millionaire shrimp tycoon. Perseus begins as an exiled child and becomes a grand hero foretold by prophecy. Each of these characters, despite their differences, share backgrounds and personal traits.

At the center of a story is a singular, identifiable heroic character, shades of the same person whether named Jack Ryan (*The Hunt for Red October*), Annie Sullivan (*The Miracle Worker*), or Chance the bulldog (*Homeward*

---

1. Michael Maltese. *Haredevil Hare.* Warner Brothers Pictures. 1948.

Bound). Despite country, color, class, or gender, the hero[2] retains the same traits and performs the same tasks at roughly the same places in each story told.

Traits of the Hero

Like The Great Story structure discussed earlier, every hero has an identical framework. Traits and actions of the hero identify him as heroic in our collective understanding. Here are some of the major traits you can find:

> » He is of royal birth
> » Little is known of his childhood
> » An attempt is made to kill him as a child
> » He is raised in exile by foster parents
> » He is gifted
> » He is idealistic
> » He is killed but is reborn
> » If he dies, it is by sacrifice
> » If he dies, he does not receive a burial
> » He does not have a successor

Not all traits are seen in every hero, but a sufficient number of them will be found—like a character-trait buffet; a little from here, a little from there, and the hero emerges. Here is an examination of each of these traits:

He is of Royal Birth

The hero is the progeny of a special bloodline. By genetics, he is exceptional. In ancient stories, he was often the direct descendant of a king or god. In modern stories, his father is someone of importance—a powerful politician, scientist, or someone highly regarded within their industry. The heroic mantle is bestowed upon him by birthright.

Little is Known of His Childhood – An Attempt is Made to Kill Him as a Child – He is Raised in Exile by Foster Parents

The hero's childhood tends to be shrouded in mystery, often with no reference to it at all. What is revealed about his youth will usually involve some concerted

---

2. Our heroic pronoun is *he* for ease of communication. Note, however, that just as the Scriptural concept of *man* is both male and female (Gen. 1:26-27) so the Story concept of *hero* can be either male or female.

effort to kill the hero as a child. Whether attempted by the villain himself or by nature, the hero begins his life of peril at a very early age.

Following this threat of death, the hero is shuttled off to a far-away land where he is raised either in a single-parent household or by foster parents. Luke Skywalker is raised by Uncle Owen and Aunt Beru, just as Harry Potter is raised by Uncle Vernon and Aunt Petunia.

He is Gifted

The hero always has a special talent that sets him apart from others. This skill is often something as grand as a superhero's powers—Cole Sear sees dead people (*The Sixth Sense*) and Neo can control the universe (*The Matrix*).

This special skill or talent plays directly into the hero's journey and will often be a key component in saving his own life or the lives of others.

He is Idealistic

The hero is always a man of honor. The universe is a place of laws and proper conduct, and the hero strives to live under those rules.

Even when he appears to be a bad man (*The Outlaw Josey Wales, Ocean's 11, Inside Job*) he still lives by a code of conduct which identifies him as a man with admirable characteristics beneath his criminal exterior.

He is Killed but is Reborn

The hero is pushed to his limits until he exhausts all options, and the result is his death, whether literal or figurative—Neo is shot by Agent Smith (*The Matrix*); Forrest Gump is caught in a terrible hurricane (*Forrest Gump*); Jake and Elwood run out of gas (*The Blues Brothers*).

Miraculously, the hero is reborn. He survives certain doom to fight another day: Neo rises, reborn as the prophesized savior; Forrest Gump survives the hurricane to find that he and Lieutenant Dan are the only shrimpers left in the region; Jake and Elwood arrive at the Palace Hotel Ballroom, sneak on stage, and play their big gig in front of a record company executive.

If He Dies, It is by Sacrifice – If He Dies, He does not Receive Burial – He does not Have a Successor

When the hero is a good man, his death is a sacrifice for his ideals. To obtain his goal, he gives his life so others may reap the rewards, such as Maximus (*Gladiator*) or Harry S. Stamper (*Armageddon*). This is also true when one of the hero's allies perishes after the Reversal scene—Obi Wan (*Star Wars*).

Today's happily-ever-after, tidy closures demand the hero live. Historically, however, it was common to see the hero perish if his death accentuated the lessons being taught.

In stories where bad traits are displayed to show their negative results (*Macbeth, Hamlet,* or *Oedipus Rex*), the hero's personal flaws bring about his doom.

The hero, generally, does not have any children; if he has one, that child is incapable of succeeding him.

Actions of the Hero

Along with personal traits, specific actions of the hero also appear in most stories. Next time you watch a movie, look for these:

> » He disguises himself.
>
> » He attends a celebration or public gathering.
>
> » He rescues an innocent from danger.
>
> » He is betrayed by a confidant.

He Disguises Himself

At some point the hero is forced to disguise himself. Superheroes and mythological gods constantly disguise themselves as normal people; to don a disguise is almost mandatory for a spy film. The hero at some point can go no further in the fulfillment of his goal without pretense to be something he is not. His heroic status, his true persona, is too good, too moral, to advance him any further down the path he must follow, so he must outwardly appear as something else.

Psychologically he wears a mask, stoops to be human: E.T. wears a Halloween costume to avoid detection (*E.T.*); Indiana Jones dons a Nazi uniform to get closer to the lost Ark of the Covenant (*Raiders of the Lost Ark*); Sir Percy appears as an old hag to rescue families from the guillotine (*The Scarlet Pimpernel*). This alternate persona reduces their heroic status so they fit into their surroundings and are, thereby, able to continue to their ultimate goal.

He Attends a Celebration or Public Gathering

At some point he will join his fellow man in celebration of life and relationship. This scene places the hero into the community of man. Despite his superior position, he is one with us and not a separate being: Bilbo's eleventy-first birthday party (*The Lord of the Rings: The Fellowship of the Ring*); the heart-warming community get-together in George Bailey's living room (*It's a Wonderful Life*).

This scene can take place near the beginning of a story; it presents our hero at his most normal and relaxed. Since his story is centered on conflict, this scene establishes that he finds pleasure in this world and is capable of enjoying it (*The Godfather*, *Schindler's List*).

Many times, the joys of a celebration will be cut short by the conflict of the story: the monster attack ends a surprise party (*Cloverfield*); relationship issues arise during a New Year's Eve party (*When Harry Met Sally*).

He Rescues an Innocent from Danger

It may seem obvious, but note that this rescue is an important feature of the heroic story. When a hero saves the life of an innocent, he shows his willingness to sacrifice his own safety for all of mankind. He reaffirms the belief that all life is valuable and that his actions are meant to save us all. Since this helpless innocent is normally a child or a damsel in distress, there is also the underlying concept of fertility and future generations being spared by his hand. Our hero is not just out for his own glory, he is meant to save us all: Spider-Man saves a dazed boy from being crushed by a hot air balloon (*Spider-Man*); Creasy rescues Pita from Mexican terrorists (*Man on Fire*).

This element can be reversed to show depravity: In a military sweep of a small village, the hero, Private Chris Taylor, has a breakdown and beats on a disabled young man then shoots at his feet (*Platoon*). This cruelty breaks the bond we have made with Chris, the hero, and reveals that his heroic nature is waning. It should also be noted that shortly after this scene, Chris stops the gang rape of a small girl and thus fulfills his heroic charge.

He is Betrayed by a Confidant

The hero is usually a likeable guy with plenty of friends and acquaintances. Despite the love others have for him, the hero can count on the fact someone will betray him. This turncoat can be his best friend: Lloyd poisons Harry with laxatives (*Dumb & Dumber*); his mentor: Doc Hudson calls the press on Lightening McQueen (*Cars*); or even his lover: Sondra abandons martial artist Mike Terry when things get rough (*Redbelt*).

Betrayal increases the tension and conflict within a story. If the hero cannot trust anyone, he is on his own. Depending upon the nature of the film's primary conflict, the betrayal may push the hero to deal with a personal flaw or lead him directly into a fight with his nemesis.

The hero has a template that defines him. When an author breaks from this template and attempts to introduce us to a lead character who does not possess these attributes, the character appears to be less than heroic. Even the vilest horror movies and lamest 1980s teenage sex comedies must have their heroes follow this character template. Whether being educational and uplifting or exploitive and stupid, we expect to see the same hero star in all our stories.

> This transformative journey from commoner to
> heroic figure is The Great Story.

This central, heroic figure has traits so similar as to make all heroes shades of the same person—whether black or white, young or old, male or female. While it is possible to look at a variety of stories and cite heroes that are missing one or more of these traits, it is not possible to cite a hero who does not retain at least some of them.

You can pull any hero out of any story and find a fit, even if loosely, into this template. The more of these attributes possessed, the more heroic the hero will appear and the stronger the story will resonate with audiences.

There is much more we need to discover about the hero, but to see him within proper context we must discuss the other characters who surround him—the other ingredients in the recipe of Story Structure. We will also take a deeper look into the Act Structure which tells his story. Once we discuss these topics, we will return to the hero and reveal his true identity.

16

The Villain—The Hero Lost

"That one may smile, and smile, and be a villain!"[1]
— William Shakespeare

E ACH STORY IS ABOUT A HERO, BUT EVERY HERO NEEDS A VILLAIN. THE villain is first and foremost the counterweight to the hero.

In every instance, the villain is at direct odds with the hero and works to undo everything the hero tries to accomplish. In a properly told story, the hero and the villain are at polar opposites and only one can remain standing when the story is done. In many of the best stories, this conflict is to the death.

The villain makes the hero, well, heroic. The villain causes conflict, which compels the hero into action, which puts the hero and the villain on a collision course. The hero never initiates the original conflict—the hero's role exists because of the villain's deeds. Without the Evil Witch's curse, Snow White would never need Prince Charming. Without the Emperor's meddling, Anakin Skywalker would have eventually worked through all of his teenage angst and become a proper Jedi.

The villain makes the hero stronger, forces him to define his morals, gives him purpose. In the Bible's book of Job, the title character would remain

---

1. "Hamlet" from *The Complete Works of William Shakespeare.* William Allan Neilson, editor. Houghton Mifflin. 1906. 903.

unchanged, unchallenged if not for the deviousness of Satan.[2] Through Satan's plot to undo Job's faith, Job becomes stronger and is given opportunity to prove his heroic qualities and, thus, glorify the Lord.

It is through the villain's obstacles that the hero grows and comes into his own. Frederic Nietzsche was partially right: what does not kill the hero makes him stronger.

The Fallen Hero

For a storyline to balance properly, the hero and the villain must each see themselves in a heroic light. The villain must provide the hero with a formidable conflict. When the villain's goals have a moral logic that is equal to the hero's, a critical mass is achieved in the story, the author has the ingredients of a strong storyline, and the audience will be on the edges of their seats.

The villain can be viewed as a fallen hero. He may have been moral earlier in life, but now he has progressed too far or allowed some tragic flaw to overcome his better qualities. The villain knows what he is doing may not be perceived as good, but he does what he thinks is right and, when asked, can clearly explain his motivation and why he considers himself heroic.

In many respects the villain is the direct opposite of the hero. Where the hero is brave, it is likely the villain will send others to do his bidding. When the hero is honorable, the villain is corrupting.

Both characters show our dual natures and the choices we have in life. Are we to follow God? Do the right thing and perform good deeds? Or do we act devilishly and corrupt and malign those around us? As we watch the hero and the villain we often see two men who have made different choices and are living out the consequences of their decisions.

Traits of the Villain

As with the hero, the villain retains a set of characteristics from one story to the next. In effect, we have the same hero fighting the same villain over and over again in all the stories we tell. The villain may have different goals and may come in different forms (not necessarily human), but the core entity is the same.

---

2. Satan does not have a beef with Job. Satan is working to undo Job's faith, sure, but his goal is to assault God. Job is a means to an end. Despite Satan's personal disinterest, Job still attains heroic status because of the conflict centered upon him.

It would seem logical for the villain to display attributes similar to the hero, but, in fact, the villain has his own sets of unique traits. These different characteristics are what make him so destructive. The villain:

» Is a solitary figure

» Is deceptive

» Is unable to change

» Appears stronger and smarter than the hero

» Has a personal army

» Lives in a lair

» Has a god complex

Not all villains have these traits, but all have some, especially the last one. Here is an examination of each of these characteristics.

The Villain is a Solitary Figure

The villain is alone in the world. Even if he has a family, his evil deeds separate him from those who would love him.

The villain's solitude is important because it clarifies his relationship with the hero. Both characters are separate from the world they live in. Both are exceptional, and this puts them both on a higher plane of existence than the rest of the world.

The Villain is Deceptive

Those who perform evil deeds do not want people to know it. The villain works in solitude and is always secretive. He desires to never alert any authority, but also his secretiveness heightens his mystery, makes him an unstable person. The only thing you can know for sure about a villain is that you cannot trust him.

The Villain is Unable to Change

In the finale of a story, the hero learns an important lesson and applies it to his conflict with the villain. Through this lesson, the hero's morality is altered, his worldview tweaked, and in the change he is strengthened. We, the audience, also learn the lesson as we witness this change in our hero.

The villain cannot go through such a change. He cannot learn a lesson, and this stubbornness spells his doom.

This doom is reinforced in a provocative way in many stories through a false resurrection of the villain. Remember that the hero goes through a resurrection in Act Three—he appears to die, literally or symbolically, then miraculously pulls through and gains a stronger heroic status. It is common to see a quasi-resurrection of the villain in the final moments of the final act as the hero confronts the villain.

The villain will beat the hero down, destroy him in almost every way. The hero seems to be without hope. Suddenly, the hero will spring back with some extra surge of energy to surely overcome the villain. The villain will appear to be dead. The scene will become quiet and the hero will breathe a sigh of relief. Without warning, the villain suddenly lurches at the hero in one final attempt to avenge his own death. This resurrection is always short-lived as the hero quickly strikes the mortal blow.

The false resurrection is intended to show the permanence of death. When the hero dies, he is reborn; when the villain dies, it is annihilation. This permanent death results from the villain's inability to change. Since he is a stubborn figure who refuses to budge, his destruction is the only possible outcome. Like a cancer, the villain must be completely wiped out to keep him from doing additional damage.[3]

The Villain is Stronger and Smarter than the Hero

In order for the hero's journey to have dramatic force, it is vital that he be in peril. No one wants to watch a hero who is favored to win or gets what he wants with little effort. The struggle of the hero is what draws us into the story. To stack the odds against the hero, his nemesis must be bigger, stronger, and better organized. The more formidable the villain, the bigger the challenge.

J. R. R. Tolkien used this to great effect in *The Lord of the Rings*. The diminutive and harmless hobbit, Frodo, takes on the satanic Sauron and all of his armies. The old adage, "the bigger they are, the harder they fall," applies here. The toppling of a great power by a heroic little figure is more dramatic, and it strongly cements the purpose of the heroic journey.

The Villain Has a Personal Army

The villain is a man of power. He is rarely a cog in a wheel but, rather, is the one who owns the wheel. The importance of his organization is that it is an extension of his efforts to attain his ultimate goal.

If he runs a corporation, that corporation dumps waste into rivers, kills small business owners, or sells dangerous products (*Michael Clayton*, *Wall Street*,

---

3. For Christians, there is an additional subtext to this rebirth/annihilation scenario. The villain is mired in his sin and refuses to turn from it. Conversely, the hero is willing to admit his weaknesses or flaws and to change, to move toward salvation. Where the hero is reborn, the self-righteous villain is left dead in sin.

Iron Man). If he leads a church, that church has deviated from Biblical standards and become oppressive (*Footloose, The Reaping, Stigmata*), or, since many screenwriters are not biblically literate, the church has deviated from the moral sensibilities of the storyteller. When the villain is an officer in the military, he breaks the rules to fit his own vision of duty (*A Few Good Men, G. I. Jane, Paths of Glory*).

The goals of the villain are achieved through the power structure he controls. Through that structure, the villain will possess an army. It can be a literal army of soldiers or it can be a vast team of faceless lawyers, but others always do his bidding. These underlings come in two different roles, the secondary antagonist and the minions.

Every villain keeps a right-hand man for protection and to do his heavy lifting. The secondary antagonist is that right-hand man. The Emperor has Darth Vader; the James Bond villain, Karl Stromberg, has metal-mouthed Jaws (*Moonraker*); the scheming Hedley Lamar employed the blundering Taggart (*Blazing Saddles*). The villain directs the action and holds the secondary antagonist in some type of bondage. [Chapter 18 will discuss this important character in more detail.]

Other members of the villain's private army are his minions. Since every villain runs some kind of operation, he must have grunts working below him. These can be simple soldiers (flying monkeys in *The Wizard of Oz*) or members of a gang (lackeys who follow Biff Tannen in *Back to the Future*). These nameless, faceless followers have no individual thoughts or actions and their only desire is to serve the pleasure of their master. They are completely disposable and tend to be horrible marksmen.

Any time you see characters on screen who work for the villain, remember: they are not independent beings. They are merely extensions of the villain and his ultimate goal. Their actions reflect the villain and are made on his behalf.

The Villain Has a Lair

The villain always lives in a dark, foreboding place—a cave, a lair. In his dark place he is alone, free to ply his evil trade in total privacy. It also reveals the beast he has become. The villain's home is a physical representation of him.

The more chaotic the villain is, the darker and more chaotic his lair. This dark place is usually the location of the final confrontation, which also usually takes place in darkness.

The Villain Has a God Complex

The villain is an interesting character because he is, ultimately, the hero unchecked. He plots his movements and follows a moral code of his own invention. He is always a totalitarian. He squelches all opposition, refuses debate, and sees his goals and morality as superior to all others. The villain is similar to all power-hungry men in his urge to refuse acknowledgement of any authority over him.

The villain replaces God with himself. Sometimes this happens literally, such as Commodus in *Gladiator*, Gozer in *Ghostbusters*, or Xerxes in *300*. The villain demands worship. He relishes the putrid fruit of sinful rebellion common to all humanity and degrades it to its disgusting worst.

The villain plots a wholesale rejection of the authority of God and establishes his own moral code. This leads him to act outside of biblical teaching. Of course, not all villains say, "I hereby reject God and His teachings and now follow my own path," but this is exactly what he does. He places himself and his goals above all things, including God.

Little Bill Daggett from *Unforgiven* makes himself the savior of Big Whiskey. His arrogance and lack of empathy become his undoing. He is a false god (it's not accidental that Daggett tries his hand at carpentry and can only manage to build an uneven and unstable house) who brings the destructive William Munny out of retirement.

Less grand villains carry this rebellion in their hearts. They are sinful and they refuse to break away from their evil nature. This is the primary flaw of the villain and the reason he is incapable of resurrection.

Monologuing

> Bob and Lucius are sitting in a parked car, reminiscing.
> **Lucius**: So now I'm in deep trouble. I mean, one more
> jolt of this death ray and I'm an epitaph. Somehow
> I manage to find cover and what does Baron von
> Ruthless do?
> **Bob**: [laughing] He starts monologuing.
> **Lucius**: He starts monologuing! He starts like, this
> prepared speech about how "feeble" I am compared to
> him, how "inevitable" my defeat is, how "the world will
> soon be his," yadda yadda yadda.
> **Bob**: Yammering.
> **Lucius**: Yammering! I mean, the guy has me on a
> platter and he won't shut up![4]

During the course of a story, there will be a moment when the villain will stop and explain his motivations and goals. He will justify his actions to the hero and thus to the audience. Even villains who appear to do evil for evil's sake (Aaron in *Titus Andronicus*) are so consumed with evil that they destroy simply for the pleasure of destroying (Amon Goeth in *Schindler's List*), will still have a moment where they need to explain themselves.

This monologue is intended to make the motives of the villain as plain as possible to the audience.

Personification of an Idea

The villain is the personification of an idea. It might be "greed is good"[5] (Gordon Greko in *Wall Street*) or "The only sensible way to live in this world is without rules"[6] (Joker in *The Dark Knight*), but within Story the villain is the ambassador for a narrow worldview that the hero must overcome. This is another reason the villain does not change. If they stepped away from their worldview, they would cease to exist. Once the bad guy is defeated, their worldview is defeated as well. There is no separating the two.

---

4. Brad Bird. *The Incredibles*. Pixar Animation Studios. 2004. Used by permission.
5. Stanley Weiser and Oliver Stone. *Wall Street*. Twentieth Century-Fox Film Corporation. 1987.
6. Jonathan Nolan and Christopher Nolan. *The Dark Knight*. Warner Brothers Pictures. 2008.

Personification of an idea also illustrates why the actions of the villain are what drive Story. His actions are the argument, the hero's are the counterargument. As previously mentioned, a story is a question and an answer. In this, the villain is the wrong answer; the hero is the correct one.

As you view films, listen for the villain's monologue. He will tell you exactly why he is in the film and will detail the real point of the film. His brief explanation is the argument which is cast aside in favor of the counterargument reflected through the hero.

Actors often prefer to play the role of the villain to the role of the hero. The villainous role is almost always more fun. We humans seem drawn to those who perform evil deeds, whether fictitious or not. We live in a fallen world full of evil, and often we allow ourselves to wallow in its depravity. Villains in film allow us to satisfy our hunger for evil. Violent films (*Friday the 13th*, *Last House on the Left, The Devil's Rejects*) also feed the same desire.

The well-written villain exposes these weaknesses in humanity. He will be a symbol of our hubris and of our inclination for evil. At his best, he explains why we need the redemption promised in Christ Jesus—and why we can never be left to our own devices.

17

The Mentor

"Behold, God is exalted in His power;
Who is a teacher like Him?"[1]

IN *THE SHAWSHANK REDEMPTION*, ANDY DUFRESNE (TIM ROBBINS) IS wrongfully convicted of murdering his wife and is sent to prison. There he is brutalized by predatory convicts and threatened by a cruel captain of the guard. As Andy learns to cope with his life behind bars, he meets Red (Morgan Freeman), an old con who is able to procure any item for the right price. Red takes Andy under his wing and helps Andy adjust to spending his remaining years behind bars. The two men forge a deep and meaningful friendship that changes both of them forever.

The hero always has a mentor. Much like a parent provides warnings and advice to a child before they leave home, the mentor helps our hero adjust to the strange, new world through which the hero must navigate to confront the villain.

The mentor is an old salt who has worked in the trenches for years and knows all the right secrets. He knows the villain, the conflict at hand, and all the players involved. Usually the mentor has specific and secret knowledge that makes him and his explanation of the new world a vital asset to the hero. His explanations inform not only the hero but the audience. Every story needs some explanation since there is usually a considerable history—known as back-story—which precedes a story's beginning point. The mentor provides

---

1. Job 36:22

these details of the past, explains what has happened and how it affects the future.

Consider the *Star Wars* scene which takes place in Obi-Wan Kenobi's home where the Jedi Master recites to Luke the fall of Anakin Skywalker and gives Luke a light saber. This pivotal scene propels Luke on his heroic journey. It also establishes for the audience the back-story for the whole series of films. Later, Ben patiently explains the Force to young Skywalker, which also gives the audience a clear understanding of the belief system of the Jedi Knights.

Traits of the Mentor

The hero usually has absent parents; they are dead, missing, or debilitated. The mentor steps into the hero's life as a proxy parent and guides him into maturation. In this role, the mentor exhibits specific traits that enhance his ability to tutor the hero.

The common attributes of a mentor are that he:

» Is old and wise

» Gives gifts

» Has a previous relationship with the villain

» Is nearly equal to the villain in many ways

» Is near death

The Mentor is Old and Wise

The mentor is the person the hero aspires to become, therefore the position of mentor intentionally places this wise man within the role of parent. This parent–child relationship reveals that the hero, while already possessing impressive skills and abilities, still has room for improvement. The hero may be strong, but he lacks wisdom. He may be quick, but he is not skilled. There is something the hero must accomplish.

The Mentor Gives Gifts

The mentor provides not only counsel, he also will pass an heirloom to the hero such as a special weapon (a light saber), knowledge (the notebook in *Indiana Jones and the Last Crusade*), or skills (self-control in *The Matrix*). This gift may not appear significant at first but it will become immensely valuable to the hero during the final act.

The Mentor has a Prior Relationship with the Villain

Often the mentor character has survived at least one run-in with the villain —and often he will carry an internal or external scar from the confrontation. In some cases, his history with the villain will give the mentor that specific pearl of wisdom that leads to the hero's victory, such as John Connor's deep knowledge of the Terminator which in turn helps Sarah Connor survive. Consider the mentor to be Mr. Encyclopedia when it comes to the bad guys within the world of the story.

The Mentor is Nearly Equal to the Villain

The mentor knows the hero must learn to fight before he can confront the villain. The mentor takes the hero to a clearing and the two face each other. The film enters into a training sequence in which the mentor puts the hero through his paces. The mentor attacks with a sword and quickly knocks the hero to the ground. The two resume and we are treated to various images of the struggle. The hero slowly improves but can never quite win. Then, at the end of the sequence, the hero overcomes the mentor, sends him to the ground, and holds his blade to the old man's throat. The hero is now victorious.

The mentor, in his role as sparring partner, prefigures the villain. When the hero defeats his mentor, whether in a sword fight or a game of chess, he demonstrates the necessary ability to defeat the villain.

The Mentor is Near Death

It is common for the mentor to be near death. This can be a literal death, such as the cancer-stricken Adm. James Greer (*Clear and Present Danger*), or a professional death (retirement), such as detective Lt. William Somerset (*Se7en*).

The mentor, nearing death, reveals the closing of the old ways and preparation for the new as heralded by the hero. The mentor has spent his life in a world plagued by the villain. He identifies the hero and prepares him to battle the evil. Thanks to the mentor, the hero overcomes the villain and sets things right. Unfortunately, the mentor often dies before he can see the fruits of his labor.

It is common for the mentor's death to be sacrificial—he lays his neck on the block and the villain drops the axe. This death comes somewhere within Act Three and marks one of the hero's darkest moments. When the mentor dies, no one is more devastated than the hero, for he has effectively lost his father. Now the hero is alone in the world, and the solitude briefly consumes him.

The death of the mentor is an important scene. When the mentor is dying, perk up and pay attention. More times than not, the mentor will be allowed a monologue. In this monologue he will impart a final piece of advice to the hero. This piece of wisdom is the final message that takes the hero through to the end of the movie.

18

The Secondary Antagonist

Dr. Holly Goodhead: You know him?
James Bond: Not socially. His name's Jaws. He kills people.[1]

THE VILLAIN IS OFTEN A PENCIL-NECKED GEEK WITH A GRUDGE. HE IS all brain and the physique of your average computer nerd. Dr. No., Grand Moff Tarkin, Lex Luthor—not men you would be scared to bump into in a dark alley. If so many villains are just weaklings with an attitude, how are they able to take on the hero so effectively? The answer is they have grunts.

The villain retains underlings to do his bidding. He has faceless minions who act as his personal army—the Klansmen (*Mississippi Burning*), Col. Tavington's Green Dragoons (*The Patriot*), or Nazi Youth (*The Sound of Music*). Of these minions, there is one who stands above all of the rest. This one is bigger, stronger, faster, meaner, and more dangerous than anyone else in the story. He is a fear-inspiring, towering figure who seems immortal. This incredible figure is the secondary antagonist.

Where the villain is the philosophical, the secondary antagonist is the physical.

The Golem

In Yiddish folklore, there is a creature known as a *golem*—a man-made, brainless slab animated by the powers of its creator. A golem never spoke, never even had a thought of its own. It was a lumbering beast of burden that

---

1. Christopher Wood. *Moonraker.* United Artists. 1979.

lived to serve the needs of its master. Traditionally, a golem was made by a powerful person, often with good intentions, then the beast would grow uncontrollable and began killing people. Eventually it would turn on its creator.

The original Yiddish creature transformed into fictional characters (Frankenstein) as well as robotic characters like the android Maria in Fritz Lang's classic science fiction film *Metropolis*. When you see a man-made creature controlled by an individual, it is a derivative of the original golem tales.

The golem character defines the role of secondary antagonist—a material being that represents the earthly aspect of the villain's philosophy. It is a creation of the villain either literally or by influence, bound to the villain often against his will or his own interests.

One of the best examples of this relationship ever put to film is in *Mad Max: Beyond Thunderdome*. The hero, Max, is arrested in a post-apocalyptic village called Barter Town. There the local residents maintain justice by putting both convicts and legal contestants into a coliseum called Thunderdome. The brains behind Barter Town is an aged little person named Master. He is carried around by a mentally disabled lunk named Blaster. Together they make one entity named Master-Blaster. To regain his freedom, Max must kill Master. In order to get to the brains, Max must first kill the body. These two roles perfectly depict the duality of the villain and his secondary antagonist.

Traits of the Secondary Antagonist

Specific traits which define the secondary antagonist are that he:

- » Is seemingly immortal
- » Is a physical threat
- » Is fallible
- » Is held in bondage
- » May turn on the villain

Each of these traits promotes the ominous stature which makes him noticeable among the other minions who work for the villain.

The Secondary Antagonist is Seemingly Immortal

In many cases, the secondary antagonist will also be shown to be resistant to death. He may have scars, or someone may tell a brief story about how the brute survived some grim situation. These aspects give the secondary antagonist a sense of being supernatural.

The Secondary Antagonist is a Physical Threat

The secondary antagonist is a physical being and his powers rely on material threats. When he attacks the hero, he does so physically, not on the more philosophical level of the villain.

When the secondary antagonist engages the hero it is always to the death, whether literal or figurative. While the hero may spare the secondary antagonist, it is understood that the secondary antagonist would never extend the same mercy.

Even if the secondary antagonist does not literally kill the hero—kills his career or goals (*Office Space, Philadelphia, Good Will Hunting*)—the end results are shown in a physical way. If the hero loses, he will lose material goods, physical treasure. The secondary antagonist is always about the material world and that is the currency in which he deals.

The Secondary Antagonist is Fallible

Even the most threatening secondary antagonist, such as Blaster from *Mad Max: Beyond Thunderdome,* has a flaw, a weakness sufficient to enable the hero to defeat him. Like David and Goliath, the respective sizes are irrelevant. Regardless of how powerful the secondary antagonist may appear, there is always something small which the hero can use to destroy the seemingly immortal character.

The Secondary Antagonist is Held in Bondage

Like Frankenstein, every secondary antagonist is the creation of a villain. This creator-creation relationship puts the secondary antagonist into a subordinate role to the villain. The secondary antagonist, even when good at heart, is held in some form of servitude either to the villain directly or to the worldview the villain represents.

In the brilliant German expressionist film *Das Cabinet des Dr. Caligari* (*The Cabinet of Dr. Caligari*) the conniving doctor retains a sleepwalking slave named Cesare. The enslaved somnambulist is the main display of Caligari's bizarre carnival act and will prophesy and murder on Caligari's orders.

This service to evil often gives the secondary antagonist a tortured soul. He is commonly seen as a once-proud man now in bondage to evil. It is too late for him. He cannot be saved. When this aspect of the secondary antagonist is handled properly, such as with Captain Barbossa in *Pirates of the Caribbean: The Curse of the Black Pearl,* the results can be poignant.

The Secondary Antagonist May Turn on the Villain

Since the secondary antagonist is held in bondage, it is possible to see the character quietly yearn to be good. This can lead to the villain's creation turning on his master.

Examples include the Omni-Droid which turns on Syndrome in *The Incredibles* and Mongo in *Blazing Saddles* who joins with Sheriff Bart to fight Hedley Lamar.

A secondary antagonist who is a turncoat differs from others within this archetype. Left to his own devices, he may have never turned to evil. It is his service to the villain's worldview that compels him to bad deeds. This character is like a gun which can be used to protect or to murder—it all depends on whose finger is on the trigger.

A well-written secondary antagonist character is a treasure to any storyline, adds depth of conflict and increased tension. Remember some of your favorite films, movies where you were left on the edge of your seat. Many times those screenplays contained a well-rounded, fully-realized secondary antagonist in confrontation with the hero.

19

Archetypes

"Archetypes are God's thoughts
before they are actualized into, or represented in, things."[1]

Heroes never go it alone. They always have allies. Likewise, villains have their minions and underlings whom they use to advance their own goals.

Just as heroic characters are drawn from one template, allies and opponents who surround the hero also maintain similar attributes and actions from one story to the next. Friends and enemies of the hero are static character types known as archetypes.[2]

Every notable character in a story fits within at least one archetype. There are miracle workers (Pvt. Jackson [the sniper] in *Saving Private Ryan*), warriors (Sir Lancelot), and innocents (Tiny Tim), plus many others. Each fits into the framework of The Great Story and retains individual attributes, purposes, and meanings.

Numerous authors and scholars have grappled with the laundry list of archetypes. Lists and descriptions *du jour* are available to anyone curious enough to research the topic. While we do not have adequate space or time to unpack it completely, we will go over some of the other archetypes you can see in today's films.

1. Gould, Kendall & Lincoln. "Archetypes" in *The Christian Review*. Vol 26. E. G. Robinson, editor. April 1861. 178.
2. Psychologist Carl Jung founded the concept of psychological archetypes. His idea purports that we, collectively, form familiar character types in our minds and these work themselves out within our stories; we use these distinctive types to explain and define elements of our world. Archetypes are innate and universal to mankind.

The Herald

> Jack Vincennes: Oh, great. You get the girl, I get the coroner.[3]

The worst thing you could wear was a red shirt when you stood next to Captain Kirk. It was a one-hundred-percent probability you would die a horrifying death.

In almost every episode of the Classic *Star Trek* series, the swaggering Kirk transported down to a planet and took along some fresh-faced ensign dressed in a red shirt. Within moments of touching alien soil, this ensign was killed in some terrifying way—poisoned, eaten, beaten, stabbed, burned, or disintegrated. One would think that after seeing the fates of their shipmates, the remaining ensigns aboard the *U.S.S. Enterprise* would consider it a death sentence to accompany their captain.

When a red-shirted ensign was eviscerated, an important element of the story was played out: the audience was shown the stakes. The audience knew Kirk and crew were at risk of meeting the same fate if they failed their mission. This death heightened tension and, without equivocation, laid out the threat to the hero—like playing poker with someone who lays a loaded gun on the table as they deal the cards. The threat is established and the stakes are immediately raised.

The herald archetype is crucial for the success of Act One. His destruction not only proclaims the consequences to the audience but propels the hero into action.

It is common for the hero to, at first, dismiss the villain. The death of the herald character focuses the hero directly onto the conflict and leaves no question as to the immediate danger that confronts the hero. This is why the herald is almost always killed in the presence of the hero.

Female Archetypes

> Most women seem to be required to pit themselves
> against men in dramatic situations, and the men get to
> pit themselves against ideas or God.[4] – Judy Davis

---

3. Brian Helgeland and Curtis Hansen. *L.A. Confidential.* Warner. 1998. Adapted from James Ellroy. *L.A. Confidential.* Mysterious Press. 1990. Used by permission.
4. http://www.imdb.com/name/nm0001114/bio. Last accessed December 2009. Used by permission.

The Damsel

Say the word *damsel* and most people see images of Snow White or Rapunzel helplessly waiting for rescue. In fact, the word "damsel," according to Merriam-Webster, means "a young woman: a young unmarried woman of noble birth." She is simply an available girl with some form of status. While this can certainly be translated into a helpless young lass tied to the railroad tracks, it certainly does not have to be that way. She can be a vibrant, smart, and independent soul who happens to be single (Margo in *All About Eve,* Scarlett O'Hara in *Gone with the Wind,* Sophie Scholl in *Sophie Scholl: The Final Days,* Kate McKay in *Kate and Leopold*).

With a male hero, this archetype is the hero's love interest. She gives the hero something to fight for and inspires his actions. Luke Skywalker is not urged forward by some grand philosophical concept. He ventures off the dusty rock he calls home because Princess Leia is in trouble.

The damsel is a mirror of society's view of young women. She is an attractive girl who is approachable and retains many of the qualities society holds as important for young women. In our culture, damsels tend to be young, pretty, athletic, independent, and have full, flowing hair.

The unstated assumption is that the damsel will pair up with the hero. "And they lived happily ever after" implies more than just "they left the evil kingdom and went on a trip to Shangri-La." Happily ever after implies marriage and children in an idyllic setting, hence, the damsel is a symbol of fertility and the successful on-going of civilization.

Damsels do have other common attributes you can look for to make this identification. She is always young—or at least young at heart. As mentioned, she is a symbol of fertility. This means she is a representative of the next generation and the future. Her youth helps establish this with the audience. Her youth also makes her vulnerable and more easily identified as someone who needs protection.

The damsel is also a beauty. Who wants an ugly damsel? If Rapunzel looked like a donkey with weedy hair, she would still be up in that tower. Likewise for Princess Aurora of *Sleeping Beauty;* she would be in a permanent catnap.

Simply put, in order for the damsel to be worth helping, she needs to be a knockout—young, beautiful, unblemished, the promise of the future and the perpetuation of civilization. She represents innocence—a lack of corruption. She typifies Eve, the mother of all humanity, prior to digging her teeth into the apple.

The Femme Fatale

There is one universal fact about men: we are weak. Take the most powerful man on earth who possesses every personal gift and talent, display the treasure of the world before him and, despite having all the money and power he can desire, he is still flimsy at his core and can easily collapse. All that is needed to topple him is one thing: a woman.

The phrase *femme fatale* is French for "deadly woman." This term succinctly describes the entire nature of this archetype. She exists purely to destroy. In essence, she is the antithesis of the damsel's virginal status. Where the damsel is young and beautiful but innocent and represents fertility, the femme fatale is jaded, sensual, conniving, and destructive. She uses sex as a snare to trap men who are foolish enough to take her bait. Femme fatales use the hero's desires to lead him into situations he would otherwise find abhorrent (cheating, stealing, murder).

The femme fatale distorts the relationship the hero should have with the damsel. With the damsel, the hero will rush in to spare her from some evil that may cause her ruin. He rides in on his white horse, saves the day, then returns home to live happily ever after (*Taken, Legend, Not Without My Daughter*).

When the damsel is replaced with a femme fatale the hero still rides in on his white horse and fights off the bad guy, but once he defeats the villain, the femme fatale sneaks up from behind and knocks him out so she can take the gold for herself (Brigid O'Shaughnessy in *The Maltese Falcon*, Evelyn Mulray in *Chinatown*, Laura in *Brick*).

The Mother

Like mothers in real life, this archetype comes in a variety of forms. The characters can be divided into two categories: mothers who do good and mothers who do evil.

Think of them as either the Wicked Witch of the West or Glinda, the Good Witch, in *The Wizard of Oz*. Both witches are older than the heroine, both have a full set of powers and knowledge to bring to the table (except the Wicked Witch employs creepy flying monkeys), and both want to affect little Dorothy on her quest to get home. The two witches are perfect examples of the two avenues a mother character can travel. Good mothers are damsels all grown up. The bad mother is the unrepentant femme fatale later in life.

Please note, my use of the term "mother" in this instance does not necessarily mean the character literally has children. I use the term as a simple means to denote age and authority.

The Good Mother

The good mother almost always exists in a story in which the hero is female. In her role as mentor, the good mother is wise, kind, and most of all nurturing (Leigh Anne Tuohy in *The Blind Side*). Physically, she is traditionally shown to be a little plump with a warm smile and gentle tone (the Fairy Godmother in *Cinderella*). This makes her naturally pleasant to the audience's eyes since she is like the ideal mothers of real life. This natural appearance gives the audience a connection with the nurturing, care-taking women in their lives.

The Bad Mother

The opposite of the helpful good mother is the villainess, the bad mother. The bad mother is often presented as past her prime, nearly skeletal or decrepit in many instances (Maleficent in *Sleeping Beauty*, Norma Desmond in *Sunset Blvd.*, Jade Fox in *Crouching Tiger, Hidden Dragon*). While she has a distinctive personal fashion and usually dresses up, she is a wasted version of what she used to be.

The bad mother is cruel and manipulative, usually to a greater degree than her male counterparts. She is endlessly power hungry and hopes to squash the heroine and achieve her own ends (Miranda Priestly in *The Devil Wears Prada*, Regina Giddens in *The Little Foxes*). Many times the bad mother is driven by her jealousy of the young, beautiful heroine. Faded in years, she takes her revenge on youth.

Other Archetypes

The Trickster

Think Bugs Bunny. The trickster is a character who lives outside the rules of mankind. He literally plays tricks and thrives on tomfoolery and mockery.

Although this character has roots in numerous ancient cultures, Native American to European, he still remains with us today. In mythology he is often presented as an animal such as a fox or coyote; today he is usually a man such as the class clown.

Jim Carrey is best known for playing trickster characters. Carrey's Ace Ventura is a sarcastic jokester who dismantles every scene he enters, lampoons authority figures, and undoes all sense of decorum or order. Ventura also uses another common trickster trait: he relies on physical gags, including lewd humor (such as literally speaking out of his rump), to make his point.

The trickster is a narrative tool used to skewer societal norms and show the incompetence of our leaders. Just as only the jester could speak freely about the king's flaws, our cinematic jester, the trickster, successfully says things we normally deem unacceptable.

The Fool

Walking hand–in–hand with the trickster is the fool. The fool archetype is different, though, from the trickster because the fool often does not know he is funny. That is the difference between Ace Ventura and Inspector Jacques Clouseau of *The Pink Panther*.

Ventura is in command of his world, mocking it, directing it. Clouseau is a bumbler, a goof. He stumbles through his investigations, falls into clues, and accidentally causes all kinds of mayhem. Where the trickster may throw a bomb, the fool accidentally sets it off.

The fool, like the trickster, mocks authority. The fool is, more times than not, an authority figure such as a police inspector, military commander, politician, or parental figure.

The fool will bungle the simplest of tasks but come out unscathed at the end. Clouseau will get his man, but he will do so unconventionally and with far greater effort than necessary. Due to this eventual success, it is common to have the fool archetype in the role of the hero.

The Rival

Everyone wanted Han Solo to be the hero of *Star Wars*. Actually, many people may be confused and think Solo was a heroic character, just as a majority of people said Jack Sparrow was the hero of *Pirates of the Caribbean: The Curse of the Black Pearl*. Both Sparrow and Solo's characters are rival archetypes.

The rival archetype is the narrative blood-brother of the hero—the mischievous, despoiling, evil twin. He retains many of the same attributes of the hero, may even have similar or parallel goals. The rival may try to move in on the hero's girl—which was a good thing in the case of Solo since Luke and Leia did not know they were siblings.

There is always one paramount reason the rival is not the hero. The rival has a flaw—a grand, massive flaw that cuts through the center of his personality. Usually this flaw involves pride, greed, or a mixture of the two. This crack in the rival's character usually leads them to fail where the hero succeeds.

When the villain woos the same woman as the hero, he is also a rival character. This, more than any other device that I know of, facilitates their contentious relationship. Men are competitive creatures and are never more cutthroat than when it comes to matters of love. A woman's affection is one of the finest treasures men know. When two equally-paired men set their sights on the same gal—well, now that is the stuff of great stories.

The Shape Shifter

The term shape shifter is not so much an archetype as it is a trait. This trait accompanies an often negative character, such as the trickster, fool, or femme fatale. Shape shifters are unstable, not only physically but also in their loyalty. In some cases these characters literally change shape and form, as with the femme fatale character Mystique (*X-Men*), who transforms herself into any shape required to reach her goal, or the fluid Odo (*Star Trek: Deep Space Nine*). Jacques Clouseau (a fool) constantly changes disguises.

The shape shifter provides stories with a sense of chaos and uncertainly. It is common for a real shape shifter to present a situation where the hero will have identical copies of an ally in front of him—one the true ally and one the villain or one of his minions (*X-Men, Terminator 2*)—and each claims to be his friend. Unable to see a difference, the hero must choose.

It is possible for even the hero character to be a shape shifter any time he dons a disguise or alters his appearance (think superheroes). The difference between a shape-shifting hero and the hero who simply wears a mask is whether or not the shape shift changes who they are. There is a stark difference between Bruce Banner becoming the Incredible Hulk and Luke Skywalker dressing up as a Stormtrooper.

In a story, every character has a purpose. The archetypes can be viewed as positions on a team. The herald, the mentor, and the secondary antagonist—each acts to compel the hero on his journey and toward his ultimate victory over the villain, in much the same way a football team will set up formations to enable the running back to break through the defensive line and score a touchdown. Everyone is set up and maneuvered to achieve the goal of the story, to deliver truth—or the appearance of truth—to the audience.

We now understand the players in a story, who they are and what they are meant to do. But how do these archetypes work to deliver a story? With the understanding that we now have of the characters, we can revisit the Four-Act Structure and take a closer look at how it all comes together.

THE RIPLEY EFFECT

Women are traditionally typecast in stories as either Eve, innocent and lovely, or as the spiteful Lilith of Jewish tradition, sexually potent and manipulative. Until recent times, these roles rarely changed. Today we find women in roles previously reserved for men in what I call the Ripley Effect.

Ripley was a transformative character first introduced in Ridley Scott's *Alien*. Scott utilized Ripley's sexual appeal and mixed it with her maternal strengths to create a modern feminist heroine. This melding of attributes created a potent concoction that made her post-masculine: she stepped outside of being defined by her relationships with men.

Ripleys are a queen bee: unique, strong, and in charge. The men around them are useful drones, there to assist her but otherwise have little impact or affect on who she is as a person.

This twisting of the heroic archetype proved to be attractive to modern audiences and led to a flood of films and television shows with more heroic female leads—*Thelma & Louise* or *Xena: Warrior Princess*.

The Ripley heroine, while popular, also has a drawback. Her independence from men leads to her becoming more masculine. One look at Sarah Connor's bulky biceps in *Terminator 2: Judgment Day* says it all. Because of this masculine trait, in recent years the Ripley character has transformed into a sometimes laughable parody of itself. Filmmakers have removed the masculine physical qualities and recast her as a ninety-pound supermodel who beats up two-hundred-fifty pound linebacker-sized soldiers (*Æon Flux, Resident Evil, Underworld, Tomb Raider*).

20

The Great Story

WE HAVE SEEN THAT THERE IS A FOUR-ACT STRUCTURE THAT SUPPORTS The Great Story. We have also met the major players who populate this story. Now we have the recipe and all the ingredients. All that is left is to mingle them and see how The Great Story comes together.

The Great Story Within The Four-Act Structure

The Great Story comes in four main sections. As mentioned earlier, each section is known as an Act. An act is a contained block of narrative that moves the story in a particular direction. These four acts can be further unpacked, for they contain many elements and actions important to the progression of Story. We will start with a quick review of The Great Story structure.

Act One is the beginning. We are introduced to the hero, the villain, and the Central Question.

---

1. World of Quotes. http://www.worldofquotes.com/author/groucho-marx/1. Last accessed December 2009.

Act Two is The Rise of The Hero. The hero begins his journey, collects his allies and tools, and heads out.

The Reversal overturns the hero's main goal and sends him reeling.

Act Three is The Fall of the Hero. Everything seems to fall apart. This culminates with the hero's death and rebirth.

Act Four is the resolution. The hero and the villain duke it out and determine who wins the central conflict.

The Dénouement is an epilogue that showcases the positive results of the hero's journey.

The Great Story in Detail

It is important to remember as we move through this litany of essentials that it is common for authors to move these elements around as they weave their stories. You will find, for example, Gift Giving or Death of the Herald often in Act One but sometimes in Act Two. For some of the elements listed, it is more critical that they are present than where in the story they reside.

Act One: Introduction

The purpose of Act One is to establish the purpose of the story—to identify the Central Question. We are introduced to the hero, villain, any surrogates, and the world in which the story takes place.

The Prologue

This is the opening of the story. We are quickly introduced to the story's world as it currently exists: the time period and environment of the story—a city, a ranch, or out in space. Often, this is an idyllic place (the shire in *The Lord of the Rings: The Fellowship of the Ring*).

The prologue is also used to quickly establish that things are amiss, as in *Star Wars* with Princess Leia's humble ship pursued by the ominous star destroyer which seems to consume the whole universe.

Introduction of the Hero

Almost immediately we are introduced to the hero and the role he plays in the world (Oscar Schindler wheeling and dealing in a nightclub in *Schindler's List*, Cinderella being abused while serving her evil stepsisters).

The introduction of the hero and his world are used as narrative tools[2] and, when written to their full effect, can be used to show a deep contrast within his life.

My favorite introduction is of Indiana Jones in *Raiders of the Lost Ark*. In the opening scene he is shown as being in command, knowledgeable, and dangerously accurate with that bullwhip. He is immediately established as an adventurer. Next scene he is shown as a mild-mannered professor who is tripped up by a flirtatious student. That is great filmmaking.

Central Question

Will the Nazis get the Ark of the Covenant? Will Rick help Ilsa escape with her husband? Who the heck is "Rosebud"?

Within the first ten minutes (and hopefully within the first three) the Central Question of the piece will be posed to the audience. This question is the reason for the story, the main dramatic thrust of the tale that will consume the hero until it is resolved.

Introduction of Villain and Central Conflict

The villain may not actually rear his head right away. Often the opening moments of a story present the secondary antagonist rather than the villain (Ring Wraiths in *The Lord of the Rings: The Fellowship of the Ring*). It should be noted that the secondary antagonist is a surrogate of the villain and will refer often to the villain so the audience understands there is a bigger fish to fry.

The Central Conflict is tied directly to the Central Question. "Will the boy get the girl?" only works if there is an obstacle—social class issues, competing suitor, an argument between the couple. This obstacle is the Central Conflict.

Where there is conflict, there is a villain at work. Within the first ten minutes of a film, the villain's plot is introduced to the audience. It is this conflict that will propel the story forward. The opening conflict may be legal issues like those that ruin Mr. Incredible and foreshadow the antagonism of Syndrome (*The Incredibles*), terrorists entering a skyscraper (*Die Hard*), or the secret distribution of five golden tickets (*Charlie and the Chocolate Factory*).

Death of the Herald

What prompts the hero into action is usually the death of someone close to him. This can be, and normally is, a physical death (Uncle Owen & Aunt Beru in *Star Wars*, Gazerbeam in *The Incredibles*, or Murron MacClannough

---

2. story-writing devices used to drive the plot forward and to shape the audience's view of the writer's fictional world

in *Braveheart*) but is often a symbolic death such as loss of station or privilege (Bobby is cut from the team in *Bull Durham*).

The scene in which the Death of the Herald occurs does not necessarily need to fall within Act One, but it should come no later than the middle of Act Two.

Refusal of the Call

The hero always has something else he would rather be doing than saving the world. He will initially turn up his nose at the idea of running off on a fool's errand. Luke Skywalker has his commitments to his uncle (*Star Wars*), Maximus (*Gladiator*) dismisses politics and the role of emperor, Neo ignores Trinity's presence on his computer monitor (*The Matrix*).

The hero is forced to weigh his options and finally comes around to doing what is right—not that the hero is amoral or does not care, he simply prefers to let things work out without causing a disruption to his way of life.

Crossing the Threshold

The Death of the Herald or other impending doom (the ship capsizing in *The Poseidon Adventure*) compels the hero into action. This change of focus provides an important scene for the hero and establishes his character by providing him with a dramatic moment.

The hero has resolved to enter the strange New World and to confront the cause of the conflict.

Act Two: The Rise of the Hero

Act Two sees the hero as he begins his journey into a strange New World. He must learn the rules of the game, get to know the other players, develop his skills and abilities, then challenge the villain for the first time.

The New World

The hero has left the safety of his home and entered a foreign land. This can be literal (Luke in Mos Eisley in *Star Wars*) or a completely new experience (the night shift in *Night at the Museum*). The new world can also be less fantastic, say the beginning of a romance (*Sideways, When Harry Met Sally, The Notebook*) or the beginning of a performance tour (*Walk the Line*).

It is important for the rules of the New World to be established. You can introduce a giant spider in a story with hobbits, orcs, and elves, but it will not work as well in, say, *Love Story*. Act Two explains those ground rules.

They can be laws governing physics (people can fly and run on tree tops in *Crouching Tiger, Hidden Dragon*) or rules of morality (Reverend Moore proclaims dancing is evil in *Footloose*). Once the rules are set down, the audience has expectations of how things will work.

During this law-giving segment, all rules are confirmed. If the storyteller tries to introduce new laws of behavior later than Act Two, the audience will feel the new rules are forced.

Sometimes a second herald meets his demise as a means of showing the rules of the New World. If a second herald character dies, it will normally impact another secondary character more than it will the hero (the murder of the advisor to Prince Edward by Longshanks in *Braveheart*).

Allies and Enemies

In the New World the hero will take on new friends and allies as counterpoints to all of his new enemies. This can also be a time when the hero, if returning to a known place or occupation, is reintroduced to old pals or nemeses (*Sexy Beast, Raising Arizona, Payback*). These relationships, rivalries, and grudges are normally all laid out in the first half of Act Two. Rules and relationships are foundational to the story's interactions.

The Mentor and the Gift

At this point, the mentor provides the hero with that special gift which will aid the hero in defeating the villain. This can be a physical gift (light saber, magical cape, or key). It can also be a piece of wisdom ("turn left to turn right" in *Cars*).

Conflicts and Tests—The Rise

With allies and enemies established, the hero begins his journey to take on the villain. Simple challenges arise with increasing consequence. These challenges often end with the hero making a new friend (Joe and Betty Schaefer in *Sunset Blvd.*) or enemy (Edmund and the Witch in *The Chronicles of Narnia: The Lion, the Witch, and the Wardrobe*). The hero is learning to walk in the New World and is gaining experience, knowledge, and support.

The First Confrontation

The hero encounters a direct underling of the villain. This can be a group of minions (Stormtroopers closing in on the *Millennium Falcon*), the secondary antagonist (the new and improved Omni-Droid in *The Incredibles*), or the villain himself (Voldemort in *Harry Potter and the Order of the Phoenix*). This clash puts the hero in direct conflict with the villain for the first time.

This is the first serious test of the hero's mettle. In most cases the hero passes this test and is established as a viable threat to the villain.

Following the First Victory

The hero often gains a critical piece of knowledge or a device as the fruit of his first victory. In a detective mystery this can be a huge piece of the puzzle or a vital lead. The clichéd scene in which we see the hero grab a dying man and coerce information from him often happens here. This victory will embolden the hero and his cohorts. Things are going well, or so they think.

The Villain's Interest is Aroused

The first conflict forces the hero out into the open. The villain, who did not take the hero too seriously, is now aware there is a definite challenger in the mix. The first victory is not a critical injury to the villain but it is a darn nasty flesh wound.

The villain then decides to take action to reduce the threat. The reaction of the villain may not come immediately and is often reserved as the centerpiece of the Reversal scene.

Reversal

Everything gets turned on its ear. Everything the hero has worked for is reduced to rubble. In most cases, this change in direction is due to the villain's reaction to the hero appearing on his radar in the previous Act.

This Reversal can be as devastating as Bryant announcing to Rick Deckard that he will need to terminate his love interest, Rachel, because it has come to light that she is a replicant (*Blade Runner*). It can also be something as benign as Judge Smails buddying up to Danny in *Caddyshack*. After Danny wins the caddy golf tournament, Judge Smails approaches the college-bound teen and asks, "I'm having a little party at the yacht club this Sunday. I'm christening my new sloop. What are you doing next Sunday?" When Danny responds he is free, Smails generously offers, "Great! How would you like to mow my lawn?"[3]

Whatever happens at the Reversal, things are never the same. The villain responds with notable impact to the hero's rise. The hero's goal is overturned. The glory of his early victories evaporates. From this point forward, the villain determines he will stop the hero by any means necessary. There can be no peace until the hero defeats—utterly destroys—the evil one.

---

3. Brian Doyle-Murray, Harold Ramis, and Douglas Kenney. *Caddyshack*. Orion Pictures Corporation. 1980.

The hero's goals will also be swapped. Rather than simply arriving at Alderaan, Luke Skywalker and crew discover the planet has been destroyed and they are captured by the Death Star.

Act Three: The Fall of the Hero

The hero hits the skids. His heroic stature is tested and it appears he is not a hero after all, only another regular guy. His earlier successes are eclipsed by a series of failures. What had risen now falls.

Conflicts and Tests—The Fall

In a replication of the tests of Act Two, the hero is given a series of tasks and challenges through which he must navigate. Still reeling from the disorienting Reversal, the hero usually fails these tests. Unlike the progressively improving but minimally rewarding victories in Act Two, the failures in this Act are grave. The hero's failure can lead to others being injured or killed.

The Death of the Mentor

At the mid-point of Act Three, there is a mini-reversal of sorts—think of it as an aftershock to the earthquake the hero experienced at the Reversal. It is usually during this mini-reversal that the mentor unexpectedly dies. Well, it is not completely unexpected—he is old and, in most cases, sickly. But it comes as a serious blow to the hero.

The death of the mentor can also occur at the opening of Act Four and function as a final push for the hero to take on the villain one-on-one (Obi-Wan Kenobi's death in *Star Wars*).

After this mini-reversal, the hero is left alone in the New World (Frodo feels abandoned after Gandalf's death in *The Lord of the Rings: The Fellowship of the Ring*).

The Second Conflict

A second big conflict hits the hero, similar to the First Conflict, but this time the hero loses and loses big. He may lose a meaningful ally (the mentor), but most importantly, the hero loses his way.

The hero symbolically is lost—he acts anti-heroically, breaks a vow or is in danger of becoming evil himself. Conflict at this point is almost always with the secondary antagonist or directly with the villain.

The Death of the Hero

At the end of the Second Conflict, the hero is killed in some sense. Normally, this is not a literal death although a literal death can occur. In most instances, the hero appears to die (Indiana Jones goes over the cliff in a tank in *Indiana Jones and the Last Crusade*). Other examples include the hero seeming to lose his legal case (*Philadelphia*) or the boy who loses the girl and goes on a suicidal drinking binge (*Wedding Crashers*). The important thing here is that the hero has lost all control and life has gotten as bad as it can get.

The Resurrection

The hero then comes out the other side of the dilemma as a new man. He is not dead, he is reborn. He snaps out of the coma, pops up from the murky depths, or seizes on the perfect legal defense. And something occurred during his death, during his low point, that reminded him of his first goals and rekindled his original passion. He was once lost, now he is found—and he is ready to get busy.

Act Four: The Answer

This is it—the end of the story. The hero is finally heroic and the villain is ready to fight. The forces of good and of evil are set and the game begins. In Act Four, all conflicts are resolved, all subplots are decided, and all players get exactly what is coming to them. At the end, the Central Question is answered and the moral of the story is expressed.

Entering the Lair

With his refreshed sense-of-self intact, allies in tow, and all comforts left behind, the hero boldly goes to where the villain resides. No more messing around. His aim is for the throat and he risks everything.

Dispatching the Minions

The villain deploys his first line of defense—a horde of faceless minions (the Immortals in *300*, the townsmen of Big Whiskey in *Unforgiven*). The hero must take out the lower-rung guys before he can get to anyone of importance. This shows us the hero's new abilities and bravery.

Dispatching the Secondary Antagonist

Once the hero has cleared the field of all minions, it is time to take on the secondary antagonist. This is usually done by using the special gift (the whistle in *Mad Max: Beyond Thunderdome*) or by his wits (tricking of Mongo in *Blazing Saddles*). If the hero overtakes the secondary antagonist by force, it will come at a huge physical cost. The secondary antagonist is a serious foe and will most likely kill at least one of the hero's allies.

If he survives, the secondary antagonist will often betray the villain. This is when we learn the secondary antagonist is enslaved to the villain in some way or that he does not respect his boss as we had assumed. This swapping of loyalties is seen at the end of *Slumdog Millionaire* when Salim turns on the thug Javed and allows the enslaved Latika to escape.

Moving Deeper into the Villain's Lair

With the defeat of the secondary antagonist, the villain is on his own. The hero also loses contact with his allies and must finish the fight alone.

The hero summons all of his courage and heads into a deep, dark place which the villain calls home (Frodo enters Mount Doom; Col. Kurtz's eerie, shadowy temple home in *Apocalypse Now;* Fletch enters Alan Stanwyk's dark home office in *Fletch*).

The Final Conflict

The hero confronts the villain in darkness. They both state their case then do battle. The villain is stronger, smarter, and richer; the hero is, well, heroic. He is sturdy and he is right. During this battle, the hero will seem to be at the point where he loses—he has a blade pressed to his throat or he is gripping the edge of a cliff with the villain glaring down at him.

Use of the Gift

The hero now uses the special gift or wisdom received from the mentor. It can be the magic sword or device, but it assures the thorough destruction of the villain. The hero rises triumphant over his foe in replication of the Resurrection which occurred in Act Three.

Death of the Villain

The villain, now defeated, drops dead. This may be literal or figurative. He could lose a critical legal case (Al Capone in *The Untouchables*) or lose the big match (*Dodgeball: A True Underdog Story*)—or, he could just die.

The False Resurrection

The Villain will attempt a resurrection similar to the hero's but will fail. A villain (Jason from *Friday the 13th*) will appear to be dead then suddenly lurch at the hero one last time. The villain struggles then suddenly drops over, dead.

This is seen in *The Untouchables* when Al Capone tries to physically beat Elliott Ness after the final verdict, or in *Unforgiven* when the townsfolk cannot bring themselves to shoot at Munny, too scared they will miss and he will come after them.

Getting the Reward

Once the villain is dispatched, the hero acquires a piece of knowledge or a treasure from his foe. Luke literally takes his father back from the Emperor in *Return of the Jedi*, Buggin' Out posts the picture of Malcolm X and Martin Luther King on the burned wall of Sal's pizzeria in *Do the Right Thing*, and Westley and Buttercup share the perfect kiss at the end of *The Princess Bride*.

The Central Answer

As the villain expires, the hero or someone close to the hero will state the moral of the story. This is a direct and, hopefully, unequivocal statement of fact. It will explain the lesson learned by the hero through his adventure. This is the Answer to the Central Question.

How will the boy get the girl? According to *Pirates of the Caribbean: The Curse of the Black Pearl* he will—but "sometimes an act of piracy is what's needed"[4] (meaning he can get the girl if he throws off normal social behavior). The simpler the moral, the stronger the story.

The Dénouement

In the end, the very end, we see the result of the hero's journey upon his world. The moral of the story is put into practice and we clearly see the results.

At the end of this story structure, you, the audience, witness a New World where the author's point-of-view is expressed and explained. An example of this can be found in *Frequency*—aged firefighter Frank Sullivan has saved his own life and spared his wife from a serial killer. The final moments of the film show Frank and his family enjoying life together, everyone safe and happy.

You were given a proposal at the beginning of the story, shown the various possible results, and presented with the final and correct answer. That is the purpose of The Great Story—to deliver truth.

---

4. Terry Rossio and Ted Elliot. *Pirates of the Caribbean: The Curse of the Black Pearl*. Walt Disney Pictures. 2003.

When I look at this structure, I see a beautiful tapestry both in fiction and in real life. Now that you have seen this structure, it is likely you will also begin to perceive it revealed in the stories you see on screen, read in books, or encounter in well-done advertising. The next time someone tells you a story about something that happened in their lives, try to identify the parts of The Great Story in their tale. When you hear a joke or view a news story, see what aspects of The Great Story appear. In many cases, it should be obvious.

Why do we identify with this story structure? Where does it come from? Since it appears inherently across time and cultures, it would seem logical to assume we were designed to respond to it. Something drives us to use this story and to recognize it as the foundation of truth. The answer to why Story resonates so deeply within us can be found in the identity of the man at the heart of The Great Story: the Hero.

21

The Hero Revealed

"To us is born a child, a son is given to us, and the rule is on His shoulder;
He is called Marvelous, Advisor, Hero, Eternal Father, Peace of Prince;"[1]

LORD FITZROY RICHARD SOMERSET RAGLAN WAS A BRITISH SOLDIER and independent scholar who produced *The Hero, a Study in Tradition, Myth and Drama.*[2] Published in 1936, Lord Raglan's book laid out characteristics of the hero found within the heights of Western and Indo-European literature. From Oedipus to Hercules to Robin Hood, Lord Raglan discovered common elements between the heroes we have both celebrated and created throughout time.

One heroic character, we will refer to him as the mono-hero, has guided generations through eons of civilization. The mono-hero has worn different names—Gilgamesh, Winston Smith, Anne Elliot, Sam Spade—and has

---

1. Isaiah 9:6, direct English translation of Martin Luther's translation of the original: "Denn uns ist ein Kind geboren, ein Sohn ist uns gegeben, und die Herrschaft ist auf seiner Schulter; er heißt Wunderbar, Rat, Held, Ewig-Vater Friedefürst;" (Luther Bibel, 1545). Used here for Luther's translation of the Hebrew *El gibbor* into the German *Held* (hero). Most English translations are "mighty God" (*gibbor*, "mighty"; and *El*, "God"). Translation of these two words have long been a point of contention between Christian and Jewish scholars due to the word *El* and whether it means "God" or "god" (as in not Yahweh). Our focus, however, is on the word *gibbor* translated to mean simply "mighty." *Gibbor* as "mighty" is in the sense of the might of a champion and holds the connotation of a hero, like the man at the heart of our stories. The use of "hero" also provides an elegant pairing of contrasts within the verse: "advisor, hero / eternal father, Prince of peace": counselor contrasts with eternal Father—both are wise but the advisor is a cold teacher of wisdom while Father denotes loving instruction; hero contrasts with the Prince of Peace in that one denotes a warrior while the other a conservator of freedom from disquieting or oppressive thoughts or emotions. This contrast reveals Jesus as a champion—willing and able to drop the hammer, but fair and patient.
2. Lord Raglan. *The Hero: A Study in Tradition, Myth and Drama.* Vintage Books. 1956.

lived in all eras in all locations. Regardless of country of origin, class, or even gender, the hero is always the same person with the same traits.

If an individual hero can be defined by identifying his unique traits and actions, it is logical to assume that we, in our storytelling, refer to that same individual. The hero and his story are the source of all stories. The mono-hero's Great Story is foundational to our search for and expression of truth.

In story, we insert a truth into a narrative structure in an attempt to prove the validity of our idea. For this structure to produce a proof of truthfulness, the structure itself must be true.

To apply truth to this structure, we, as a society, use The Great Story to demonstrate the validity of our idea. We look at The Great Story as being true, and we hold other tales up to it to show our ideas are also true—hold a copy up to the original to prove the copy's worth. If the narrative structure, itself, is inaccurate, the expanse of human culture has based itself upon a lie. The Great Story must be true if there is to be any plumb line for truth.

The desire to know the identity of the hero has, for ages, captivated people interested in the study of societal customs, traditions, and cultural beliefs. If The Great Story and its hero are consistent, as it appears they are, then the Story and the hero must be identifiable. Folklorists and other scholars have labored to explain the various traits of the mono-hero and his monomyth. In Chapter 15 we discussed some of these basic traits:

» He is of royal birth
» There was an attempt to kill him as a child
» Little is known about his childhood
» He is raised in exile by foster parents
» He is gifted in some way
» He is idealistic
» He is killed but is reborn
» If he dies, it is by sacrifice
» If he dies, he does not receive a burial
» He does not have a successor

We also detailed central events in the hero's story:

» Disguises himself
» Attends a celebration or public gathering
» Rescues an innocent from danger
» Is betrayed by a confidant

Lord Raglan's Thesis, Heroic Traits, and ... Who is He?

Lord Raglan produced a list of twenty-two characteristics which seem to build the ultimate hero. Lord Raglan's list has been widely attacked by intellectuals as being false and incomplete, but it is still taught and studied by story geeks and screenwriters around the world.

Lord Raglan admitted his list could be incomplete and did sheepishly offer the caveat that his list was arbitrary in its construction. In defense of Lord Raglan's work, I state first that despite the continual haranguing against its scholarship, his compilation has never been displaced by any more definitive list. Over seventy years of study and no one has dethroned Lord Raglan's list of twenty-two traits.

Lord Raglan's work, with all its scratches and dents, is a viable vehicle for study. Until it is successfully replaced, it will remain the definitive work on the subject of the person of the hero. I intend to look at Lord Raglan's twenty-two heroic characteristics and then offer my opinion on whom I believe this man to be.

Lord Raglan's Proposed Template of 22 Heroic Traits:

1. The hero's mother is a royal virgin.
2. His father is a king.
3. His father is a near relative of his mother.
4. The circumstances of his conception are unusual.
5. He is reputed to be the son of a god.
6. At birth, an attempt is made to kill him.
7. He is spirited away.
8. He is reared by foster parents in a far country.
9. We are told nothing of his childhood.
10. On reaching manhood he returns to his future kingdom.
11. He is victorious over the king, a giant dragon, or a wild beast.
12. He marries a princess.
13. He becomes a king.
14. He reigns uneventfully.
15. He prescribes laws.
16. He loses favor with his subjects.
17. He is driven from his throne.
18. He meets with a mysterious death.
19. He dies at the top of a hill.
20. His children, if any, do not succeed him.
21. His body is not buried.
22. He has one or more holy sepulchers.

In *The Hero: A Study in Tradition, Myth and Drama*, Lord Raglan compared the mono-hero to a number of history's literary and legendary figures. He intended to prove that our legendary figures were just that—legends—not real people. His contention was that anyone who fit this framework did so as the result of human molding rather than reality.

To his credit, Lord Raglan found a structure that fits most known Western heroes and he does express his point in a respectable way. His premise is solid enough; I believe his conclusions are faulty.

When we take Lord Raglan's list and apply it to some notable fictitious figures we can see how many heroic traits they each hold:

> » Apollo (11 traits)
> » Robin Hood (13 traits)
> » Perseus (18 traits)
> » King Arthur (19 traits)

Couple the heroic character with civilizations' widespread use of the Four-Act Story Structure and a pattern emerges in the stories we have told ourselves throughout time.

Why do we do this? What is it about this structure that we find so alluring? What causes men from many nations, ages, and religions to defer to it? And if we are so compelled to use this heroic frame, why do we not know who this mono-hero is? We know details about the man; we know what he has done. This solitary heroic figure just needs to be identified.

I believe the hero is Jesus Christ and that The Great Story is the story of the Bible.

Dundes, Raglan, and Price

In his dissections of legendary heroes, Lord Raglan ignored the person of Jesus Christ. I believe it safe to assume that Lord Raglan did this to avoid unsettling confrontations with his church, publisher, or conscience.

Other studies have been done on identification of the mono-hero in the person of Jesus Christ, the major project being University of Berkley professor and folklorist Alan Dundes in his work, *Hero Pattern and the Life Of Jesus: Protocol of the Twenty-fifth Colloquy.*[3] Is the heroic structure the blueprint for Christ? According to Dundes and others, the answer is a resounding no. Dundes finds only seventeen of the heroic points in the person of our Savior. Then again, Dundes follows with a relentless rant which sexualizes the Christ in a

---

3. Alan Dundes. *Hero Pattern And The Life Of Jesus: Protocol Of The Twenty-fifth Colloquy, 12 December 1976. In Quest of the Hero.* Otto Rank, Fitzroy Richard Somerset Raglan, and Alan Dundes. Princeton University Press. 1990. 179.

way I am certainly not going to go into here. Suffice to say, he sees Freudian sexual connotations within the crucifixion, of all things.

Excesses aside, Dundes offers a vigorous debate against Jesus' claim to Lord Raglan's heroic traits. Dundes lays out the life of Jesus and scores the Nazarene with only seventeen of the traits. He cites items such as number 12, He marries a princess, as being why Jesus fails to match up to Raglan's heroic template. He also disputes points 2, 3, 11, and 20.

Scoring seventeen of the twenty-two traits makes Jesus more heroic than Apollo (11) but less heroic than Oedipus (21). Oedipus garners the most traits of anyone, which makes him Dundes' most heroic character in existence.[4]

Dundes's refutation of the heroic stature of Jesus has become a cornerstone for those who wish to cast Christ in a mythological light. Christian skeptic, humanist, and Professor of Theology and Scriptural Studies at the Johnnie Colemon Theological Seminary, Robert M. Price, is author of *The Incredible Shrinking Son of Man*. He states in another of his works, *Deconstructing Jesus:*

> One does not need to repair to the epistles to find a mythic Jesus. The gospel story itself is already pure legend. What can we say of a supposed historical figure whose life story conforms virtually in every detail to the Mythic Hero Archetype, with nothing, no "secular" or mundane information, left over? As Dundes is careful to point out, it doesn't prove there was no historical Jesus, for it is not implausible that a genuine, historical individual might become so lionized, even so deified, that his life and career would be completely assimilated to the Mythic Hero Archetype. But if that happened, we could no longer be sure there had ever been a real person at the root of the whole thing. The stained glass would have become just too thick to peer through.[5]

I believe there is error in the thinking of both Dundes and Price. Mythic literature is perfected in a way the Gospels are not. Myths and mythic literature are intentionally idealized and are clearly not written as history. A close examination of the Gospels reveals something startling. The Gospels are history—the true crime story of humanity.

It is ludicrous to argue that Jesus was a humdrum, normal guy onto whom we have foisted the heroic archetype to serve our own purposes. He is presented in the Gospels in a historical context, not as a hero of folklore.

---

4. Oedipus fulfilled a prophecy which said he would kill his father, marry his mother, and bring disaster on his city and family.
5. Richard M. Price. *Deconstructing Jesus*. Prometheus Books. 2000. 260–61.

Critics do not accept the possibility that The Great Story and its hero are devices the Almighty Creator designed into our souls for a purpose. Yet, The Great Story is a tool we use to discern truth because it is the ultimate truth—it is given to us by God. We know it, we react to it, we use it every day whether we realize it or not.

Myths from ancient times resemble the story of Christ because they are a premonition of what was to come. Like a blind date being told to watch the crowd for the woman with a red rose in her lapel, God placed in our hearts a way to recognize His coming and to identify Him—the One who is Truth.

Our intrinsic need for God and the human hunger for telling this story are one in the same. When we tell a story, we express our desire for the clarity of the Lord. English author and scholar J.R.R. Tolkien wrote the following during the process which led his friend C. S. Lewis to salvation:

> Now the story of Christ is simply a true myth: a myth working on us in the same way as the others, but with this tremendous difference: that it really happened: and one must be content to accept it in the same way, remembering that it is God's myth where the others are men's myths; i.e. the Pagan stories are God expressing Himself through the minds of poets, using such images as He found there, while Christianity is God expressing Himself through what we call "real things." Therefore it is true, not in the sense of being a "description" of God (that no finite mind could take in) but in the sense of being the way in which God chooses to (or can) appear to our faculties. The "doctrines" we get out of the true myth are of course less true: they are translated into our concepts and ideas of that which God has already expressed in a language more adequate, namely the actual incarnation, crucifixion, and resurrection.[6]

All other heroes are merely faded copies of Jesus. My children put on my boots and stomp around the house; in the same way, we dress up our heroes in Jesus' traits and pretend to touch divinity. This may explain why we insist our heroes be more than just normal people. They are extra-ordinary. They are super-human, more like God than like us, and they tell us how to live.

How does Lord Raglan's list of twenty-two traits match up when we look at the life of Jesus Christ?

---

6. Joseph Pearce. *Tolkien Man and Myth: A Literary Life.* HarperCollins. 1998. 60.

Jesus Christ and the Heroic Traits

Trait 1: The hero's mother is a royal virgin

The mother of Jesus, Mary, was a virgin (Isa. 7:14; Matt. 1:23–25; Lk. 1:27, 34) and she traced her lineage back to King David (Matt. 1:1–16, Lk. 1:27). She was betrothed to Joseph, also a descendant of King David (Lk. 3:23) and would have adopted Joseph's lineage—a family line which led directly back to God (Lk. 3:38). Mary is thus the definitive "royal virgin."

Trait 2: His father is a king

The Most High God is Jesus' father, and it is fair to consider God to be king. Throughout Scripture God is known as the Most High, the Almighty, the Creator of all, and LORD.

In Isaiah chapters 40 through 48, God offers shining promises of blessing for those who trust Him and dark judgments upon those who turn away from Him. He also details His ability to control nations and their leaders, continents and kings, and to deliver His people.

> Even from eternity I am He; and there is none who can deliver out of My hand; I act and who can reverse it?
>
> I am the Lord, your Holy One, the Creator of Israel, your King (43:13, 15).

In Luke 1:35, the angel Gabriel tells Mary that it is "the power of the Most High" who will overshadow her to bring forth the Son of God. This Scripture correlates directly with Isaiah 9:6–7:

> For a child will be born to us, a son will be given to us; and the government will rest on His shoulders; And His name will be called Wonderful Counselor, Mighty God, Eternal Father, Prince of Peace. There will be no end to the increase of His government or of peace, on the throne of David and over his kingdom, to establish it and to uphold it with justice and righteousness from then on and forevermore. The zeal of the LORD of hosts will accomplish this.

In the New Testament, Jesus repeatedly states that His Father's home is the kingdom of Heaven (Matt. 6:10; 7:21; also 13:41, implied).

Trait 3: His father is a near relative of his mother

Almighty God was Jesus' father, but the man Joseph was the legal father of Jesus here on earth. Both Mary and Joseph (Jesus' step-father) were of the lineage of King David and, since they came from the same small town (Nazareth), could have been cousins or other close relations.

Trait 4: The circumstances of his conception are unusual

For a virgin to conceive a child is about as unusual as things get (Matt. 1:18–25, Lk. 1:34–38).

Trait 5: He is reputed to be the son of a god

As mentioned before, the hero is always the progeny of a special bloodline. His superiority is in his ancestry. In reference to Jesus, He is *the* Son of the only true God, but since it is always best to give references:

> And when the [Roman] centurion, who stood facing him, saw that in this way he breathed his last, he said, 'truly this man was the Son of God!' (Mk. 15:39),

> I have seen and have borne witness that this is the Son of God (Jn. 1:34), and

> So they all said, 'Are you the Son of God, then?' And he said to them, 'You say that I am' (Lk. 22:70).

Also Matthew 26:63–64, Matthew 27:43, and toss in Mark 3:11 for good measure, where even His enemies said it is true.

Trait 6: At birth an attempt is made to kill him

Just as Pharaoh ordered the killing of all newborn boys in an attempt to wipe out the infant Moses, Herod, King of Judea, heard of the coming of the Christ, a new king, and called for the death of all male children under two years of age within the vicinity of Jesus' reported birth (Matt. 2:16). This event has become known as the slaughter of the innocents.

Trait 7: He is spirited away

Keeping with the tradition of all great heroes, the baby Jesus was spirited away in order to spare His life. Joseph, warned by an angel of the coming slaughter of the innocents, fled Bethlehem and secured Mary and the baby Jesus in Ancient Egypt (Matt. 2:13–15).

Trait 8: He is reared by foster parents in a far country

Again we come to the details of Jesus' parentage. Jesus is the son of God, not of Joseph. To raise a child not his own qualifies Joseph as a step-parent—and they were still away in Egypt. When King Herod died, Joseph returned to

Judea only to learn that the area was ruled by a harsh and bloody king. So Joseph took his family to Nazareth in the north (Matt. 2:19–23).

Trait 9: We are told nothing of his childhood

Nothing is known of Jesus' childhood except that He grew, became strong, and increased in wisdom (Lk. 2:40). There is a thirty year gap in His history during which time we are given only one glimpse of the adolescent Jesus in Luke 2:41–51: He was twelve years old and already debated with the priests and religious leaders.

All other records of His childhood are non-canonical, unsubstantiated apocryphal works.

Trait 10: On reaching manhood he returns to his future kingdom

Jesus stated many times "The kingdom of heaven is at hand" (Matt. 3:2, 4:17, 10:7). He taught on aspects of the kingdom which were both present among them and to which He would return after His purpose on Earth was completed.

The people's recognition of this was seen during Jesus' return to Jerusalem. The people exclaimed, "Save us!" and "Blessed is He who comes . . . the King of Israel!" (Jn. 12:13).

Trait 11: He is victorious over the king, a giant dragon, or a wild beast

Jesus defeated the temptations of Satan (Matt. 4:1–11), but Satan was decisively defeated by Jesus' sacrificial death on the cross (Col. 2:15, Heb. 2:14). We can assume it is permissible to call the devil a "giant dragon" since he is called "the red dragon" in Revelation 12:3 and "the great dragon, the serpent" in Revelation 12:9. Note that Satan is also referred to as a roaring lion (1 Pet. 5:8), a snake or serpent (Gen. 3 and 14, 2 Cor. 11:3), the Ruler of this World (Jn. 12:31, 14:30, 16:11), and the Prince of the Power of the Air (Eph. 2:2), indicating Jesus' victory was over a king, a dragon, and a wild beast.

Trait 12: He marries a princess

No, we will not stoop to *The Da Vinci Code* shenanigans, but this is another point at which some people are tripped up. Too often people concentrate on Raglan's verbiage. The emphasis on the word "princess" is misplaced; the phrase can be simply, "He marries." If a woman marries a man of royal parentage, she automatically becomes royalty herself, *a la* Diana, Princess of

Wales. Since this bride is marrying the son of a king, she becomes a princess. If we accept this trait as being "He marries," we can turn to Matthew 9:15 to see Jesus refer to himself as being the bridegroom. The church is his bride (Eph. 5:25–29). Revelation 19 gives the details of the wedding.

Trait 13: He becomes a king

When Jesus entered Jerusalem, the people called out, "Blessed is the King of Israel!" (Jn. 12:13–15). Jesus stated to the Jewish Council of elders in Luke 22:66–70 that they would "see the Son of Man coming on the clouds"—a direct reference to His authority and ascension to the throne of His ancestor, King David. This claim to be king, to be God, was what solidified their charge of blasphemy against Him and made Him, in their eyes, worthy of death.

In John 18:33–37, Jesus accepts the title of King:

> So Pilate entered his headquarters again and called Jesus and said to him, "Are you the King of the Jews?"
>
> Jesus answered, "Do you say this of your own accord, or did others say it to you about me?"
>
> Pilate answered, "Am I a Jew? Your own nation and the chief priests have delivered you over to me. What have you done?"
>
> Jesus answered, "My kingdom is not of this world. If my kingdom were of this world, my servants would have been fighting, that I might not be delivered over to the Jews. But my kingdom is not from the world."
>
> Then Pilate said to him, "So you are a king?"
>
> Jesus answered, "You say that I am a king. For this purpose I was born and for this purpose I have come into the world—to bear witness to the truth. Everyone who is of the truth listens to my voice."

Trait 14: He reigns uneventfully

Jesus ministered to multitudes but did not reign as a traditional ruler. He had no armies and did not seek power other than what He already retained as the Son of God. He did not even retaliate when unjustly struck (Jn. 18:19–23).

Trait 15: He prescribes laws

Jesus reigned as the king of "the kingdom of heaven which was at hand" (Matt. 4:17) there in their midst.

He demonstrated His rule over demons, disease, defilement, defectiveness, death, money, nature, and physical needs. When He spoke, He was immediately obeyed by howling winds, angry waves, and frightened demons. Even his enemies confessed that He was "teaching with authority."

He revealed that He needed nothing other than Himself to have and to be ultimate authority, therefore we know He intended His words, His instructions, His rules, and His precepts to be obeyed.

Trait 16: He loses favor with his subjects

The crowd who had worshipped Jesus as He entered Jerusalem became the people who scorned Him and rallied to demand his execution (Mk. 15:5–15).

Trait 17: He is driven from his throne

Jesus was arrested by the Romans (Lk. 22:47–53) and charged with blasphemy by the Sanhedrin (Mk. 14:63–65). These actions forward Jesus toward His crucifixion, an execution reserved for only the most vile and traitorous criminals. His earthly ministry over, His claims to be the Son of God are dismissed and he begins the torturous ending of His time on earth.

Trait 18: He meets with a mysterious death

According to Luke 23:44–46, at the time of Jesus' death,

> darkness came over the whole land until the ninth hour, for the sun stopped shining. And the curtain of the temple was torn in two.

Matthew 27:51–53 records that at the moment of Jesus' death,

> The [thick tapestry] curtain of the temple was torn in two from top to bottom and the earth shook; and the rocks were split, and the tombs were opened; and many bodies of the saints who had [died] were raised and coming out of the tombs after His resurrection they entered the holy city and appeared to many.

The earth heaved, the sun went dark, the three-inch-thick curtain was ripped apart, starting from the top; godly people already dead and buried suddenly sprang to life. These supernatural events qualify as being mysterious and strange.

Also, no one, not even His closest friends had any expectation that He was to die so soon—even though He told them many times.

Trait 19: He dies at the top of a hill

The hero's death atop a hill elevates him physically at this critical moment. His elevation represents an ascension, being closer to the heavens above.

Jesus Christ was crucified and died on the hill of Golgotha, "The Place of the Skull," Mount Calvary. This is noted in Matthew 27:33, Mark 15:22, Luke 23:33, and John 19:17—one of the few times where all four eyewitness retellings duplicate each other.

Trait 20: His children, if any, do not succeed him

Again, we will dispense with *The Da Vinci Code* nonsense and firmly state that no, Jesus had no descendants. Those who are called the children of God and, indeed, are said to be joint-heirs with Christ (Rms. 8:1,7, Gal. 3:29, Titus 3:7) will never be able to succeed the One who is the Ancient of Days, the Alpha and Omega, the Everlasting One; nor could they ever be qualified to sit upon His throne.

Trait 21: His body is not buried

Following His death, Jesus' remains were interred in a borrowed tomb, sealed with a boulder, and guarded by a Roman cohort posted to keep watch for three days lest His followers tried to steal the body (Matt. 27:59–66); yet the tomb could not hold Him. He destroyed death, physically, bodily arose, and walked out of that tomb alive. His body is not buried but He sits at the right hand of God Almighty, interceding for those who call upon Him (1 Pet. 3:22).

Trait 22: He has one or more holy sepulchers (tombs)

For many Christians, the sites of Jesus' death and burial are holy places; pilgrimages are made to them, candles are lit beside them, voices use hushed tones when visiting them. The Church of the Resurrection, also known as The Church of the Holy Sepulcher, is the holiest site for many within Christendom. A Church is built over the spot where many believe Jesus Christ was crucified.

Jesus Christ gets a perfect score using Raglan's model. We are able to ascribe each of the heroic traits to Jesus without manipulation. This places Jesus Christ as the only figure, fictional or historical, able to fulfill all twenty-two traits.

Heroic Activities

Likewise, if we examine the common heroic actions, Jesus' time on earth lines up with them as well.

Disguises himself

Jesus disguised Himself as a man during His whole time here on earth. If that seems too simple to fit the criterion, we can also look at verses such as John 8:59: "At this, they picked up stones to stone him, but Jesus hid himself, slipping away from the temple grounds." The implication is that Jesus altered His appearance to work His exit through the seething crowd.

Attends a celebration or public gathering

Jesus attended a number of public gatherings, the Sermon on the Mount being one example. The fact is He *was* a living, public event wherever He went.

A specific example of His attendance at a celebration can be found in John 2:1–11, the wedding at Cana. On the third day of festivities, they ran out of wine. His mother, Mary, told Jesus of the shortage. He instructed servants to fill six stone jars with water; when they poured from the jars, the water had become from one hundred twenty to one hundred eighty gallons of fine wine. This was His first public miracle and one which provided pleasure and joy to the party-goers as they celebrated a union of love.

Rescues an innocent from danger

Jesus directly saved a number of people. Among a number of fortunate souls, He exorcized a demon from a boy in Mark 9:14–29: promptly following the Transfiguration, a boy was brought to Jesus; the child was frothing at the mouth and his body was rigid. It was explained that the boy had been cursed his whole life as the demon tried to kill him. Jesus exorcised the demon and the boy's life was spared.

Is betrayed by a confidant

Judas Iscariot was one of Jesus' closest followers (Matt. 10:14). Judas was possessed by Satan (Lk. 22:3) and betrayed the Son of God (Lk. 22:47–53). He sold Jesus to the Jewish high priest for thirty pieces of silver. It is significant that our phrase for ultimate betrayal, the Judas kiss, comes from the life of Jesus.

Does the detailed matching of these lists instantly prove that Jesus is the hero of our stories? No, but I do know that every set of traits, attributes, and elements assigned to the heroic archetype do specifically match the life of Jesus Christ.

We use the hero's story as a means of determining truth—Christ is Truth (Jn. 14:6, 18:37). I do not believe it presumptuous to notice a relationship between Christ and the Heroic Archetype.

Please note that Raglan's framework is not somehow "canonical"—it is not equivalent to Scripture. Remember also that Lord Raglan avoided reference to Christ Jesus when he published his studies. And Lord Raglan's points could be warped by his study of many false-Christ examples in mythologies.

It is far more important at this point in the discussion for each of us to be able to answer Jesus' question in Luke 9:20:

"But who do you say that I am?"

A Fictionalized Christ?

In his dissection of the character and story of *Christ, The Hero Patterns and the Life of Jesus,* Alan Dundes mentioned that Lord Raglan had avoided discussion of Christ in *The Hero: A Study in Tradition, Myth and Drama* because he feared implying Jesus was fictitious.

Lord Raglan told Professor Albert B. Friedman that of course he had thought of Jesus in connection with the hero pattern, but that he had no wish to risk upsetting anyone and therefore he elected to avoid even so much as mentioning the issue.[7]

Dundes posits the notion that since Jesus scores so strongly with the twenty-two traits, his life must have been as fictitious as the other heroes mentioned in Raglan's book (Heracles, Dionysus, Zeus, and King Arthur). This argument does not stand up, however. The hero character and His story is one which resides in the unconscious mind of everyone on earth, throughout all time. The narrative structure must come from some place and must have a meaningful purpose.

Even those who are not Christian should look at the existence of this structure, this language. It is blindness to assume it is not within us for a reason—like traveling to Mars, finding a Bible laying in the dirt, then shrugging your shoulders and saying, "Look at the naturally occurring but completely uninteresting phenomena. Best ignore it and keep looking for

7. Alan Dundes. *Christ, The Hero Patterns and the Life of Jesus, Part III of In Quest of the Hero.* Princeton University Press. 1990. 180.

aliens." The narrative structure is within us, it is a part of who we are as a species. It must be there by design.

Since The Great Story tells the tale of a single individual, it is logical to assume it points to a single individual. As I have mentioned, this can lead some people to claim that Jesus was dressed up in godly clothes in order to prepare Him for worship—that He lived and died and then, after the fact, the apostles inflated His story to make Him more "god-like" than He really was. That argument assumes we are capable of knowing how God should look and behave. Since the men of Jesus' time did not have the hindsight we employ today, how could they know which elements to insert into Jesus' life story to make it so compelling? I believe we can safely assume that a bunch of Galilean hillbillies did not have full comprehension of the details of Homer and Sophocles.

For Dundes's theory to be accurate, any fictionalization of His life would have occurred immediately following His death. Could Paul and the other New Testament writers have been imbued with sufficient knowledge of narrative, mythology, and public relations to know how to prop up the story with these elements on the spot? Been able to create a story which would resound so brilliantly over the millennia and transform the lives of billions of people?

Furthermore, the story would have to coincide with the numerous eye witnesses at the time and with the authorities and enemies of Jesus who would have loudly condemned the vaunting of a homeless cult leader as the Son of God.

The easiest and most obvious answer is, generally, the accurate one. In this case, the answer is right in front of us. Our opinions of what God should act like, the concepts of what we consider heroic, are within us for a reason and that is to give us the ability to identify God when He reveals Himself to us.

For centuries, missionaries have noted that on being introduced to cultures previously untouched by civilization, the indigenous peoples retained stories strikingly similar to that of the story of the Christ. Much like the Ancient Greeks and Romans had developed multi-layered pantheons of gods and goddesses, untouched cultures exhibit natural yearnings for higher beings to explain the world.

The introduction of the Biblical Gospels has been the key to lifting cultures into spiritual and socio-economic positions where they begin to experience healthful, beneficial standards of living—as if an isolated group of people were using a tool incorrectly, then someone demonstrated its proper function.

Jesus Christ was not a phantom of our collective imagination. He lived. He died. He was bodily resurrected from the dead. His life altered the destiny of humanity as no other figure before or since.[8] It is not some amazing coincidence that Jesus' life matches all heroic traits, events, and structures of the mono-hero archetype. I do not believe in blind coincidences. Again, coincidence is God being obvious.

The completeness of the character of Christ Jesus sets Him far above all other heroic figures. His perfect heroic status is the standard; all others are imitators. As scholar J.R.R. Tolkien stated, "the story of Christ is simply a true myth . . . *it really happened.*"

> Our opinions of what God should act like, the concepts of what we consider heroic, are within us for a reason and that is to give us the ability to identify God when He reveals Himself to us.

---

8. For more on the historical evidence of Jesus Christ, see these works by Josh McDowell: *Evidence that Demands a Verdict* or *More Than a Carpenter.* These works were important in my conversion.

22

The Great Story is
the Greatest Story Ever Told

"Life is God's novel. Let him write it."[1]
—— Isaac Bashevis Singer

ONE FANTASTIC ELEMENT OF STORIES IS THAT THEY TRAVEL WELL. Many of the stories we commonly tell have been around for centuries if not millennia. Stories, properly constructed, can live for generations and influence entire civilizations.

Egyptian hieroglyphics tell stories. At some point, the Ancient Egyptians worked their images into stone, images intended to carry an event in story form. The same can be said for Assyrian and Phoenician cuneiform. These have survived the centuries and still inform us today.

In much the same way, Charles Dickens sat at his desk and wrote *A Christmas Carol*. This work of his creative imagination has been passed down from generation to generation, not only to entertain but to provide valuable lessons of generosity and love for our fellow man as being the heart of the Christmas season (again, all cemented with Dickens' Christian worldview—a point lost by our secular culture).

In like fashion, the Gospels and the story of the Bible, itself, are a gift from God passed down from one generation to the next.

If Jesus Christ is the Hero whom we mimic in our stories, it is natural that His story would be The Great Story. The Gospels deeply affect us because

---

1. *Voices for Life: Reflections on the Human Condition*. Dom Moraes, editor. Praeger Publishing. 1975.

His story is the root of all stories. It is the original and the greatest story ever told.

Eden is attacked by evil and falls (Gen. 3). Having chosen to remove themselves from God's protection, fallen humanity is attacked, scattered, and enslaved by the villain, the Father of Lies (Jn. 8:44). Christ Jesus is born, the Prince of Peace (Isa. 9:6), and enters the fallen world to save his bride (Lk. 2: 21–39, Jn. 1:14), is killed (Matt. 27:45–56), and is resurrected (Lk. 24:1–12). He will come to finish His story by completing the defeat of the Father of Lies and usher us back to our natural place under God (1 Pet. 2:25).

Jesus' path is the greatest epic known to man. The Bible tells a story that expresses the truth of Jesus' sacrifice and the salvation of mankind. The story of Jesus has transformed millions of lives and shone the light of hope on all humanity. More than any other story or any other figure in either the real world or the world of fiction, the events of Jesus' life have changed the world forever.

I look at The Great Story's structure and the mono-hero and I see the hand of God. To me, this is elegance. When The Great Story plays out, it is like complex harmonies performed by skilled musicians—beautiful and transcendent to the human soul.

Tools and Proofs

The Great Story is a tool, a mode of communication the Lord God crafted so He could speak to us. This tool is used as an identifier of His Son.

We all know this structure; we react to it naturally. It is imprinted on our psyche. When the Gospels are told, we hear the structure but not as a piece of fiction. It is the relay of history—the mono-hero who revealed Himself in the flesh.

Often when people first hear the story of Jesus, they equate it to a light that clicks on in their heart, as though they had struggled with a complicated mathematical equation their whole life then someone whispered in their ear, "You forgot to carry the two," and the whole proof fell into place.

In my case, I was as lost as a man could be. I was bitter, petty, and completely self-absorbed. In other words, I was a perfect example of the results of following the direction of today's Western culture. When the scales fell from my eyes and I saw existence through the light of Christ, all things were transformed. And my story is far from unique.

We know the Gospels to be *The Greatest Story Ever Told* (1965), so it makes sense for us to use it as the measure for all other stories. We can use it not only as a standard for proper story structure but, more importantly, to decipher accurate, godly moral teaching. As the various elements of a story tick by, the easiest way to decide if the story is well written is to map it against the story's structure. If it matches, the story is probably sound. If a segment is missing, too long, or out of place, its break from the structure creates dissonance.

This does not mean we should have Christ as the literal center of all our stories. Even though we reference the structure of His life and story, it is preferable to have a heroic character stand-in for the Messiah because Story is not just a repeat of the story of Christ, it is a retelling of aspects of truth and reality that we need to hear—justice will prevail (*The Scarlet Pimpernel*), there is hope for something greater than we know and experience (*The Pursuit of Happyness*), peace is attainable when pursued through righteousness and truth (*Silverado*), we can find joy in simple pleasures (*The Ultimate Gift*), and love does conquer all (*Beauty and the Beast*).

Jesus Christ is the fount of Truth. He is the Light, and He is the Way. His life is the expression of God's love for us and the path of our redemption. By His path all truth can be discovered and we follow His truth as the moral compass for our lives. Even Jesus did not place Himself in the starring roles of His parables and stories. He replaced Himself with logical surrogates so the stories made sense to us mortals.

When we use a mortal man as our hero (Oskar Schindler, Jefferson Smith, or Marty McFly), we model actions and message upon Christ, Himself. It is the truths, morals, and ideals of Christ that are important.

We run into trouble with Luke Skywalker not because his name is not Jesus or even because he does not do good works. He is a moral character, but his morality is not Scriptural. Ultimately he promotes a Buddhist-animism hybrid (the Force is a part of all living things, which apparently includes plants and animals). The anti-scriptural religious tenents proposed in the film are the core problem Christ-followers must grapple with when viewing our generation's most enduring myth, *Star Wars*.

Developing a Christian Cinematic Worldview

Christ's life found in the Gospels should be used to measure truth. It is crucial that we take all stories, despite the teller or what they seem to say, and hold them up to the light of Christ. Every story, even the most banal, meaningless tale, contains a truth it wants to impart. We must use the teachings of Christ to discern if that message is true and worthy of our attention.

The Great Story comes from God but, like any other tool, it can be used by Satan to deceive and destroy. The same narrative that gives us moral tales —*It's a Wonderful Life, Henry Poole is Here, The Chronicles of Narnia: The Lion, the Witch, and the Wardrobe*—can also create *Porky's, Pink Flamingos*, and *The Texas Chainsaw Massacre*.

How then should we use this story structure? To have the structure and characters in our minds when we watch any film gives us a foundation upon which to build. Since we know many aspects of a film are consistent despite the genre, we can build a reliable guide to determine what a filmmaker says and if the message is worth a listen.

Most people, other than hapless film geeks such as myself, never consider sitting down with a pad of paper to write out the Four-Act Structure as it plays out on screen. For the normal person, knowing the structure exists is half the battle.

During the next film you watch you will spot the herald, mentor, and secondary antagonist. You do not have a choice now. They are in your head to stay.

While distracting at first, you will find over time an added depth to your movie viewing. You will begin to see patterns in how the characters and structural elements are presented. You will begin to spot instances where the various parts are handled well and other times when they are fumbled. If you pay attention, you will also begin to see how these elements work to make or break a production.

Before we go any further, I have an assignment for you. Once you have seen The Great Story played out in front of your eyes, you will see movies in a new light and, likewise, respond to them in different ways, so, believe it or not, I want you to put this book down. Well, wait to finish this chapter and then put it down.

Your Assignment, Should You Choose to Accept It

Find your favorite movie or at least one you know well. For me, in a pinch I pick one of the five movies my children watch in a perpetual loop. (I have been subjected to these movies so many times I can recite Pixar like scholars quote Shakespeare.) Watch the movie as you normally would and see if the elements of The Great Story pop out at you. Do not search for them, just watch the film and see if they appear. The likelihood is strong that this movie, which you have seen a dozen times, will now be seen through new eyes. In my opinion, my friends, that is the definition of cool.

Once you have watched that movie in this new way, rejoin me in Section Three and we will explore what to do next.

Watching Film: The Right Way to Sit There and Do Something

23

Changing the World from Your Recliner

"Never doubt that a small group of thoughtful, committed citizens can change the world; indeed, it's the only thing that ever has."[1]
— Margaret Mead, anthropologist

THE CRUDITY AND CRUELTY WITH WHICH OUR SOCIETY AMUSES ITSELF saddens the heart. The impulse to detach ourselves from that ugliness is understandable. Some Christians would even say that to turn our back on this hideous culture is the righteous thing to do. When we see a woman mired in addiction or we are approached by a homeless man, it is tempting to keep walking and pretend they are not our concern. But heed my words: there is a devastating wake-up coming for those Christians who turn their backs on the entertainment industry.

We find ourselves on the outside of our culture looking in, unable to make any impact since the post-modern movement expanded in the late 1960s when movies went from uplifting, sweeping films such as *Ben Hur* and *The Ten Commandments* to a dead standstill. The dramatic voice of our faith was muted as waves of disinterested, secular-minded, young filmmakers descended upon the scene.

---

1. Nancy C. Lutkehaus. *Margaret Mead: The Making of an American Icon.* Princeton University Press. 2008. 261. Used by permission.

The Greatest Story Ever Told was replaced with *Godspell* and *Jesus Christ Superstar*. The true tale of Christ's sacrifice for man's sin was watered down to fit the cultural needs of unwashed hippies and their love of loose morality. While the Jesus of 1965's *The Greatest Story Ever Told*[2] may have been a laughably stoic Swede,[3] the false messiahs of *Jesus Christ Superstar* (Aug. 15, 1973) and *Godspell* (Aug. 24, 1973) were executed on their crosses never to return. Fade to black. Roll credits. No resurrection equals no Messiah equals no redemption for mankind.

> There is a devastating wake-up coming for those Christians who turn their backs on the entertainment industry.

Filmmakers recast Jesus in their image, a mere human who dispenses a few good one-liners then fades into the archives. In other words, the first thing modern Hollywood did was kill Jesus Christ. Since then, Christians have wandered the desert looking for a new home.

The spoiled fruits of the 1960s radical movement have poisoned our culture. Most of today's youth were raised in a completely secular society. Like the wayward Jews who turned to the golden calf while Moses was atop Mt. Sinai, today's young people willingly follow any trend that comes along. They have been weaned on so much trash that Art, symphonies, and Shakespeare are foreign to most. They are culturally retarded and completely ignorant of or disinterested in the heritage stolen from them.

All of us were taught that great Art is for the elites; we have bought the notion that pop culture is best for us commoners.

When people use the word *culture*, it invokes a number of images. Some people imagine wealthy snobs who examine abstract works in a sterile art gallery. Others envision beret-wearing wimps who offer each other knowing laughs and snide comments at a downtown coffee shop.

But the word *culture* is more than haughty jerks trying to impress one another. The definition includes you and what you enjoy. Effete coffee sippers like to believe they define the culture. They do not. We, common individuals, are the ones who ultimately decide.

Historically, culture was settled by the upper levels of society and it trickled downward, a cultural pyramid with a small, select group at the top and a thick base of average folks at the bottom. It was taken for granted that those at the top of the pyramid were the important ones. They are essential, I do not deny that, but I believe the masses at the bottom are just as vital to culture.

---

2. nominated for five Academy awards
3. played by famed Swedish actor Max von Sydow

As an artist needs an audience, a culture needs patrons. Without support from the masses, a widespread movement cannot sustain itself. Leaders need followers, and if the base refuses the direction of those at the top, the elites must listen. When leadership overreaches, it becomes the job of the people under their care to compensate. Even the most brutal dictatorships fall when the oppressed organize against it. The powerful only rule as long as the people allow them to remain in control.

Change does not have to spring from the elites then filter down to the masses. It is just as possible for it to rise from the base of the civilization and move upward. This direction is most exciting—an upward-moving cultural shift that works entirely counter to everything that happens today. A cultural change that bubbled up from the masses would inherently be a revolutionary movement.

Christ-followers have the tools to spark this revolution at any time. Our society is starving for real direction and real leaders. Yes, the *status quo* holds Christians in disdain and severely mocks and destroys anyone who attempts to bring morality back into the marketplace. But that does not mean we turn and run. It means we stand and fight.

The moral are maligned because they threaten the *status quo*. When we teach people they are loved, that they deserve dignity and respect, they become harder to control—you cannot sell crud to someone who believes they are above being debased. In turn, those who bring trash into the marketplace will finally be marked as the filth merchants they are.

The problem with our society is not only that people buy and sell garbage. The deeper problem is that people do not see themselves as being worth anything better.

A Revolution

We own this culture, and we control its destiny. We saw a grassroots revolution in the 1960s and '70s that removed God from the culture. Christ-followers must educate themselves, do the hard work, focus the culture back towards God. Under God, our culture can be revitalized because under Him and only under Him can humanity flourish.

The movement back to God will not come from the elites. It must come from the base, the audience, us. The problem at that point is that most Christians have been raised in the feeble church-goer subculture or have partaken in the secular media with little restraint.

I believe we need to forge a new path. We need to discard the Christian subculture that flourished during our exile from the mainstream. It has not spawned a viable and life-changing movement, and it is not likely to do so in the future.

Biblical truth is the one and only truth, and it stands on its own. Our arguments, our worldview can stand up to any opposing argument or worldview. When we allow godly culture to be separate from the mainstream, we have ceded the argument to our opponents. We refuse to show up for the debate and thus lose by default. Our opponents are free to cast us in any light they see fit and, unopposed, are able to define the world at large.

In America, most of our opponents are secular humanists. The world, to their eyes, is a miserable place. Life is not important, there is no design to the universe, there is no set morality or truth. Existence is meaningless in a secular world since there is no reason to care about anything. History becomes a series of casually-related events; values become fluid; the pain and embarrassment of others becomes entertainment. The cultural masters value nothing so they create nothing of value. If existence is meaningless, then it is logical to pursue moments of shallow amusement and ecstasy.

But Christ-followers understand we are more than our pleasures. We are created by God for His purposes and exist due to His love. Every life and every moment in our lives is precious and has purpose. We are worthy of respect.

If Christ-followers get down to the business of creating Art, we can bring the richness of our faith to the world. Rather than continue our fledgling sub-genre, Christ-followers must enter the ranks of the industry and bring Biblical truth to the masses.

The secular culture tells us the exact opposite of what Christ taught. It tells us man is no more important than his temporary urges. The simple establishment of the elementary concept that life is valuable, set in the context of several successful Art and movie productions, would be a game-changer.

Change in the culture comes when Christians change how they relate to it. We can begin to flex our market muscle by applying pressure both internally and externally. Bit by bit, just as the secular movement grew over the decades, our movement can take hold and begin to flower.

Those in power today propose the universe is nothing; we offer the glory of God. Which argument do you think would win the hearts of Common Man?

Many Christian filmmakers know how to make movies, but most Christian audience members have no idea how to watch them.
To change our culture, we must be informed.

We now understand The Great Story Structure and how it relates to the Gospels. This gives any Christian a simple foundation for reading a film. But we need to explore how Christians watch films and how we can determine if a film expresses biblical truth. Next, we will discuss how we can watch films with keener vision and make wiser judgments regarding the movies we choose to support.

24

Does this Hollywood Blockbuster Make Me Look Fat?

"We rarely repent of having eaten too little."[1]
—— Thomas Jefferson

SHOULD I SEE THIS MOVIE? — THAT IS THE ONE QUESTION THAT OFTEN precedes most peoples' night at the movies. The question has several meanings depending upon where you stand. The non-Christian could mean, "Do I have time to see this movie?" or "Do I really want to watch another chick flick?" or "It's got Ben Affleck in it. Do I really want to watch him pretend he can act?"

Christians, when they pose the question, can mean these things as well. They can also mean, "Will this film sully my soul, sour my resolve, and propel me on a theological downward spiral through which I will eternally plummet?" (We Christians tend to have deeper considerations than our average, non-believing peers.)

Christians rightfully look at film through the lens of their faith. We know that the consumption of some films will indeed harm us or worse, insult God. This concern is a serious issue for Christians since it is nearly impossible to make it through twenty-first century life without interacting with film or television to some degree.

---

1. Thomas Jefferson. *Jefferson's Ten Rules* as published on the Library of Congress website: http://www.loc.gov/shop/index.php?action=cCatalog.showItemImage&cid=19&scid=148&iid=3849&PHPSESSID=f6578ab1e1a3ec132. Last accessed December 2009.

A majority of American Christians live normal lives. They work hard and do their best to relax when they can. This relaxation usually involves media consumption.

It is common for church-goers to put a good face on their viewing habits. How? Walk into a church and begin a discussion about television shows or movies. Responses will come from those who proudly exclaim they do not watch anything, or they only watch G-Rated films. While it is a positive attitude to want to avoid what tempts you, many Christians have become comfortable throwing out the baby with the holy bathwater.

The healthy percentage of people I have talked to about media, though, interact with it on a continual basis. Many hold deep reservations about what their children watch but, when pressed, reveal they do not hold the same standards for their own viewing habits. Publicly they will scorn the foulness of Hollywood and then go home and watch *CSI: Crime Scene Investigation* display a murder investigation of a transsexual stripper shot outside an S&M juice bar. They often know that what they are watching is wrong, they just think it is wrong for everyone else.

There is another group that sees no contradiction in watching *Inglorious Basterds* on Saturday night then hopping over to church on Sunday morning. They squat in front of the cultural fire hose with their mouth wide open—no discernment whatsoever, it *is* just a movie, after all.

In truth, this libertine approach is not generally a hallmark of those who are strict in their faith but, rather, is seen in CEO Christians—Christmas and Easter Only.

You Are What You See

Watching film is like eating food. The often misquoted line from Jean Anthelme Brillat-Savarin, "Tell me what you eat and I will tell you which you are,"[2] shortened to "You are what you eat," applies here. You are what you see.

What you put into your body and mind defines who and what you are, it feeds your soul. Someone who eats whatever they want whenever they want it becomes fat, lazy, and in turn is stupefied. Watching anything that comes from today's entertainment industry is no different than eating fast food every day. Everyone loves a cheap burger once in a while, but if you eat them all the time eventually your heart will burst out of your chest.

---

2. Jean A. Brillat-Savarin. *Physiologie du Goût*. 1825. Principles of the Professor No. IV. http://www.gutenberg.org/files/22741/22741-h/22741-h.htm. Last accessed October. 7, 2009.

Conversely, if you starve yourself at the banquet before you, constantly fret about tasting anything too sweet, you will waste away emotionally and intellectually.

There are keys to proper nutrition and good eating habits. Likewise there are proper ways to consume media. A moderate view is best for most people. I say *most people* because some are sensitive to certain content and should adopt a stricter approach. The pornography addict, for example, should avoid all media which may elicit sexual urges. Those prone to violence should leave horror movies alone. The first step to a moderate approach of movie-viewing is to realistically assess your own predispositions and boundaries.

If you believe something will cause harm or lure your mind in an unhealthy direction, it is wise to avoid it. With film we should be as careful as when we consider what book to read, which television show to watch, or whether or not it is worth talking to the lady down the street who pukes out gossip at you like a mother bird feeds her young. First John 4:1 tells us to "test the spirits, whether they are from God." Making judgments is good. When you stop making those determinations, viewing gets wonky and sin enters the picture.

Christ-followers walk a tightrope in regard to the best way to handle modern media. We want to remain faithful, but we also want to relax, have fun, and be able to relate to those around us. It is not wrong for us to want to be a part of society and enjoy the fruits of our civilization—how else are we going to meet those in it and speak to their need for Christ? The longing for good Story is not where we run into trouble. Where we often go astray is with the limits, or lack of limits, we place on our own entertainment.

WHAT DO WE CALL CLEAN?

Jesus says in Mark 7 that *"nothing that enters a man from the outside can make him 'unclean.'"* In that context the subject matter is food. Jesus later states that all foods are clean and *"What comes out of a man is what makes him 'unclean.'"*

My claim that you are what you see, i.e., what you take in through your eyes and ears, may appear to be counter to this teaching.

The consumption of media begins when each viewer decides what they will see and if they will continue to watch. These choices are directed by our faith, but our nature also leads us to sin. The mode of entertainment is not the issue. Our motives for participation and our reactions to what we consume are what should concern us.

If a man accidentally arrives on the homepage of a pornographic website, he has not sinned, even though the site itself is clearly sinful. When he lingers or clicks into the site, then he has sinned.

A woman reads a book with themes about suicide. She has had issues with violent thoughts in the past and knew when she picked up the book it might elicit more suicidal fantasies. If she knew it was likely the book would cause her to harm herself, it was sinful for her to even crack the cover.

25

Does God Call For Us to Become Ned Flanders?[1]

"I have to admit I enjoyed *Bruce Almighty*.
I wish I had some way to excuse myself,
but I don't. Now, of course, I feel incredibly guilty,
but I know it was a sin that has been covered by His blood."[2]
—— "Samantha"

PROTECTION FROM TEMPTATION, FROM SLIPPING INTO SIN ARE CONSTANT battles for every Christ-follower. Some of us are weak and the slightest push in a particular direction leads to a fall. Conversely, we are prompted by the Holy Spirit to refrain from luring other people into sin. These issues pose a constant discussion in Christian circles: What is permitted while walking the Christian life?

---

1. Ned Flanders—a character from the popular prime-time cartoon *The Simpsons*. Flanders is a ridiculous parody of the out-of-touch, happy-at-any-cost Christian who is so heavenly-minded they are useless here on earth. He is the exact opposite of his neighbor, the gluttonous simpleton, Homer Simpson.
2. "Samantha," commenter responding to Tim Challies' review of *Evan Almighty*. June 15, 2007, 11:01 a.m. http://www.challies.com/archives/articles/evan-almighty.php Last accessed November 2009. Used by permission.

Protection from Temptation

Our excessive leisure exposes us to more temptation than previous generations faced. Advances in technology and other sciences ease our lives and we find that, like Chaucer said, "Idle hands are the devil's tools."[3] If you do not have to keep crops alive or fend off disease and invading armies, you will have more spare time. More spare time means more opportunities for temptation.

In reaction to the influx of media experienced during the last fifty years, many Christians have opted to take the road of least resistance. To them, "walking with Christ" means living in a self-imposed cloister. These Christians believe that non-Christian-flavored media is sinful by nature and must be avoided.

If you choose freely and for good reason to avoid these things, I support you. Many of us are burdened by weaknesses and anything we can do to shield ourselves is good.

However, this position often derives more from a stance of legalism than an acknowledgment of Christ's love and a desire for purity. Those of you who blindly follow this doctrine with no investigation into the issues, well, you and I disagree.

Christians often speak of cinema in the context of how they relate to it as individuals and not of its place as a part of this world. We do not live in bubbles, though it seems many Christians want to. We live in this world. It is part of our job to help clean things up. Film can and will help to accomplish that work.

Test and Know Your Limitations

What of verses such as Psalm 11:5, "The Lord tests the righteous, but his soul hates the wicked and the one who loves violence"? Or perhaps Romans 12:9, "Love must be sincere. Hate what is evil; cling to what is good." Other verses urge us to only view what is beautiful. I agree with those admonitions. Those verses should be tightly clung to whenever we review our entertainment choices. But we must not simply decide that what is "good" or "beautiful" always equates to a sanitary view of the world.

In my opinion, sanitizing this world to make it appear sinless is a lie. Yes, there is beauty in this world, but there is also sin. We are to "take captive every thought" (2 Cor. 10:5) and "Test everything. Hold on to the good" (1 Thess. 5:21). We cannot do that by simply avoiding unpleasantness without consideration.

---

3. Attributed to Geoffrey Chaucer. "Tale of Melibee." c.1386. Translated from the French treatise "Le Livre de Melibee et de Dame Prudence."

Conversely, we should be very careful of the choices we do make and how they will impact us. One does not need to hold up *Saw IV* or *Zombie Strippers* for testing—it should be obvious what the verdict will be.

The more delicate choices are where we often lead ourselves astray. Some of us can handle seeing *The Wrestler* or *We Were Soldiers*, some of us cannot. It falls to each of us to understand our limitations and live in a way that honors God.

Some people may be concerned about the presentation of sinful behavior in film. Their avoidance of movies is not based on a fear of being misled but upon concern that they would be supporting evil behavior by the purchase of a ticket. When we discuss films like *Jason Goes to Hell* or *Make the Yuletide Gay*, it is correct to be concerned about what you support. Life, however, is not always black and white.

> We live in this world. Part of our job is to help clean things up. Film can and will help to accomplish that task.

The portrayal of sin to teach a moral lesson is not necessarily sinful. I will go further and say that sometimes it is necessary, such as in the case of *Schindler's List* (see Chapter 26). Where the line can blur is with a film like Clint Eastwood's *Gran Torino*.

In *Gran Torino*, Eastwood portrays Walt Kowalski, a cranky, widowed, Korean War veteran retiree. Walt has a loose mouth when it comes to his opinions, in particular about people of other races and nationalities. Walt is a blue collar guy and not religious at all. Walt's dialogue is very rough, he spews racist jokes and, more importantly, he casually blasphemes. I wrote a review of the film praising it for being a brilliantly written character piece with an intelligent approach to racism and forgiveness. I was criticized for my praise because of the film's use of harsh language, in particular the blasphemy. How could I recommend a film where the main character takes the Lord's name in vain?

I have met more than one Walt Kowalski in my life. The speech patterns found in Nick Schenk's script match exactly how Kowalski would talk. Yes, men of Kowalski's background, age, and temperament are known for taking the Lord's name in vain. To pretend otherwise is to avoid the ugly truth of our sinful natures. The striking thing about the film is Kowalski's unfiltered dialog. The reason it has such resonance is because it is real.

Kowalski's abuse of the Lord's name is also a sign of his corruption, in the same way his racist jabs at his neighbors reveal his bitter soul. His blasphemies are not celebrated or gratuitous, they are a symptom of his fallen nature.

There are people who believe that allowing blasphemies into a movie is beyond what should be allowable and provides grounds for avoiding the film altogether. I ask: If it is wrong to show someone who uses the Lord's name in vain (presumably because it breaks a commandment), is it okay for us to view other commandments being violated? Is it permissible to watch people being murdered? The actor, himself, does not kill, so it is not as if we watch an actual murder. In the context of the film, however, we witness the sin as if it happened.

Moreover, while Eastwood actually says the words, he may or may not actually mean them. He plainly offers a representation of someone blaspheming. Just like an actor who pretends to murder someone is not guilty of murder, an actor reciting dialog is not necessarily guilty of blasphemy when done within proper context.

> ## What we must be careful to avoid
> ## is the celebration or promotion of sin.

That is where you will find that the above-listed cautions—not breaking a commandment or leading others to sin—will have the most affect.

Whether or not there is a love for showing and experiencing violence is the difference between the violence in *Saving Private Ryan* and the violence in *Hostel*. If a production blurs the distinction between the right and the wrong (*The Dark Knight*) or drops all pretensions and comes out on the side of evil (*Ocean's 11*), we should tread very lightly, if at all.

Suburban Christianity

It is important both to keep tabs on what tempts you and to not allow fear to run your life—both of which have created a lifestyle for many Christians that I call Suburban Christianity.

Fear of being tempted has become a self-serving racket meant to put Christians in a strange, self-imposed, victim role where they are constantly taunted by the evil culture outside their door. As though our God was not exciting or all-powerful, many Christians feel compelled to overstate the potential dangers of this world and they include films and television shows. Suburban Christians portray the world as completely nasty and scary and act as if they cannot take the slightest breeze of discomfort. Again, I do not promote involvement in temptation. I am talking to the person who cowers away from *The Lord of the Rings* because Gandalf uses magic.

Too often Christians are so concerned about covering their own theological backsides that they cannot effectively speak to those outside the church walls. We are to "Go, therefore, and make disciples of all the nations, baptizing them in the name of the Father and of the Son and of the Holy Spirit, teaching them to observe all things that I have commanded you" (Matt. 28:19–20). How can we do this if we are too frightened to tackle our own DVD players?

Colossians 3:2 tells us, "Set your minds on things that are above, not on things that are on earth." We are to keep our eyes on our prize and not the Oscars, but if a Christian fails to connect to the culture in some fashion, they will not be able to speak the language of those around them.

We live in an entertainment-based culture. People discuss television shows and movies the way previous generations spoke of the weather. Many people hold complete conversations using little more than movie quotations and references. If Christians turn away from the culture, they lose the ability to understand what is going on around them. If we do not know what is going on, if we do not speak the language, how can we possibly expect to have an effective mission?

In Acts 17:16–23 Paul preaches in Athens. What does he do? Athens is a cultural capital lost in a swamp of theological musings. At the time, numerous idols were erected and worshipped. The place, while beautiful and vibrant, was spiritually dead. Paul does not meander in, see the pagans, and run away crying. He enters Athens, investigates, takes the time to understand their philosophies and arguments, then proceeds to reach their hearts by speaking their cultural language.

> While Paul was waiting for them in Athens, he was greatly distressed to see that the city was full of idols. So he reasoned in the synagogue with the Jews and the God-fearing Greeks, as well as in the marketplace day by day with those who happened to be there.
>
> A group of Epicurean and Stoic philosophers began to dispute with him. Some of them asked, "What is this babbler trying to say?" Others remarked, "He seems to be advocating foreign gods." They said this because Paul was preaching the good news about Jesus and the resurrection. Then they took him and brought him to a meeting of the Areopagus, where they said to him, "May we know what this new teaching is that you are presenting? You are bringing some strange ideas to our ears, and we want to know what they mean." (All the Athenians and the foreigners who lived there spent their time doing nothing but talking about and listening to the latest ideas.)
>
> Paul then stood up in the meeting of the Areopagus and said: "Men of Athens! I see that in every way you are very religious. For as I walked around and looked carefully at your objects of worship, I even found an altar with this inscription: TO AN

UNKNOWN GOD. Now what you worship as something unknown I am going to proclaim to you" (Acts 17:16–23).

Paul, a man of strong faith, was able to engage a non-Christian culture on its own terms. He worked to understand the culture then acted to turn it toward Christ. What would have been the result if Paul had picked up his blocks and gone home like many Christians today demand that we do?

Let me again explicitly state I am NOT saying Christians should immerse themselves in crass culture. No. You do **not** need to see the *Saw* films; you do *not* need to sit down and watch a boxed set of *Sex in the City*. Rather, we must make careful attempts to understand the wider culture in which we live.

It is not sinful to consume material
which does not cause harm
in order to remain relevant to this society.

Scared of being tempted? Frightened of a trial of faith? Pray. Trust the power and promises of the Almighty, then get up and lean into the storm and persevere—and stay in prayer. We should not search out sinful behavior, but we must not avoid confronting it when it appears. If your faith is strong, you can be exposed to opposing worldviews and not be swayed. Trust the Lord's promises, learn to read culture, to see opposing worldviews, then ask the Lord and trust Him to provide ways for you to address those errant views so that many people will be saved.

26

Purpose, Truth, and Content

"Art is a collaboration between God and the artist,
and the less the artist does the better."[1]
— Andre Gide

THE EFFORT TO PAY ATTENTION TO A MOVIE WHILE WATCHING IT, LET alone to deconstruct its various elements, may seem too cumbersome. If you do not want to think about structure and character, you are not alone. To keep track of everything eats up a lot of brain power and becomes a distraction. So, to bring things down to brass tacks, I suggest you focus on three aspects of any film you watch:

Purpose ~ Why was the film made?

Truth ~ What is the film saying?

Content ~ How is it saying it?

These three aspects and the questions they pose speak to most of the concerns Christians should have about watching movies.

To watch a film is like being chauffeured. To determine the *purpose* of a film is like understanding that (a) you are in a car and (b) it will take you to a certain location, say, to the store. To determine the *truth* of the film is like understanding which store is the intended destination. There is a difference between a grocery store and an adult book store.

The *content* of the film is the (c) pathway you take to reach the destination. Are you taking the direct route or driving through the rough part of town?

---

1. Craig Detweiler and Barry Taylor. *A Matrix of Meanings: Finding God in Pop Culture.* Baker Academic. 2003. 278. Used by permission.

Are the windows down so you can enjoy the breeze, or does the driver (filmmaker) have the windows up while they are smoking and flatulent?

A closer look at these three aspects of a film can enable us to develop an ability to determine which films are healthy and which are toxic sludge.

Purpose ~ Why Was the Film Made?

To know the reason a film was made is essential to your determination of its worth and its inclusion on your viewing list. The purpose explains the production's existence.

Does the storyteller push a political or social agenda (*Fahrenheit 9/11, Blood Diamond, An American Carol*)? Does he cater to violent natures (*Rambo, Natural Born Killers, Henry: Portrait of a Serial Killer*), exhibit sexual content for a quick buck (*American Pie, The Girl Next Door, Zombie Strippers!*), or produce a film to inspire viewers toward virtuous actions or attitudes (*The Straight Story, Cinema Paradiso, The Blind Side*)?

To know the purpose of the film can help you guard against productions which intend to lead viewers astray from their beliefs.

Often the purpose of a film is obvious and can be verified before you see the picture. Films like *Milk* or *Fahrenheit 9/11* have clear messages they intend to deliver, and most of us get the hint before we buy the ticket. We can read reviews and interviews or peruse a film's website and other marketing materials to determine the filmmaker's motivations.

At other times, identification of a film's purpose is not so easy for many audience members. Even after a film is released and reviewed by critics, some films' purposes may still seem masked.

Case Study: Avatar

James Cameron's landmark film *Avatar* was released in December 2009 to near-universal critical praise. The film introduced us to the latest advancements in cutting-edge camera systems, three-dimensional footage, and performance-capture technology. Audiences were treated to a strange planet named Pandora filled with bioluminescent jungles and a race of tall, primitive, blue cat/Smurf/elfish humanoids called the Na'vi.

The film (supported by merchandizing link-ups with McDonalds, Mattel, JEM Sportswear, Abrams Books, Ubisoft, and HarperCollins) enjoyed a top-notch marketing campaign for its launch. With the marketing push and media's fawning praise, the film raked in over $600 million in worldwide gross during its first week[2] and gave the production the highest ranking non-sequel opening in cinema history.[3]

The story of *Avatar* is a simple one. Humans have come to Pandora to plunder the planet of its natural resource, a mineral called unobtainium. The largest deposit of this mineral resides under the sacred lands of the Na'vi, the aforementioned big blue kitty-looking people. The hero, Jake Sully, a paraplegic Marine, enters into a program established by the corporation that hopes to displace the tribal blue-kitty people. The program will have Jake take over an avatar—a fully biological replica of a Na'vi that he will control remotely with his mind and body. Essentially, it is a living puppet. Jake is promised that the corporation will pay to have his legs repaired if he helps move the Na'vi off their sacred lands.

Jake enters into his avatar persona and before long becomes involved with the Na'vi. In particular, he falls in love with a young female Na'vi named Neytiri. As Jake becomes accepted into Na'vi culture, he begins to feel at home with their primitive ways. When the corporation loses patience and moves in, Jake's Marine brothers confront the tribesmen and Jake is forced to choose sides in the conflict.

To moviegoers, this film was a feast for the eyes that offered amazing three-dimensional effects and photo-realistic animation previously unseen by general audiences. The story, while lacking in originality or depth, was easy to understand and digest—a simple tale of good guys (Na'vi) and bad guys (Humans), right verses wrong. But the film had another side. With *Avatar*, Cameron pushed the thematic struggle between our desire for technology versus our humanity.

Humans arrive on Pandora with a mechanized army and drilling equipment. These Humans, despite all their technological advancements, have lost their humanity. Only the alien race of Stone Age blue kitties has retained the values of decency and integrity.

To be certain, James Cameron was intent on making a fun movie. He also deliberately created a movie that would alter audiences' thinking. In response to the question, "What do you want people to take away from this film, other than '3-D is awesome' and 'Action is cool'?" Cameron replied:

> Number one, 'I had a great time at a movie theater.' That's the thing they should take away—'I got my 15 bucks worth. That kicked ###. My mind is blown.' That's goal number one.
>
> Goal number two is that, 'my emotions are still working. I cried because I felt something.'

---

2. http://boxofficemojo.com/movies/?id=avatar.htm. Last accessed December 29, 2009.
3. http://boxofficemojo.com/alltime/world/worldwideopenings.htm. Last accessed December 29, 2009.

> And goal number three is, 'Why was I crying again? Oh yeah, because that tree fell.' A slight shift in perception, if that's possible.[4]

What perception was Cameron intent on shifting? Earlier in the same interview he provided a glimpse of those motives:

> And now with climate change pretty much dooming the coral reef habitats over the world over the next fifty years, which not enough people are talking about, I do feel a sense of outrage, in the sense that as an artist it's kind of my responsibility to create a warning and remind people.

> People need to be reminded from every direction. Maybe people want to go see a film for pure entertainment and not to think about it, not have to feel guilty—I'm not trying to make people feel guilty, I just want them to internalize a sense of respect and a sense of taking responsibility for the stewardship of the earth, and I think this film can do that by creating an emotional reaction.[5]

Adding to Cameron's environmental agenda is the presentation of the Na'vi in the noble savage motif.[6] The Na'vi are idealized to the point of being angelic in nature, are wise, patient, clean, and healthy. In contrast, the infiltrating Humans are bitter, broken, and destructive. Humans have abandoned an Earth despoiled by their lifestyles, and Pandora does not fare much better once they claim residence.

Cameron inserts other elements that should be of even more concern. Some critics have noted racist overtones.[7,8] The Na'vi display a culture reminiscent of African and Native American tribal peoples, and the Na'vi characters are almost entirely portrayed by African-American actors. The Human characters are almost all Caucasian and performed by actors of European ancestry.

[*Spoiler warning*: the next two paragraphs reveal elements essential to the storyline.] Cameron presents, on one hand, the hapless tribesmen—all minorities—who are spared only by the actions of "a great white savior." On

4. David Chen. *The Filmcast Interview: James Cameron, Director of* Avatar. December 18, 2009. http://www.slashfilm.com/2009/12/18/the-filmcast-interview-james-cameron-director-of-avatar. Last accessed December 28, 2009.
5. Chen. Ibid
6. "a mythic conception of people belonging to non-European cultures as having innate natural simplicity and virtue uncorrupted by European civilization ; *also* : a person exemplifying this conception"
7. Will Heaven. *James Cameron's Avatar is a Stylish Film Marred by Its Racist Subtext*. December 22, 2009. http://blogs.telegraph.co.uk/news/willheaven/100020488/james-camerons-avatar-is-a-stylish-film-marred-by-its-racist-subtext/. Last accessed December 2009.
8. Annalee Newitz. (*Is* Avatar *Racist?) When Will White People Stop Making Movies Like* Avatar? http://www.freerepublic.com/focus/f-news/2412025/posts. Last accessed December 2009.

the other hand (and at the end of the film), Jake only becomes respectable and whole when he literally sheds his white, human skin and permanently adopts his blue, avatar body. He leaves behind his "whiteness" to become a minority so that he can save himself.

This viewpoint of the film—that imperialist, European whites dominate African and Native American peoples—was not accidental. At the 2009 Comic-Con convention in San Diego, California, James Cameron was asked: "Sam Worthington, who plays Jake, said in an earlier interview that an element of the script is about bullying. How does that work into the story?" Cameron answered:

> I mean really, our cultural history for the last 5,000 years is about bullying. I've got the men, I've got the weapons, I've got the armor, I've got the ships and the cannons and all that stuff, and you don't. You've got bows and arrows. Your s##t is mine. That's how it works. That's what this country's based on, the musket versus the tomahawk. You've got the oil, we're coming. So it is a form of bullying.

> It's about the cultural interface and how one culture always buckles to another culture. Very seldom are we so enlightened that we're culturally inclusive of the culture that's getting hammered and displaced. So this is about a culture that fights back and says, "No, no, no. You don't get to do that."[9]

Can someone slip ol' Jim a note regarding the history of Attila the Hun, Idi Amin, or the Ottoman Empire?

If racial politics and blanket condemnations of European expansion were not enough, the process which transforms Jake from Human to Na'vi introduces serious theological elements. The Na'vi are pagans. Ancestral worship mixed with prayers to Nature are the central tenants of their spiritual life. Jake, our hero, decides to abandon his humanity and, through a sacred tree that contains the spirits of the Na'vi ancestors, he transfers his soul from his natural-born human body into the man-made avatar body. The lesson communicated? Our soul is malleable, transitory, and alterable at our command rather than specifically designed, created, and directed by God.

The average audience member probably left the theater thinking they had watched a movie about poor natives fighting another in a series of mean corporations. In fact, they had actually swallowed a significant serving of anti-humanity, anti-European, environmental paganism dressed up in likable, blue-kitty fuzziness.

---

9. Fred Topel. *SDCC: James Cameron Reveals* Avatar's *Genesis*. July 24, 2009. http://scifiwire. com/2009/07/sdcc-james-cameron-reveal.php. Last accessed December 2009.

A frustrating aspect of discovering the purpose of a film is that too often we discover it too late. The average filmgoer normally has neither the time nor the inclination to research what James Cameron (or any other filmmaker) has brewed up, much less has delved into filmmakers' personal worldviews.

> To determine the purpose of a production
> is the hardest aspect of being a responsible
> audience member, and it is often a consideration
> left unattended.

It would be easy for me to belligerently insist that you exert some effort to research the motivations behind films, but I know for the vast majority of readers that is simply not going to happen. So, I would like to propose that you take some simple steps to give at least a little thought to this aspect of a film and to look at the history of the folks involved in its production.

Use a Filmmaker's History

For example, James Cameron has spent his career making movies about the abuse of technology and how it relates to our humanity. In *The Terminator,* a killing machine is unleashed to hunt down Sarah Connor and it mindlessly mows down scores of bystanders in the process. In *Titanic,* the grand ship was a technological marvel and testament to the ingenuity of mankind—until it found an iceberg bobbing along in the ocean. In *Alien,* a spaceship's crew is left to the mercy of a frightening, murdering alien with acid for blood, and the crew's struggles to stay alive are sabotaged by one of their crewmates—an android with orders to defend the dangerous beast.

It should not be surprising that *Avatar* follows in this same vein. It is unusual for a filmmaker to deviate very far from their established successes. Even famous directors like James Cameron must locate financing for their projects, and it is easier to find millions of investment dollars when the producer can promote the new project as being similar to the previous ones which made tons of cash.

Directors, producers, and actors are usually comfortable working within specific genres or handling particular subjects. Can you see Wes Craven making an adaptation of *A Tale of Two Cities?* Clint Eastwood portraying Puss-'n-Boots? Okay, Eastwood as Puss-'n-Boots could be fantastic, but the point is that Hollywood rewards talent that can be branded. We know that if a film bears Wes Craven's name, it will be a horror film. We see Quentin Tarantino's name, we know we are in for a campy blood-fest. See Will Ferrell? We know to stay home.

Attempts to decipher a film's purpose should lead you to look at the filmmaker's private life. An actor who is politically active usually becomes involved with projects which promote their ideals. For example, Matt Damon is open about his liberal politics. It has not been surprising to see a number of his choices in projects reflect this aspect of his life, including *Che: Part Two* and *Syriana*. Does this mean that every Matt Damon film will promote liberal politics? No, of course not. It is not out of line, however, for the audience to acknowledge his tendency to employ his fame and professional success to forward his own agenda.

There is a reason that during presidential-election years we see an increase in star-studded films with political themes. In 2004, the year of the Bush-Kerry presidential race, came the release of *The Manchurian Candidate, Fahrenheit 9/11, The Day After Tomorrow, The Stepford Wives, The Terminal, The Bourne Supremacy,* and *Team America: World Police*—all with overt or subtextual political themes.

Finally, to unearth a film's purpose, simply use your head. It should be obvious that a story about the apocalypse which stars Arnold Schwarzenegger (*End of Days*) or Demi Moore (*The Seventh Sign*) will not have Scriptural integrity at the forefront of its agenda.

Despite the difficulties, I must say it is best to do your homework before you go to the theatre. Do not be lured by the marketing or by what you hope the film will promote. It is crucial for every Christian to be alert and aware of what someone wants to whisper into your ear while you sit in the darkness of a cinematic experience. We must always pay close attention while we watch.

Truth ~ What Does the Film Say?

"I believe that unarmed truth and unconditional love will have the final word in reality. This is why right, temporarily defeated, is stronger than evil triumphant."[10]—Martin Luther King, Jr.

A film critic looks at many different aspects of production when he reviews a film. He studies the director's use of light, editing, and movement. He reviews shot placement and the choice of transitions. There is the acting, design work, and script to consider as well. A film is a multilayered event which melds facets of many different art forms and sciences together to impart a story. Of all of the various elements that can be found in a film, there is one that stands above all else—truth.

A film dispenses truth as it answers its questions. When I speak of *truth* I am not concerned with the delivery of facts such as "water is wet" or "Madison is the capital of Wisconsin." What we must look for is moral

---

10. King, Martin Luther Jr. Nobel Peace Prize Acceptance Speech of Dec. 10, 1964. http://www.
     mlkonline.net/acceptance.html. Last accessed October 2009.

truth. Are the film's moral statements true? Does the story present the right answer to the right question?

Quentin Tarantino is a clever filmmaker. He has a sharp eye and is a skilled screenwriter. In fact, I believe Tarantino is the most gifted screenwriter of his generation. His characterizations and dialogue can be masterful at times. I could explain all day long the technical and artistic reason why *Pulp Fiction* not only works but exceeds most other films. It is a brilliant piece of cinema. But the core of the piece is rotten. Its existential viewpoint, its criminal heart, makes it unworthy of full praise. I do not recommend the film because it is immoral and promotes not only criminal behavior but criminal thinking. (*See* a fuller discussion of *Pulp Fiction* in Appendix A.)

Most film critics do not concern themselves with looking at the worldview of a movie. They concentrate on the aesthetics and how much pleasure it provides.

Christian audiences must be aware of what is being said, must look beyond the ornamental elements in a story and be conscious of the structure underneath. This structure, The Great Story, gives us a consistent foundation from which to work. We can watch a film, locate specific aspects, and use them as guideposts through the filmmaker's cinematic journey.

Use Film's Structure

Much like a house has a support beam which extends across the frame and supports the weight of the building, The Great Story has a support structure to hold the weight of Story. This central beam is the easiest way to tell if a film delivers a solid, moral story. Remember that all stories can be simplified to a question followed by an answer. That is the support beam and where we find the morality being promoted. Locate this and you determine whether or not the story is treasure or trash.

The question is proposed during the opening minutes of the film. Will the boy get the girl (*Forrest Gump*)? What are the wages of revenge (*Munich*)? Dude, where's my car (*Dude, Where's My Car?*)? The expanse of the story is where the writer offers alternative answers to this central question, all of which lead to his real answer delivered in the final scenes. Forrest wins Jenny's heart in the end (but she has AIDS, tough luck Gump), assassinations deprived Israel of the moral high ground (or at least that's what Spielberg thought), and the dudes find the car after locating the Continuum Transfunctioner (it makes sense in the context of the film—which you should never bother watching).

The moral of the story normally comes during the final minutes of the film. A character, usually the hero or mentor, is given prominence on screen and recites the moral lesson learned through the journey of the hero. Such was the final shot of *Spider-Man*.

Peter Parker, having defeated the villainous Green Goblin, had a choice to make. Would he take the high road and remain Spider-Man, knowing his heroic status would require a life of solitude? Or would he choose to be common, settle for being just plain old Peter? Mary Jane, Peter's love interest, says the words he dreamed of hearing: "I love you, Peter Parker." At this moment he stands over the grave of his mentor, Uncle Ben. Peter tells her that he cannot say he loves her. He walks away from a "normal life." At this moment, he closes the film with the narration: "Whatever life holds in store for me, I will never forget these words: 'With great power comes great responsibility.'" He chose duty over his heart.

Judging the moral truth of a film is not always so cut-and-dried. Our ability to judge can be clouded by our desire to be entertained. If a film is well made, we can easily disengage our minds and forget to consider the message. Even when we are swept away by the excitement of a film, we must stay aware of all aspects of what we are seeing.

> **Our ability to judge can be clouded by our desire to be entertained.**

Case Study: The Matrix

A prime example of this is the Wachowski Brothers' *The Matrix*. The film follows Neo, a computer hacker, who is approached by a gang of leather-clad revolutionaries. They show Neo that what he thinks is reality is actually a complex computer program run by machines called the Matrix. Neo also learns he is the prophesized savior of humanity. Neo and company then do battle with a computer program named Agent Smith within the world of the Matrix.

The film is loaded with Biblical references:

» The hero's name is Neo, "New"—he is the "new man." The name is also an anagram for "One." He is "The One."

» At one point someone says to Neo, "Hallelujah. You're my savior, man. My own personal Jesus Christ."

» Neo's mentor, Morpheus, has a ship named Nebuchadnezzar, a connection to Nebuchadnezzar II in the Book of Daniel. Morpheus shares his name with the Greek god of dreams and King Nebuchadnezzar II was afflicted with horrible dreams.

» Neo's love interest is named Trinity.

» Symbolically, Neo can be seen as Jesus Christ, Morpheus as God, and Trinity as the Holy Spirit.

» Neo (Jesus) is betrayed by Cypher (which means 'zero'). Cypher exchanges his loyalty for the savor of his old life in the Matrix, just as Judas traded his for silver.

» Agent Smith, a computer program, describes the original form of the Matrix as being like Eden. It was trashed when they learned humans needed a flawed (sinful) world in which to live.

» Morpheus' ship bears the words "Mark III, No. 11" a reference to Mark 3:11: "Whenever the unclean spirits saw him, they fell down before him and shouted, "You are the Son of God!" This is meant to give clear connection between Neo and Jesus Christ (Jn 1:49).

» Neo is gunned down and dies. He is then resurrected and is a transcendent figure able to overpower the illusions of the Matrix and take command of the world. He is godlike.

» Hidden in this death and rebirth scene is another clear connection between Neo and Christ. After being killed, it takes Neo exactly 72 seconds until he is reborn. This is intentional. The 72 seconds correlates with 72 hours (three days).

Many Christians, hungry for approval from the cinema, see these references and immediately cling to the film as being Christian. In reality, the film, while inventive and influential, is hardly a Christian allegory. In fact, it is defiantly anti-God.

The Matrix is a hodge-podge of philosophy and theology dressed up in a beautiful package. Like a supermodel with Tourette's syndrome, it may look nice but what it has to say is troubling. Despite the Christian gloss, the movie itself is an ode to nihilism and the power of self-realization via Hinduism.

Brothers and filmmakers Andy and Larry Wachowski, dip into the Hindu concept of Maya. Maya is a belief that since God made everything, everything is God. A stone is as much a part of God as you are. A stick is no different than the tree from which it fell. Material differences are an illusion and Maya is the network of universal impulses that binds everything together (this should all start sounding like The Force from *Star Wars*). Maya is, through this line of thought, actually the Matrix. We see a spoon because Maya pushes our perceptions of reality that way. We live inside of Maya and need to break down our perceptions of reality to actually experience the universe as it truly exists.

But what of all of the Biblical references? What of the savior character coming to save the world? Is not Neo a Christ figure and are not the computers actually Satan, and the Matrix our sin-filled world? *The Matrix*, as with many other films, appears to be one thing while actually being something completely different.

Be Alert to Scriptural References

When a film uses Biblical quotations or makes direct, Christian references, always be on guard. When a filmmaker uses the Bible to forward his own ideas, he takes on a responsibility similar to that of a pastor or priest—he speaks from a position of authority in relation to the Word of God. That is a dangerous business (*see* 2 Peter 2:1–9).

Use of Scripture directly or in allegory does *not* make a story or film Christian. The presence of Scripture does *not* mean the presence of righteousness. Satan was very comfortable (mis)quoting Psalm 91:11–12 when he tempted Christ (Matt. 4:6). What is important is the *context,* the reason for Scripture's use.

The purpose of *The Matrix* was not to offer a clean, Christian allegory. It was not created to honor Christ. In fact, I argue *The Matrix* was made to deny Him in typical post-modern fashion—to explore the pliability of human consciousness and the thin veil of reality. There is no truth, no depth to what we perceive or experience in the film, no basis for morality. Characters given special knowledge of the Matrix were morally sanctioned to gun down any ignorant, innocent bystander. Neo was a false Christ delivering a false message.

While the compulsion to enjoy products of our culture is understandable, we must always remain on guard. *The Matrix* is a fun film that delivers a steady dose of unbiblical philosophy.

Responsible viewing comes down to conscience and accountability before God. Once you, as an audience member, are aware of what you are seeing and have the tools to identify the sham of the disposable paradise—agenda, product placement, and propositions—you are more protected than the average person.

If an angel walked into your room right now, you might do whatever he told you to do. Now what if, before the angel appeared, you were told that Satan was going to come disguised as an angel (2 Cor. 11:14)? Your reaction would be different, not because the angel's words were different but because you were now aware of the dangers involved. You would know better than to take the messenger at his word.

Watching film is no different—knowledge is power.

We must hold all things up to the light of Christ, to hold Him as our standard. Only then can we decide if a film's truth-message makes the grade.

The Matrix falls outside of Christ's teaching. In my view, some of us can still see the film as long as we keep this in mind. Again, as long as we understand the snake oil salesman is selling us snake oil, the impact of his pitch is thwarted. As long as we understand that the film is proposing low morality or offering a false savior, then its ability to influence us is greatly diminished.

To Watch or Not to Watch

But that brings up another question: If a film is outside of Christ's teaching, why should we watch it at all? This is where each of us must make our own choices. Many will decide that if a film is outside of biblical teaching, they must refuse to watch it. Others will decide to watch it for its entertainment value but will do so with the knowledge it does them no good and promotes poor values.

I tend to fall into the second group, although I understand the actions of the first. With films like *A Fish Called Wanda, Dumb & Dumber,* or *Blazing Saddles,* which all have questionable material and certainly fall outside of Biblical teaching, I do not watch them to gain support for my beliefs. I am responsible to understand they can have a corrosive effect on my belief system if I watch them without thinking, without acknowledging their potential to mislead.

The typical football game on television is rife with questionable content. When I sit down on Sunday afternoon to watch my beloved Green Bay Packers, I am confronted by numerous commercials which attempt to lure my attention with sexual imagery; cheerleaders hop around on the sidelines; commentators speak of the players and coaches as if they were demigod gladiators. As a Packers fan, each season I see fawning displays of worship at the shrine of Vince Lombardi, his iconic image presented in a fashion usually reserved for the saints of the church. These displays clearly do not represent positive support of Christian lifestyles and biblical thinking, yet our faith is rarely questioned when we sit down to watch the NFL.

It is crucial for us to keep tabs on our reactions to anything we see— watching with a Christian mindset and keeping tabs on temptation. Just as a Christian can watch a football game with all of its questionable ornamentation, he can sit down to watch a stupid comedy. Some people may balk at a film's immorality. They may decide it is something they refuse to see. That is their right and their choice.

It does not fall even to critics like me to decide what is appropriate for you. You must define that for yourself. My mission here is to give you the tools and direction to make a responsible decision.

 As long as you can watch
and still keep your faith in place
and your heart clean,
then you are watching responsibly.

Content ~ How Does The Film Say It?

"There are always trends: One year it seemed every film had someone urinating. Another year everybody was throwing up."[11] — Joan Graves

In the old days (and I cannot believe I refer to the early 1980s as "the old days"), the PG-13 Rating did not exist. Back then films got an R-Rating for any nudity or use of the F-word. R-Rated films came in two flavors: Hard Rs and Soft Rs. *Friday the 13th* was a Hard-R; *An Officer and a Gentleman* was a Soft-R. The former was loaded with graphic violence, open drug use, and sexual content; the latter had its share of sexual content and harsh language, but it was a story intended for adults. Back then, the R-Rating was common to see, particularly in the late 1970s to early 1980s.

During the 1980s, a shift occurred in the content of films. Films intended for family viewing began to display rather graphic material. Steven Spielberg films, in particular, sported a number of questionable items. [*Warning*: the next several sections contain graphic language and descriptions.]

In *Gremlins*'s audiences witnessed a woman brutally stab to death an evil gremlin then stuff another of the mischievous creatures into a microwave oven where it struggled until it blew up. In Spielberg's *Indiana Jones and the Temple of Doom*, a shaman plunged his hand into a living man's chest and pulled out a still-beating heart.

Concerned citizens and activists began to pressure government to intervene. The music industry also stepped into the fray, under assault by citizens' groups and government officials for the irresponsible materials they shoved into the marketplace.

Hollywood Creeps Created Ratings Creep

The MPAA existed to prevent government intrusion, so they concocted a new rating to relieve some of the pressure. They introduced PG-13 in 1984. This new rating was intended to bridge the gulf between the family-friendly PG Rating and the adult R Rating.

The result was ratings creep. PG-13 became the niche for what had been Soft-R films. Content that would, before, earn an R Rating was now commonly seen in PG-13 films. Also, what had been regulated to PG-13 has become merely PG, and what should be PG films are now given a G Rating. This erosion of our standards is documented in a study of films released between 1992 and 2003 by researchers at the Harvard School of Public Health.[12]

11. Joan Graves [head of the Motion Picture Association of America (MPAA) ratings board] discussing "ratings creep" and how social mores change from year to year. In Discretion Adviser: As head of Hollywood's movie ratings board, Joan Graves keeps parents in the know. Sonja Bolle. *Stanford Magazine*. July/August 2008. Used by permission. http://www.stanfordalumni.org/news/magazine/2008/julaug/show/graves.html. Last accessed December 2009.
12. Harvard School of Public Health. *Medscape General Medicine.* July 13, 2004.

Ratings creep is a self-propelled descent into depravity. The industry allows more and more adult material into family fare. Some people complain about the lurid material, but it continues to worsen. Over time we become jaded and give filmmakers freedom to push harder against the envelope—harsher materials, greater vulgarity, more adult themes in what used to be considered family entertainment. The slide down that slope has brought us to accept pornographic references as non-issues in children's films and commonplace in television commercials.

> **We lost our sense of shame.**
> **We are without modesty.**

Shrek and *The Cat in the Hat* are littered with blatant sex jokes. In *Shrek*, the villain is said to be compensating for something because of his oversized tower. In *The Cat in the Hat,* the hero holds a picture of the children's mother, it unfolds like a centerfold, then he gasps lustfully as his hat suddenly goes erect.

I do not say development of the PG-13 Rating was the sole cause of the descent into depravity. I *do* say it was a notable contributor to the fall. We lost our sense of shame. We are without modesty.

All generations and cultures struggle with what is and is not acceptable within the public sphere. At this time in our culture, we seem more concerned with exploration of what we can get away with before we get into trouble.

Christians tend to be more concerned with breasts and swearing than with poor theology. In our pornographic culture, this is understandable. I wish I could tell you things were going to change—they will not, at least not on their own.

I often compare our culture to a drug addict. Sometimes you must let an addict hit bottom before he will finally admit his problem. Unfortunately, as our current culture hits the bottom of the barrel, this generation of movers and shakers only dug down deeper.

What about all this foul content? Are we to watch the nudity, sex, drug use, cursing, or violence? I do not have a clear answer on the subject of sex and violence. It is too dependent upon your personal level of tolerance.

Some people can watch the nudity in *Titanic* and only be marginally affected; others will obsess over it. Some people can witness the horrors of *We Were Solders* without having nightmares; others will suffer for weeks.

As we continue on this topic, remember: personal responsibility and accountability before the Lord mean that you must determine for yourself and your family what is and is not permissible viewing. If you are a parent, let Ratings Creep alert you to the need to preview anything you let into your home or in front of your children. The industry has no concern for them or for you.

Sex and Violence—Viewing the Unwatchable

Jesus called the crowd to him and said, "Listen and understand. What goes into a man's mouth does not make him 'unclean,' but what comes out of his mouth, that is what makes him 'unclean.'"[13]

In the comedy *Tropic Thunder,* a group of actors and a film director enter an East Asian jungle to shoot a war film. During their shoot, the director steps on a landmine and is blown to smithereens. The lead actor, believing the horrific death to be fake, picks up the dead man's decapitated head and posts it on the end of his prop rifle. While he explains that the head is a fake, it is not; the actor sticks his hand inside the dangling neck of the decapitated head, wiggles it around so guts fall out, then he licks the blood off his fingers. This is all done as comedy.

In *Beetlejuice,* the titular character is an undead sex offender shown happily entering a whorehouse in the afterlife. At one point the belligerent ghoul screams, "Nice f###ing model!" and grabs his genitals, accompanied by the sound of a bicycle horn. This moment was only seen in the original theatrical run of the film and was removed from the VHS and DVD releases. The film was rated PG and marketed to children. It went on to spawn its own Saturday morning cartoon series.

In *Iron Man,* the hero, Tony Stark, seduces a liberal news reporter, beds her, then has her thrown out of his mansion the following morning. He also has stripper stewardesses on his private jet who dance on a stripper's pole and serve liquor to him and his friend.

The presence of sex, violence, and swearing has been an issue within the entertainment industry for decades, and the debate will not be resolved any time soon. Where the line should be drawn for appropriate viewing of sex and violence has been a battle for every Christian and a matter of debate within the church.

Some people have a zero-tolerance policy. Any nudity, any reference to sex, or any violence is sufficient cause to not watch, read, or even hear about it. For other people, almost no consideration is ever given to content of any kind. Whatever is on, is on, and it does not matter to them. There are people who attempt a more moderate approach—which, if not handled properly, can lead to becoming jaded.

I do not believe it is sinful for an adult to view nudity, sexual behavior, or violence, or to hear cursing, *provided it is in the proper context.* To say that viewing these elements is sinful is, I believe, errant since each of these transgressions is clearly referenced, in detail, in the pages of our own Scriptures. The mere presence of these elements is not what makes them sinful. It is the context of their presence which should concern us.

---

13. Matthew 15:10

Sex

I will begin with the subject of sex since that is the most sensitive topic I deal with when discussing the Arts. My general rule is that sex scenes in films are rarely needed. In almost all cases, they are gratuitously used and frivolously displayed.

If you watch a sex act on screen, you should probably question what you are watching. In almost no case is the display of sex done with discretion. We do not need to see the actors naked and rolling around.

It is possible, however, for the act of sex to be an important part of a story and I would never say it must all be abolished. My concern is the actual showing of the act.

We run into trouble in this society in regards to sex because it has been removed from the moral structure which should define it. Prior to the late 1960s, plentiful references were made to sex but they were kept within the moral framework of marriage. Even when there were situations where people were acting lustfully or acting sexually outside of marriage, the moral framework still hung over their behavior. In today's films, this context has been removed. Today, sex is just another part of life, like going to work, eating lunch, or receiving a text message.[14]

Even the topic of sexual intercourse outside of marriage should not be avoided in film, provided it is done in the proper context. Too often characters hop in the sack with one another without a second thought, even in films geared to families or teens (*Batman*). Referring to sex in the context of being something that happens between a married couple is best. If it is shown as happening outside of marriage it is vital for the filmmaker to acknowledge it as a bad decision, just like in real life.

Nudity

Nudity in film is another aspect of human sexuality which troubles many Christians. Unlike the act of sex, I can cite numerous examples where nudity, even full-frontal nudity, is not only acceptable in a film, but critical to telling the story. The presence of nudity in a film can offend some Christians. I know of many Christians who have seen a naked breast in a film and felt guilty for years. As with all questionable content, if nudity is an issue for you, do not watch it. Avoid all movies with nudity.

The presence of a naked person, however, is not instantly sinful. To make this argument is to say that many of the classics of Western Civilization are sinful. Is Michelangelo's "David" or the ceiling of the Sistine Chapel sinful? They both display full-frontal nudity. It is not the nudity which is sinful, but the context of that bare skin.

14 If you listen, you will hear today's teens talk about it in these terms.

Two movies that contain full-frontal nudity of women taking showers are *Porky's* and *Schindler's List*. Both are R-rated films but there is a stark difference. *Porky's* intended to illicit lust in the audience; *Schindler's List* intended to show the horrors inflicted upon the victims of the Holocaust and the cruelty of their Nazi captors.

A Christian who refuses all nudity in film casts out the good with the bad for the sake of simplicity or fear. I, personally, consider *Schindler's List* to be a brilliant film. It is a moving piece that juxtaposes the worst of mankind with what is good in the human heart. Spielberg's frank imagery is needed to make his point. While Spielberg is not a Christian, we can still look at his work and its effect in the light of Jesus and say his film, with all of its graphic scenes, follows Ephesians 5:11: "Take no part in the unfruitful works of darkness, but instead expose them." Spielberg fully exposed the evil of the Nazi regime by his clear representation of the crimes committed and the impact felt by their victims. We, as an audience, are made aware that these events were more than just paragraphs in our history books but were actual, horrid experiences of living people, children of God, who were slaughtered by the minions of the devil. Casting aside a film such as this over a simplistic, self-imposed rule is done out of laziness or fear, not righteousness.

Violence

The context of violence is also a consideration when watching a movie. Again, I turn to *Schindler's List* as an example. The movie is a litany of human misery and cruelty. In nearly every scene someone is hung, shot, beaten, or tormented. The story could not be told without the horrifying violence.

This same litany of violence is shown in Eli Roth's *Hostel*. In that film, a group of American college kids are lured into a remote city in Eastern Europe, kidnapped, and sold to disturbed people who pay money to be able to torture people to death. Yes, this is the plot of an actual movie.

Roth could not tell his story without showing the slow, painful torture of his characters any more than Spielberg could avoid it to complete his great work. Just as with sexual content, the difference here is a matter of context. *Hostel* is a disgusting, perverse piece of torture pornography that would never have seen the light of day in a culture with any shred of dignity. Conversely, *Schindler's List* is a masterwork that should be required viewing for all high-school seniors.

Playing "Cops and Robbers" or "Doctor"?

I tend to take a somewhat lighter view of non-graphic violence than I do of sex. Human sexuality is a more sensitive subject because it speaks to the core of a person's humanity. When we talk about a child's "innocence" what are we talking about? What removes this innocence? Sexuality.

Committing an act of violence does not necessarily have the same coarsening effect. Would you rather have your children play "Cops and Robbers" or "Doctor"? It is not good for children to watch or commit violent acts. Our children hitting one another is not acceptable. I would say, though, that it is far more important to keep sexual material away from their eyes.

Mild violence is generally permissible, even for younger audiences, provided its intent is to teach a moral lesson (*The Chronicles of Narnia: Prince Caspian*) or, when done for evil purposes, that evil is punished (*The Princess Bride*). I would much rather my children watched mild violence where the good guy punishes the bad guy within a clear, moral framework (*The Incredibles*) than ever have them see even mild sexual content.

Many instances of violence committed by movie heroes are included without any moral context other than the hero wants it done, as in most Bruce Willis movies. Violence crosses the line, in my estimation, when it is gratuitous and gory. We have all seen older films and television shows where a cowboy was shot, grabbed his chest, and slumped over. That was on-screen violence. Today, that same scene would probably show the cowboy being shot, a mass of blood erupting from his chest, him screaming as he flies backward and lands in the dirt gasping for air, then the hero slowly walks over to him, recites some ironic line befitting the moment, and mercilessly pumps more shots into the dying man. That is gratuitous on-screen violence.

I do not dismiss violence as something of no consequence. Viewing graphic violence has a deep impact on both a person's psyche and their soul. With the first violent scene someone sees will come a shock to their physical system as their eyes are opened to the reality that they live in a rough and often unjust world. How parents, mentors, or the individual handles the situation will determine how that person thereafter relates to the world around them. A subsequent, continual diet of violence has the same corrosive effect as a diet of sexual content. The more violence you watch, the more desensitized you become. The more desensitized you become, the more gratuitous or bizarre content you are willing to watch. Be vigilant and aware of that slippery slope.

27

Morality Points

"I learned a lot about morality from fiction, from movies."[1]
—— Rob Morrow, actor

M Y PROPOSAL THUS FAR HAS AN OBVIOUS PROBLEM: BY THE TIME YOU get the Answer to the Central Question you have already digested the entire film. What if the ultimate Answer is immoral or ungodly? Then what?

Christ-followers have the tools to handle ungodly proposals and you probably will not be terribly harmed by one experience, but there are ways to determine the quality of a film without being forced to stick around for the ending. Here is where our understanding of story structure and characters of The Great Story comes into play.

We enter into a film with the knowledge that we will be presented a structure broken into four equal parts with a reversal in the middle. We also know the story will be populated by specific archetypes who each perform predictable tasks at specific moments within the story.

We can use this knowledge to identify key moments or common interactions in films and use these as stopping points—*Morality Points*—to evaluate what is on screen. At each of these morality points we face our own fork in the road: whether to continue to ingest or decide enough is enough.

We will begin by identifying important components of characters and their actions.

---

1. Ken James. "The Emperor's Club" Interviews: Rob Morrow as Charles Ellerby. 2002. http://www.christiananswers.net/spotlight/movies/2002/theemperorsclub-i-morrow.html. Accessed November 2009. Used by permission. Rob Morrow played FBI Agent Don Epps in CBS-TV's *Numbers*.

Character Introductions

Pay attention to how each character is introduced, particularly the hero. The old adage "you only have one chance to make a first impression" is true. Filmmakers meticulously craft how their characters are presented. In the initial seconds of an introduction we are given cues on how we are to feel about this person. The director will manipulate our perceptions to drive our emotions for or against a character.

In the opening shot of Hitchcock's *Lifeboat,* we discover a ship has been destroyed in the middle of the ocean. The smokestack of the ship sinks below the surface, bodies bob in the waves, debris juts to the surface. Among the ruin, a single lifeboat floats above the wreckage. Soon we realize a woman is sitting in the boat. Once we get a closer look, we see she is not just a woman but a very glamorous woman dressed in fashionable clothing. She sits impatiently perched in the lifeboat as if she is waiting for the valet to return with her car. The woman looks down and sees a run in her stocking. She sighs in frustration. With horror and devastation around her, it is the run in her stocking to which she reacts.

Hitchcock's careful sequencing not only set up the foundational facts of the film—the ship is sunk and all that is left is a lifeboat—but with her dress, demeanor, and reaction to her circumstances, we are given the basic facts regarding fashion columnist Connie Porter.

During a film's opening, observe how the director attempts to manipulate his audience. Does he attempt to have us quickly denounce someone we might normally approve of, or to be apathetic toward someone we would otherwise have empathy for, such as Connie Porter? Does he want us to support someone we might normally loathe, such as the scavenging, untrusting Mad Max in *The Road Warrior*?

During an introduction, the filmmaker is forced to make moral distinctions for the audience—to reveal their beliefs and intents to their audience.

In the same way you can learn a great deal about someone by the type of friends he has, you can tell much about a film and its maker by the character given the heroic role. A writer or director vouches for their hero character—they are plainly stating that this is the kind of person you should emulate.[2] For the Christian, the reaction to this introduction is simple: We should ask, "How much does this character reflect Christ?" Does the hero character adhere to Biblical standards or does he follow an ungodly path?

---

2. The purpose of some movies such as satire or black comedy is to point out an inappropriate personal or cultural characteristic. In these films, the hero is not intended to be emulated but rather is to show how we should *not* be and why.

Character Names

What is in a name? Quite a bit actually. A character's name can elicit deep emotional responses and provide insight into personality. We make assumptions about a person based on their name. It is fair to assume we would all rather get into a fender bender with a guy named Orville Lipschitz than one named Max Buttkicker.

When you are introduced to a character, make note of their name and consider the writer's intentions. Screenwriters will often attempt to manipulate our thoughts regarding a character by giving them a name that can sound ominous (Nurse Ratchet), ridiculous (Sheriff Buford T. Justice), or a mixture of the two (Snake Plisskin).

It is common for the hero to have a larger-than-life name, one clearly stating he is a man's man, for example, like John Rambo, Sam Spade, or James Bond.

James Bond is a great example. His name is one of the most recognizable in modern Western Civilization. His first name is always the formal "James," never Jim, Jimmy, or Jimbo. The use of James gives him an air of civility if not haughtiness. His last name is a short, thud of a word, but it is a marvelous word that conjures strength, reliability, security, usefulness. When he introduces himself as "Bond. James Bond," his formal, family name becomes a replacement for "Mister." In effect he introduces himself as Mister Holds-Things-Together or Mister Strength. Not bad for two syllables.

A hero's name does not always give the sense of power. With today's penchant for anti-heroes—rudderless half-men cast in the heroic light— we often have a main character given a name that signifies a dork, a lout, or a loser.

Travis Bickle, the smoldering assassin in Martin Scorsese's *Taxi Driver*, has a name that tells us he is never going to amount to much. The awkward sounding combination of his first and last names warns us this guy is not cut out for heroic work.

We find the same result in *The Usual Suspects*' Verbal Kint. Verbal? His name is Verbal? He is a criminal and his name means "to blab"?! Not a great handle to carry around in the underworld. He is cast as the weak one in his group of thieves and his name states it is the appropriate place for him, particularly since the other men in his crew have names like Dean Keaton and Michael McManus. Who is the tough guy? Mr. Kint or Mr. McManus?

A writer may attempt to use our reliance on names to capture our approval of someone we would never normally like, or to loathe someone we should respect. It may seem a minor detail, but the name has deep impact on how we perceive that character and on how we are willing to interact with them.

A charismatic character with an attractive name, Jack Sparrow for example, makes it easier for us to ignore things like his constant thieving and lying and his references to his history of rape and murder.

Occupations

Other than soldiers, cops, crooks, and spies, most heroes do not make ends meet by being a hero. They usually have day jobs. Indiana Jones was a history professor, Andy Dufresne (*The Shawshank Redemption*) was an accountant before his incarceration, and Navin Johnson (*The Jerk*) was both a gas station attendant and a carnie before he became an inventor.

As in real life, a character's job says a great deal about who they are and what we can expect from them. We see a teacher on screen, our initial reaction is trust and we assume they are intelligent and somewhat compassionate. If we see a garbage man, right or wrong we assume he is not so bright and perhaps a little boorish. These assumptions may not be fair, but they play a role in how we define each other.

In film, a character's job will be a primary definition to the audience of who that character is. Once again, if we look to Travis Bickle of *Taxi Driver*, we see a shiftless young man who performs a job that is shown as meaningless. This tells us he is not a man of vision or high expectation.

Note, too, that the actual job is not as important in discerning the filmmaker's intent as how that occupation is presented.

> The way an occupation is shown on screen
> will explain to you
> how the filmmaker defines the world.

Are the police shown as brutes willing to bend rules (*American Gangster*)? Is a nurse shown as a living saint, calmly and patiently healing the sick (*Band of Brothers*)? Is the President of the United States represented as a wise leader and great statesman (*Deep Impact*)?

The way an occupation is shown can also manipulate how we think of certain lines of work. Wesley Gibson (*Wanted*) is tormented by his menial life inside an office cubicle. He sits hunched over his desk, barely tolerating his coworkers and manager. The film goes to great lengths to explain to the audience that Wesley's work is meaningless and therefore his life is without value. He is a shell of a man—until he learns his father was a great assassin and an order of assassins recruits him to join their ranks. Then, and only then, does he become someone worthwhile.

The two sides of Wesley are summed up by his mentor, Sloan:

> "It's a choice, Wesley, that each of us must face: to remain ordinary, pathetic, beat-down, coasting through a miserable existence, like sheep herded by fate—or you can take control of your own destiny and join us, releasing the caged wolf you have inside."[3]

In the trailer for the film, the first part of this quote is played over images of Wesley working in an office. In the view of the filmmakers, someone who works in a cubicle is a meaningless cog with no real worth. The audience gets this message either consciously or subconsciously and, since a vast majority of the audience members probably spend most of their time in an office, they are learning it is *they* who are without value. Someone watching *Wanted* will not automatically feel they are a pitiful waste, but add this dribble to the steady drip and it does reinforce the perception that ordinary work is somehow loathsome and empty.

Combine this film with other productions which show average office work as dehumanizing and miserable (*Office Space, The Matrix, The Incredibles, Fight Club, Joe Versus the Volcano*), and a motif emerges which impacts how we view office work. This manipulation is one way a film works to undermine our current values and our appreciation for other people's labor.

Character Flaws

Heroes are larger than life. They are super-human. Each is a notch above the rest of us, someone we want to emulate. They are, as I have mentioned, Christ-like and therefore reflections of God. Like the gods of the world's polytheistic religions, our modern heroes are not God—they are god-lite. What keeps them from being God? They are each afflicted with a flaw.

Every great hero has his Achilles' heel. Indiana Jones is scared of snakes, Fletcher Reede (*Liar, Liar*) is consumed with his work, and Tony Stark (*Iron Man*) is a drunk. Their flaw makes them human and reduces them to our size so we can identify with them.

Such is also the case with Jesus Christ. He is God who willingly came down to our level. He became one of us to stand in our place and shed His blood in ransom for our souls. His "flaw" (if you will permit my use of that term in this context) is His humanity, His mortality. He Who is God became flesh with a definite capacity to feel pain and loneliness, to hunger and thirst, to die; those were His weaknesses. He was tempted by Satan only because He became flesh, a man, and He identified Himself among us because we are unable to identify or even recognize Him (Heb. 4:15).

---

3. Michael Brandt, Derek Haas, et al. *Wanted*. Universal Studios. 2008.

In the end, Jesus overcame temptation, indeed overcame mortal death and is now at the right hand of the throne of God—the Christ, our Ultimate Hero (Heb. 8:1, 12:2; Eph. 1:20).

While we may not have much in common with a suicidal, nearly-psychotic cop such as Martin Riggs, many of us can identify with his addiction to cigarettes and his attempt to quit (*Lethal Weapon 2*). Even if we do not smoke, his petty attempts to quit smoking allow us brief moments of humor and commonality with the over-the-top character.

Flaws are not only for heroes, either. Villains have them as well. The difference is that a villain's flaw (Kahn's thirst for revenge in *Star Trek: The Wrath of Kahn*) will consume him, while a hero can overcome his flaw (Scottie Ferguson's fear of heights in Alfred Hitchcock's *Vertigo*). The hero copes with his flaw; the villain embraces his and allows it to command his motivations.

Take note of character flaws as they are presented. What is the hero's main flaw? How is it handled? Is the flaw truly a flaw or something stated as being a flaw that, in truth, is a strength?

Will Turner in *Pirates of the Caribbean: The Curse of the Black Pearl* is a proper, good, young man. He believes in right and wrong and in social order. His adherence to the social good is his main "flaw," the thing which keeps him from being able to attract Elizabeth Swann. Only after he sheds his social standing and his morality to become a dreaded pirate like his father, does he manage to get the girl and become truly heroic.

> When you find that the hero's character
> flaw is something that would Scripturally be
> considered an attribute, you know to be careful
> of what you are watching.

Forks in the Road

Life is a series of choices. Every day we choose between right and wrong, good and evil, smart and stupid. Sometimes the choices in life are obvious events where we know our decision will have a huge impact: Do I say "yes" to the marriage proposal? Do I take this job? Do I put my house on the market?

The hero normally has one or more instances in a film in which he is given a yes-or-no moment and his morality comes into play. You can note these moments because the action will pause and the hero will be shown pondering his decision, even if it is for a brief moment (Joe pauses on his first time up the stairs in *Sunset Blvd.*). Does Deckard reveal to Rachael that she is not actually a human but rather a man-made replicant (*Blade Runner*)? Does Frodo remain loyal to Samwise or does he succumb to Gollum's lies (*The Lord of the Rings: The Return of the King*)? Does Detective Mills kill John Doe or does he allow the villain to live and the wheels of justice to dole out their punishment (*Se7en*)?

Many times these forks in the road occur within the final act and are the moment at which the hero takes on the value learned during his resurrection scene at the end of Act Three. There are times however, such as with *The Lord of the Rings: Return of the King*, where the decision continues to deepen into the final conflict in the final act.

> As a rule, any time the action stops in a film you should be on guard because something important is being delivered to you.

Be it a narrative element or a morality point, when a moment reveals a stark choice being made it is very important to pay attention to what happens. At these moments we learn the character of the hero and the morality peddled by the filmmaker. These moments teach us to laugh at violence and revenge as we watch Arnold Schwarzenegger decide to drop a man to his death (*Commando*) or learn mercy and forgiveness when we see Bruce Wayne pull Henri Ducard up from the cliff's edge, sparing the villain's life (*Batman Begins*).

Killing and Being Killed

Any time the hero kills someone, pay close attention. Killing and death are normally handled with little concern in modern films. It is common to see heroes mow down dozens of faceless bad guys with no moral consequence whatsoever. With movies like *The Wild Bunch*, *Rambo*, or *Death Race*, one expects death and killing to be treated with passing interest. One should not need to think too hard about these types of films to determine whether or not they follow a biblical standard—the movie is called *Death Race*, after all. I think we can assume it is not a movie Jesus would pick for his collection.

The aspect of killing in a more serious film is another matter. Films such as *Million Dollar Baby*, *Paths of Glory*, or *Goodfellas* all wrestle with the subject of killing by suicide, war, and murder, respectively. When someone is killed in these films, there are very specific circumstances set up with clear moral frameworks to support them.

In *Million Dollar Baby*, the young boxer, Maggie (Hilary Swank), becomes paralyzed. Her trainer, Frankie (Clint Eastwood), must decide whether or not to pull the plug on her life support system. His choice to either kill the woman or to allow her to languish in her hospital bed is not treated lightly and prompts the audience to make their own moral choice along with Frankie.

> The issue of death is serious. When treated seriously in film, it can lead to great drama. It will also be a clear moment where a filmmaker decides to value or devalue human life.

When you see a prominent killing or death in a film, take note of the circumstances. Discern what the event is saying.

Reaction to Death

It is common for someone close to the hero to die at some point. In many cases it will be a loved one (the herald) during Act One. This death will shatter the hero's world. The hero is shown in a moment of grief (Mal in *Silverado*), even sometimes shown standing over the coffin at a funeral (*The Green Mile, Watchmen, The Third Man*) or over the corpse itself (*Tombstone*). The hero's reaction to this death is important—the way in which it motivates his decisions and actions can shed light on the Biblical bent of the piece. Is the hero driven to violent revenge (*Unforgiven*)? Or is his reaction to forgive (*End of the Spear*)?

Reaction to Opposition

At the heart of the story is the central conflict between the hero and the villain. Their goals are diametrically opposed and only one of them can remain standing. We are asked to take the hero's side in this conflict and we usually do so without question. The villain is the villain, after all, and he must be stopped.

While we cheer for the hero, how does he oppose the villain? Does he approach conflict in a Scriptural manner (*The Patriot, Pride and Prejudice*)? Does he just go in guns blazing (*Taken, Payback, Sin City*) or does he allow opportunity for the villain to change his ways and try to reason with the bad guy, to offer him an avenue other than the road to perdition (*Shane, The Dark Knight, Star Wars III: Revenge of the Sith, Schindler's List*)?

Only the most heroic are able to extend a helping hand to those who would do them harm. A true hero reflects the patience and forgiveness of Jesus as he works to correct the villain rather than simply destroy him.

At each of these film moments, these morality points, the hero is revealed to us. He is shown to be a worthy leader of men, a Christ-like man, or he is shown to be a criminal in heroic clothing. We must keep a watchful eye on how the hero both acts and thinks throughout a film because it is him we are meant to emulate.

If his choices are not aligned with Biblical thinking, we must reconsider whether or not the film is worth watching. Even if we choose to continue to watch the film after we determine he is clearly not a Christ-like hero, it is important for us to recognize him for what he is. We then understand that his story and his philosophy are unscriptural, and we can interpret the characters and the film with the skepticism they deserve.

28

Freedom of Choice Means the Freedom to be an Idiot

"God judged it better to bring good out of evil
than to suffer no evil to exist."[1]
— Saint Augustine

O N THE WAY INTO WORK, I SAW A BUMPER STICKER THAT EXCLAIMED,
"Jesus save me from your followers." This blunt insult contains a lesson.
When you take on the title *Christian*, you take on the name of Christ. You
become part of His body, the church. You are Jesus' representative to all the
people with whom you cross paths.

Ask any secularist what they think of Christians and invariably you will find
us described as controlling zealots, unrealistic do-gooders, or theocrats. The
stereotype of the hyperventilating, micromanaging Christian has not been
artificially synthesized. It has its root in reality.

Christians have a long and somewhat pathetic history of trying to force the
square-shaped peg of this world into our nice round theological hole. The
image of Christians protesting a movie is not an unfamiliar sight. *The Da
Vinci Code, The Last Temptation of Christ, The Golden Compass,* and even
the Harry Potter movies have irked Christians to some degree. But when we
protest, do we help or hurt our cause?

Many of our arguments and most of our tactics are outmoded. The general
tone of many Christian leaders toward our culture seems more appropriate

---

1. Horton Davies. *The Vigilant God: Providence In the Thought of Augustine, Aquinas, Calvin, and
Barth.* P. Lang. 1992. 34. Used by permission.

for problems that afflicted us twenty years ago. When a media company releases a product we find offensive, say *The Golden Compass*, what is our reaction? Christians whine and threaten. We write articles in Christian publications (both public and private) to warn of bad content and try to organize protests against the offending material.

With *The Golden Compass*, a storm of anger erupted over the film's disparagement of the Christian faith (and Catholicism in particular) and was a media story for weeks. The rancor of Christian leaders was repeated in mainstream sources such as *Time, Newsweek,* and *USAToday.* The author of the film's source material, Phillip Pullman, was interviewed heavily about his works and questioned about his motives when writing the children's books. A controversy ignited, the media conglomerates built up their marketing campaigns, and interest in the film's release skyrocketed. When the film finally hit theatres, it bombed—brought in less than $70 million in the American box office. Christians breathed a sigh of relief and knew their efforts had sunk yet another subversive work of the corrupt filth-mongers in Hollywood.

In reality however, the Christian caterwauling may have had less effect than originally thought. The film found new life on the international market where it brought in over $255 million. Considering its $180 million price tag, under Hollywood accounting the total take of $325 million was not enough to make this a profitable venture and the film is still considered to be a disaster based on the expectations of what could have been.

The point here is that the Christian reaction to the film, while it seemed relevant, actually had very little to do with the film's overall lack of success. Certainly, the removal of the Christian audience took a chunk from the opening weekend grosses, but the overall failure of the piece probably had to do with the fact that *The Golden Compass* was just a poorly made film. If the movie had been better produced, it is unlikely that all the Christian complaints in the world could have kept it from becoming a success. Even a moderately well-made film that received such treatment from Christians (*The Da Vinci Code*) still made a notable amount of money at the domestic and international box office.

Christians did not stop *The Golden Compass* from hitting theatres and they did not cause it to fail. As the piece hits DVD, online rental, and cable, the marketing chains will reignite and the books, toys, and posters will be seen once again. The film, even though it underperformed, can still expect a long life in rentals—well into the next decade.

Our warnings helped inform the flock, which is wonderful and needed. It did not, however, do much outside of our church walls. Our actions' lack of potency outside of our own sphere of influence should tell us our current tactics will only take us so far; and that is not far enough.

It may seem a noble ideal to control the media, to make our voices heard, to tell filmmakers what they can and cannot release into the mainstream of our society. The fact is, that is a fantasy. Times have changed. Protests and complaints may have their place, but we must understand they are not effective tools to bring about notable, Kingdom change. At best, our protests become footnotes to the history of a film, but at what expense?

What can we do? How can we actually affect the culture?

> The best thing a Christian can do
> to change society is to simply be
> a daily, devoted Christ-follower.

When we choose to extend our faith-life to the films we rent and purchase, we show our walk with Christ. Sounds odd? It is true.

How would you feel if you entered your pastor or priest's living room and saw a rack of DVDs that included *Friday the 13th*, *American Pie*, and *Austin Powers: The Spy Who Shagged Me*? Most of us would immediately question the man's fidelity to his Lord as well as his respect for his position in the church.

We make a statement with the films we choose to see, and those films eventually express themselves in our daily lives. Our entertainment choices should be molded by our faith because our entertainment feeds our souls. When you settle for lurid materials that speak to our basest natures (*Saw* or *Borat*), you lower yourself and the reputation of Christ to that level.

Even then God is pro-freedom, including the freedom to do the wrong thing. God demands certain behavior, but He always keeps it an issue of choice. Noah was allowed to decide to descend into drunkenness, Esau was given opportunity to take revenge upon Jacob, Peter was permitted to confront his personal prejudices and choose not to submit to them.

The human ability to individually decide is a gift that provides opportunity to be closer to God. An automaton who never had any option but to stay with God cannot rightly say it is capable of love, hate, or any other real emotion. One of God's blessings is our ability to express our gratitude and love back to Him. This can only be done with the blessing of freedom—the freedom of choice.

This blessing has its downside, however. If we can choose to love and obey God, we can also choose to be disobedient and to scorn Him.

The Bible makes clear that some of us will remain dutifully aligned with God while others will fall to the wayside. God has determined who will live forever and who will die. When Christians overplay their role and make severe demands on behavior—make godly choices not an issue of voluntary conversion but a matter of compulsion—we step away from the teachings of Christ and inch toward religiosity.

Conversion through force has no value because there is no choice involved. Paul did not enable Christianity to flower across the ancient world by condemnation and control; rather, he engaged people, challenged them, and ultimately led them to Jesus. We must do the same.

There are obvious restrictions which should be placed on filmmakers; clear examples are public sex acts, child pornography, or the use of real footage of death and torture for purposes of entertainment. To deal, though, specifically with mainstream entertainment, I believe a more tolerant approach is best.

Yes, this means things like *Wolf Creek, Saw,* and *Hostel* will be produced and released. For many Christians, the dangers of having these films released to the public is too much to bear. I understand this view, and I am sympathetic to it. However, we do little to halt this type of content if we run it underground. It is vile, devilish stuff and anyone who views it is likely to be deeply troubled by the experience whether they realize it or not. The point is that if this content is restricted, it will not cease to exist. It will simply go underground—away from our ability to address the inaccuracies and threats its messages pose to our society.

The impulses fed by this type of content will still be here. It is the impulse, the initial sinful thinking which must be addressed.

I look at it this way. Despite the fact that pornography is a multibillion dollar business, most adults understand that it is a corrosive poison to our society. This horrid medium feeds a perceived need, however, and millions of men and women feed from its sickening banquet every year. What if we banned the production and distribution of all pornography tomorrow? What if the federal government enacted strict anti-pornography laws and the pornographers were all sent to prison. What if, in addition, we included restrictions on the display of extreme acts of violence—no more gory violence allowed. A large segment of the church would probably applaud.

Before long, those films would appear on the black market (which already exists) like ants on a bowl of sugar water. Secret strip clubs would sprout up.

How would the government be able to define what was pornographic? Who would make the choices? Church leaders? If so, which church? Would Protestants want the Catholic Church deciding what content was permissible, or vice-versa? What of agnostics and others? Should they be held against their will to the moral distinctions of the Faithful? How long would they allow that to stand?[2]

---

2. U. S. Prohibition in the 1920s should adequately answer that question.

The attempt to control is a slippery slope. When examined, the issue is not the creation of pornography. The issue is the demand for it.

One Sunday, our congregation was shown a video—a short film of a man sitting at his computer. He surfed the Web out of boredom and stumbled across a pornography site. He looked at the tempting images and his eyes widened. Suddenly, the man violently struck his computer monitor and sent it crashing to the floor. He destroyed his computer. Out of breath, he returned to his chair, a satisfied smile on his face. Then this verse faded onto the screen:

> If your hand causes you to sin, cut it off. It is better for you to enter life maimed than with two hands to go into hell, where the fire never goes out. And if your foot causes you to sin, cut it off. It is better for you to enter life crippled than to have two feet and be thrown into hell. And if your eye causes you to sin, pluck it out. It is better for you to enter the kingdom of God with one eye than to have two eyes and be thrown into hell (Mk. 9:43–47).

The message said that man was righteous for destroying his computer because it caused him to sin. But the fact is that it was not an act of piety; it was an act of idiocy. The man's computer did not cause him to sin any more than my sister's homemade chocolate-chip cookies cause me to be fat. If I find my mouth watering over a plate of cookies, I do not destroy her stove. The material object is not responsible for our decision. The verse does not call us to blame external forces for our internal problems.

Christians are to pluck out our eye if it causes us to sin. Notice this is our own eye, not someone else's eye. The responsibility for our inclination toward sin and sinful thought rests within us, not on society at large. The man who destroyed his computer had little strength toward resolution of his pornographic urges. He may have removed the instrument through which he acted out the momentary, sinful desires, but in its absence his sinful thoughts and impulses remain because they were still unresolved. Only after the man recognizes his issues, admits his sin and his need to change, then turns to Christ Jesus for help can he say he is on the road to removal of the sin in his life.

We need to change the focus of our concern.

> It is not the choices we have available
> which are the problem.
> Our troubles lie in the choices
> we are inclined to make.

29

Less Christian Art, More Christian Artists

"Ladies and gentlemen: as communicators of the human word, you are the stewards and administrators of an immense spiritual power that belongs to the patrimony of mankind and is meant to enrich the whole of the human community."[1]
— Pope John Paul II

CHRISTIAN CULTURE IS OFTEN THE ENEMY OF QUALITY. INDEPENDENT Christian film, in particular, has a history of being seriously and deeply flawed—routinely dismissed by secular critics and audiences as intellectually vacant and disconnected from reality. Unfortunately, even the harshest criticisms of Christian film tend to be true.

Christian films are often more embarrassing than inspiring but, to be fair, things have improved. Production values are increasing and some serious shops are attempting to make quality productions. Within the past ten years we have gone from unwatchable disasters (*The Last Sin Eater, The Omega Code, Joshua*) to the more impressive *The Nativity Story, Luther, Beyond the Gates of Splendor, Bella,* and *Heart of Texas*. And, lest we forget, there is also Mel Gibson's little film, *The Passion of the Christ*.

As Hollywood has seen financial and cultural muscle begin to develop within the Christian film community, they have worked to market products in our direction. Our ranks have, likewise, tried to cater to our tastes. This has led to more investors. More money leads to better-looking product.

---

1. Address of His Holiness John Paul II to the People of the Communications Industry, Registry Hotel (Los Angeles). September 15, 1987. Used by permission of Libreria Editrice Vaticana.

With the attention the Christian community has gained over the past decade, money and marketing are no longer issues. When the Kendrick brothers can push out a film with a $10 million budget and gross over $30 million at the box office, we can no longer claim that Christians are not making headway in the film industry. Yet even in the face of these improvements, the term *Christian film* is still synonymous with substandard production values, stilted dialog, and childish plots. Why is Christian film no more than a side note to modern culture? Why are Christians left behind?

Throughout the 1960s, heavy-handed Christian values were overthrown by the hippie generation. Christians retreated, overwhelmed by the burgeoning social changes. But church-goers still wanted the pleasures of modern culture—only without the tempting content and foul philosophy that muddied the entertainment. Our reaction was to slowly build a cultural wall around ourselves, complete with self-prescribed content filters and an isolationist attitude.

This cocoon was a comfy, safe place for Christians, but the cocoon became a time capsule. We spent decades discussing what we hoped the world was like rather than dealing with how things are.

Our isolation also bred generations of well-intentioned but poorly-trained artists. Instead of playing with the big boys, Christian filmmakers have remained in the minor leagues. Christian audiences learned to accept substandard artists who make substandard works—we no longer have any expectations of quality. The situation is no different from expecting a church youth group play to compete with off-Broadway productions. We are ill-equipped and out-matched.

Today, even with the financial successes we have seen, we are on the outside looking in. You can have the huge budget, skilled and experienced technical crew, and a firmly executed marketing plan, but if you film a pedantic script with summer-stock-reject actors, your "better looking product" is simply lipstick on a pig. Throw in Christian film's inherently agenda-driven plots and dialogue and you have lipstick on a preachy pig.

The Christian film genre is rooted in delivering an agenda. Films are not allowed to develop organically but are designed to meet the church's outline, to produce films that are stodgy and forced.

The fact is that the average Christian film is more pushy and sanctimonious than the global-warming agenda movies that hit the market during the past decade.

Violence is almost non-existent, salty language never happens, unmarried people never struggle with lust, and evil is never very bad because showing various forms of sin is not allowed. By movie's end, everyone is converted quite nicely with no residual issues. Life is reduced to an after-school special with prayer thrown in for good measure. For me, this is where the dry heaving begins.

Restrictions on content are there, presumably, because people believe it to be biblical. *We must not let actors kiss or use swear words, after all.* I disagree. Such restrictions would bar me from producing a movie accurate to Scripture, itself. It is a tough argument to think modern Christians cannot handle a simple kiss or rough language when God allowed Joshua to slaughter thousands behind the crumbled walls of Jericho, or permitted Moses to execute his own people following his descent from Mount Sinai.

It is wrong to blame only the artists and producers for the saccharine muck that lines the walls of Christian bookstores—like being mad at the chef for offering no variety after demanding he serve you nothing but macaroni and cheese. We, the audience, are to blame for the failure of Christian culture. Christian artists cater to us, give us what we want, what we prefer— and Christians' expectations have tended to *not* stress biblical truth, moral clarity, or technical achievement but rather a watered-down, unrealistic view of the world.

Christians are not the only audience trained to not expect quality. Audiences in general have had their tastes dumbed down to accept the pitiful, disposable paradise of the corporate cinema. This is not meant as a snobbish slam against the average person, we simply are not taught the Arts in this society. Lack of education coupled with the tsunami of crud flowing at us on a daily basis has left us unequipped to discern the good from the bad from the ugly.

Americans, in general, are expected to accept Hollywood's false and disposable paradise as a relevant, important aspect of life. We are born on a fabricated, cultural treadmill, constantly chasing new releases while the latest celebrity gossip hangs just out of reach—given the illusion of doing something but never making progress.

Christians have nothing to lose as modern culture falls. We are the direct beneficiaries of the coming cultural implosion. When the self-destruction of our secular culture is complete, we must be ready to offer a viable alternative to today's smutty nonsense—and we have something genuine to offer which secularists can only dream of: Truth. Life in Christ feeds the hungry spirit and gives definition to life. No amount of existential claptrap will ever compete with the nourishing truth of Christ.

To Bear His Name

"I don't deliberately write 'Christian stories,' just as I don't bake 'Christian cookies.'"[2] — Jeffrey Overstreet

Can Christians cut through the haze of celebrity, corporate culture, and the Christian subculture to present God's truth to the world? As with all problems, the solution can be found in the Bible.

First Samuel 17 is a famous section of Scripture. The youthful David stands up to Goliath, the master of the battlefield.

> And there came out from the camp of the Philistines a champion named Goliath of Gath, whose height was six cubits and a span. He had a helmet of bronze on his head, and he was armed with a coat of mail, and the weight of the coat was five thousand shekels of bronze. And he had bronze armor on his legs, and a javelin of bronze slung between his shoulders. The shaft of his spear was like a weaver's beam, and his spear's head weighed six hundred shekels of iron. And his shield-bearer went before him.[3]

Goliath stood on the front lines mocking his enemies. David, probably a young teenager, appeared at the fomenting battle to deliver a message from his father to his brothers. David overheard Goliath's arrogant, offensive taunts and volunteered to take on the behemoth. At first, David was equipped just as Goliath was.

> Then [King] Saul clothed David with his armor. He put a helmet of bronze on his head and clothed him with a coat of mail, and David strapped his sword over his armor. And he tried in vain to go, for he had not tested them. Then David said to Saul, "I cannot go with these, for I have not tested them." So David put them off. Then he took his staff in his hand and chose five smooth stones from the brook and put them in his shepherd's pouch. His sling was in his hand, and he approached the Philistine.[4]

David approached the dangerous warrior and took him out with a rock thrown from a common sling. For all of his bluster and despite his reputation, expertise, and power, Goliath was defeated by a kid with good aim.

The entertainment industry is a Goliath which we must confront, but we must not prepare for the fight by dressing like our foe. We need not mimic

2. John Ottinger. Weaving the Colors: An Interview with Jeffrey Overstreet. In *Grasping For the Wind*. January 22, 2008. http://www.graspingforthewind.com/2008/01/22/weaving-the-colors-an-interview-with-jeffrey-overstreet/. Last accessed March 9, 2010. Used by permission.
3. 1 Samuel 17:4–7. A shekel equals approximately 0.025 pounds, therefore the weight of Goliath's mail coat equaled 125 pounds and his spear head weighed 15 pounds.
4. 1 Samuel 17:38–40

Hollywood to defeat it. We must trust God and rely on Him to provide and to lead.

What would have happened if David had stayed suited in unfamiliar trappings? He would have played to Goliath's strengths and the giant would have made mincemeat of him. David, rightly, rejected the king's armor and relied on his own skills. He trusted in God and relied on his own experience as a shepherd. He used what he knew—the sling. Not armor, not spear, not sword.

Hollywood produces quantity. We cannot compete with them on that field, it would be suicide. David's sling, for us, is quality. Hollywood can feed the masses, but they cannot sustain them. If we produce fine food for their minds and their souls, the audiences will come.

People have a natural hunger for knowledge. They desire truth no differently than they desire water and nutrition. We, as Christ-followers, are the keepers of truth. The Bible is the fount of knowledge. We have the truth; all we need to do is tell it. If we remove all of the fancy glitz and deliver the truth, we can take on the whole entertainment industry. Our generation can change the culture. It is as simple as David's stone.

> We do not glorify God by making lousy movies. Christians should never be satisfied with wallowing in mediocrity. We must demand the best and only the best. We need great films.

Recent Christian film releases are superior to their previous counterparts, but we do not need good movies—we need great movies. If a film claims to be Christian, it was supposedly done for the glory of God. We do not glorify God by making lousy movies. Christians should never be satisfied with wallowing in mediocrity. We must demand the best and only the best. We need great films.

A two-pronged approach is needed; the focus should be on two separate groups: artists and audience. Artists are partners in the development of a movement, but the audience is often the forgotten entity. Without an informed, alert public, who will hold the artist accountable? Who will keep him or her in line and focused?

We have the makings of a movement that can change this culture. I honestly believe this. But I also believe the first step toward establishing the groundwork for a vibrant, relevant cultural movement based on Scriptural thought is to stop producing "Christian films" or "Christian music" or "Christian art" and simply have Christ-followers who create great Art.

Culture is much like a garden. You must keep it healthy and growing or the weeds take over. With a little work on our part, we can learn to cultivate a healthy culture that will flower over time and bear fruit. It is not the artist who is the gardener, it is the audience. We are responsible for which artists take root and grow, and which ones die on the vine. We must maintain the need for a moral and just culture. We also must demand quality.

We must be open about our faith. That is why it is far more important for the *filmmaker* to be identified as Christian rather than his work labeled as such. Even a pagan can make a movie and label it Christian.

When a Christ-follower produces a film that speaks to Biblical truth and morality, he has made a Christian film. The product itself should not carry the label; the artist is the Christ-follower. His fruit will bear His name.

30

Practice Extreme Moderation

*"If you find honey, eat just enough—
too much of it and you will vomit."[1]*

USE THE WORD *MODERATION* AROUND SOME PEOPLE AND YOU MAY AS well paint yourself red and wear horns and a forked tail. To them moderation translates to unfettered tolerance or gross compromise.

I understand the negative reaction to the concept of moderation when it comes to culture. Many films and most television offerings are corrupting; little is created from a Christian perspective. To act *moderate* in the face of the entertainment industry seems like listening to the devil for the sake of hearing him out.

Many Christians, however, are already eagerly engaged in the culture. They go to church, attend Bible studies, and are involved in church activities, but in their off time they watch movies and television like everyone else.

Christian leaders often speak to the culture from outside while their flock already lives on the inside, buying DVDs and waiting in line to see new releases.

Christians more involved in their faith perhaps try to be cautious in what they consume, but they still have to watch whatever is available. It is an uncommon Christian who is fully sealed off from this culture.

The question for Christians is not if we should be involved in culture. The question is how should we be involved? How should we then approach film? What is the right thing to do regarding the movies we watch?

---

1. Proverbs 25:16

I believe it is vital to the survival of this society for Christ-followers to get involved. It is not possible for us to minister to society if we do not understand what the culture is doing—rather like doctoring a patient without knowing their symptoms.

Christ-followers are people—rational, dynamic, contributing members of society who want to live a right, i.e. Christ-like, life. When people see us doing the right things, even if they find it annoying, it reminds them there is indeed a standard of right and wrong. Their annoyance with us who choose to do right is rooted in their knowledge that there is a moral code they should follow. They do not want that reminder, and when we bring it to the forefront they are forced to confront their own actions and decisions.

We must begin the reformation of this civilization that has far more important work to do than celebrate its own loins. But what can you do? How can the average, everyday Christian impact society? You change the world around you by first establishing yourself on solid ground.

First, we must take seriously film and all other forms of entertainment. What we view does matter.

Secondly, we must begin to view films through a Scriptural lens. Christians are uniquely equipped by Almighty God to combat the negative materials spewed from the film industry. We must re-train ourselves to view Art with discrimination, regardless of its form.

While a majority of Americans say they are Christian, our culture is wholly secularized. In effect, Christians in America live in enemy territory. As the ungodly culture seeps deeper and deeper into the fabric of our society, Christ-followers know that what we believe is not accepted by a majority of the people around us.

Even those who consider themselves Christian may not be active in their faith and can become a strange hybrid known as a secular-Christian—someone completely encased in secular life but who, when pressed, still gives lip service to Jesus. They seem to say, "I'll take the salvation. You keep the rules." But James says,

> But be doers of the word, and not hearers only, deceiving yourselves. For if anyone is a hearer of the word and not a doer, he is like a man who looks intently at his natural face in a mirror. For he looks at himself and goes away and at once forgets what he was like. But the one who looks into the perfect law, the law of liberty, and perseveres, being no hearer who forgets but a doer who acts, he will be blessed in his doing (Jms 1:22-24).

C hrist-followers must help people see that our worldview is the Way.

> Jesus said to him, "I am the way, and the truth, and the life. No one comes to the Father except through me" (Jn 14:6).

> But this I confess to you, that according to the Way, which they call a sect, I worship the God of our fathers, believing everything laid down by the Law and written in the Prophets (Acts 24:14).

C hrist-followers must practice what they preach and lead by example. The culture turns around when you—I mean YOU—turn around. We do no one any good when we complain about society's depravity then quote *Borat* to our church friends over dinner. If we cannot control ourselves, who are we to demand the same of others? This starts with you, in your home, doing the right thing even when no one is looking.

To Discern Beauty Among the Squalor

Entertainment and the Arts have intrinsic value. As children of the Most High God we must learn to boldly stand in support of filmmakers who choose to honor integrity, Christ-like values, and excellence because as we become better consumers of media, we build a better foundation for all of society. Common, everyday Christ-followers can compel a revolution in the Arts of today's Western culture.

For this movement, the artist's duty is clear: create Art that professes the virtues found in Jesus Christ. Speak truth and do so in a historical context. Enliven the world with beauty. Artists—whom we allow to have massive influences upon society—must be prompted to create products which feed the mind and speak to the soul.

The audience's role, however, is not so clear-cut. Modern audiences have lost the ability to discern right from wrong, beauty from squalor. We must be able to quickly, astutely identify excellence.

> Finally, brothers, whatever is true, whatever is honorable, whatever is just, whatever is pure, whatever is lovely, whatever is commendable, if there is any excellence, if there is anything worthy of praise, think about these things. What you have learned and received and heard and seen in me—practice these things, and the God of peace will be with you (Phil. 4:8–9).

Too often today we devour fattening cakes and glazed donuts and are no longer able to take pleasure in the natural sweetness of a pear.

Romans 14 states that each of us is equipped with our own set of tolerances:

> As one who is in the Lord Jesus, I am fully convinced that no food is unclean in itself. But if anyone regards something as unclean, then for him it is unclean. If your brother is distressed because of what you eat, you are no longer acting in love. Do not by your eating destroy your brother for whom Christ died. Do not allow what you consider good to be spoken of as evil. For the kingdom of God is not a matter of eating and drinking, but of righteousness, peace and joy in the Holy Spirit, because anyone who serves Christ in this way is pleasing to God and approved by men.
>
> Let us therefore make every effort to do what leads to peace and to mutual edification. Do not destroy the work of God for the sake of food. All food is clean, but it is wrong for a man to eat anything that causes someone else to stumble. It is better not to eat meat or drink wine or to do anything else that will cause your brother to fall (Rom. 14:13–21).

It would be far too simplistic for me to declare which films are safe for Christians and which should be avoided. Christians are individuals. One choice does not fit all. What I find abhorrent, you may find acceptable and vice versa.

Though tastes are as unique as the people who have them and we are each held responsible to decide according to our unique and individual walk with Christ, we must also be aware of our impact on the lives of those around us.

The Freedom of the Faithful

We must decide not to put any stumbling block or obstacle in a brother's way. If my watching *Dog Day Afternoon* or *The Wild Bunch* will lead someone astray or even cause them to stumble, then I must reconsider my choice. All Christians must pay attention to what they are doing and how it affects anyone around them. First Corinthians 10:23–33 tells us how:

> "Everything is permissible"—but not everything is beneficial. "Everything is permissible"—but not everything is constructive. Nobody should seek his own good, but the good of others. Eat anything sold in the meat market without raising questions of conscience, for, "The earth is the Lord's, and everything in it."
>
> If an unbeliever invites you to a meal and you want to go, eat whatever is put before you without raising questions of conscience. But if anyone says to you, "This has been offered in sacrifice," then do not eat it, both for the sake of the man who told you and for conscience sake—the other man's

conscience, I mean, not yours. For why should my freedom be judged by another's conscience? If I take part in the meal with thankfulness, why am I denounced because of something I thank God for?

So whether you eat or drink or whatever you do, do it all for the glory of God. Do not cause anyone to stumble, whether Jews, Greeks or the church of God—even as I try to please everybody in every way. For I am not seeking my own good but the good of many, so that they may be saved. — Paul

Personally, I rely on 1 Corinthians 6:12–13 when I choose films both to watch and to review.

"Everything is permissible for me"—
but not everything is beneficial.

"Everything is permissible for me"—
but I will not be mastered by anything.

"Food for the stomach and the stomach for food"—but God will destroy them both.

The body is not meant for sexual immorality, but for the Lord, and the Lord for the body. —Paul

These verses deal specifically with sexual immorality, but I believe the concepts also extend to other facets of our lives. Sexual behavior itself is not sinful; it becomes immoral when done outside of a godly marriage. In this light, I find this admonition useful as I decide how to consume media.

> It might be acceptable to watch most films,
> but it is the context of our decisions
> which make them good or bad choices.

The standard above is hard to maintain. My mind is part of my body; the Holy Spirit is in my mind as well as my stomach. This is why I continue to return to the film-equals-food analogy. What I allow to be taken in by my brain is no different than what is taken into my stomach. My body, my mind, is not meant for immorality but for the Lord. I need to ask constantly, "Am I doing this for God, or am I doing it for myself?" If the answer is not "for God," I have some explaining to do.

The most interesting portion of 1 Corinthians 12, to me, and the part that slips by without much notice, is, "but I will not be mastered by anything." We are allowed to partake in our culture. We can engage it, check out what it has to say. We must, however, not get drunk on its offerings. That is extreme moderation.

We must avoid being drawn into the marketing culture and the promises of the false, disposable paradise. We must be on guard against offering any form of worship to celebrities who are often presented as demigods. In other words, we can consume films as long as they do not consume us.

> Do not let my heart incline to any evil,
>   to busy myself with wicked deeds
>   in company with men who work iniquity,
>   and let me not eat of their delicacies!
>   — David (Ps. 141:4)

> Live as free men, but do not use your freedom as a cover-up for evil; live as servants of God. — Peter (1 Pet. 2:16)

This is further explored in 1 Corinthians chapter 8:

Food Sacrificed to Idols

Now about food sacrificed to idols: We know that we all possess knowledge. Knowledge puffs up, but love builds up. The man who thinks he knows something does not yet know as he ought to know. But the man who loves God is known by God.

So then, about eating food sacrificed to idols: We know that an idol is nothing at all in the world and that there is no God but one. For even if there are so-called gods, whether in heaven or on earth (as indeed there are many "gods" and many "lords"), yet for us there is but one God, the Father, from whom all things came and for whom we live; and there is but one Lord, Jesus Christ, through whom all things came and through whom we live.

But not everyone knows this. Some people are still so accustomed to idols that when they eat such food they think of it as having been sacrificed to an idol, and since their conscience is weak, it is defiled. But food does not bring us near to God; we are no worse if we do not eat, and no better if we do.

Be careful, however, that the exercise of your freedom does not become a stumbling block to the weak. For if anyone with a weak conscience sees you who have this knowledge eating in an idol's temple, will not he be emboldened to eat what has been sacrificed to idols? So this weak brother, for whom Christ died, is destroyed by your knowledge. When you sin against your brothers in this way and wound their weak conscience, you sin against Christ. Therefore, if what I eat causes my brother to fall into sin, I will never eat meat again, so that I will not cause him to fall (1 Cor. 8).

Those around us who are wrapped within the secular culture are the ones distracted by idols. If my watching a film will confuse them further, I should not do it.

In the course of reviewing movies, I see a great many films I otherwise would never touch. With my spiritual support system in place and my years of experience and knowledge of cinema and Story, I can view most films without harming myself. But I do not invite others to tag along when I view rough movies like *Funny Games* or *Vacancy*. My tolerance is high where others will probably not fare as well. I watch these rougher films for a purpose and am careful not to draw others into the experience if I believe it will lead them astray. When I write my reviews of these kinds of films I am very clear about what someone will see. I do my best to warn against viewing them.

Do not make the mistake of thinking that since you have the freedom of choice you are free from consequences. We are allowed to stand before the banquet of human creativity, but we must choose with discretion and great care. Act as if your soul depends on it. It does.

31

Onward Christian Audiences

"Leisure is time for doing something useful."[1]
——— Benjamin Franklin

W<small>E LIVE IN A CAPITALIST SOCIETY, SO THE CHOICES OF AN AUDIENCE</small> will guide which producers survive—an awesome power when you realize its reach. A filmmaker can make a thousand movies, but if no one shows up to watch them, he will fail. If another director makes a single film that everyone loves, he will succeed. We are in control of who thrives in the cinematic marketplace. It is time for us to use this power to direct our society back towards the paths of our Lord.

Positive Action

When Christians serve their communities, it is normally by cleaning up after disasters, stocking food shelves, working in a soup kitchen, transporting the elderly, or being present for people in trouble. Perhaps we should also consider serving our communities in cultural ways.

Rarely have I been impressed with the results of protests and boycotts. While these tactics have their place, I believe positive action is frequently more effective. Urging people to do the right thing is always preferable to demanding they stop doing the wrong thing. Let me illustrate.

A hotel was built at the end of a pier which thrust out into the ocean. After a few mishaps occurred from guests fishing from their windows, management

---

1. Benjamin Franklin. *The Way to Wealth.* Leavitt, Trow & co. 1848. 3. [Full quote is usually cited as "Leisure is time for doing something useful; this leisure the diligent man will obtain, but the lazy man never."]

placed this sign in each room: "Do not fish from this room." Can you guess what happened? Fishing from the rooms increased exponentially; hotel guests who would never have thought to fish that way suddenly experienced the delights of snagging a trophy from the comfort of their own room. So management considered the problem again and posted a new sign: "Enjoy the view." Fishing incidents dropped to almost none.

Too often we are seen as condemning rather than being a loving people who offer realistic, positive, hope-filled alternatives. We must work strategically at the local and national levels to provide encouragement. We can recast our role in society from one of moral traffic cops to being valuable leaders.

Buycott

One positive action which Christ-followers can take is the *buycott*. Christians specifically target and champion Christ-friendly products, companies, and services.

If a radio program, television show, or film promotes a Scriptural viewpoint, buy from their sponsors then tell that sponsor you use their product because of the friendly values they support. Remember, films have commercials in them called product placements.

The buycott is preferable to a boycott since it promotes good works and provides much needed capital to artists and sponsors.

For too long, Christians have simply reacted to the cultural onslaught. Re-examine the last forty years. Has our reactionary mindset worked? No. We succeeded only in watching while the culture and people around us fell down the slippery slope to total debauchery and depravity. People around us live lives filled with hopelessness. When we boycott, we restrict and can easily be marked as repressive, uncaring censors.

Lobby Local Theatres and Video Stores

Church groups concerned with cultural matters can request local movie theatres carry films that support a Christian worldview. If there is a specific film they would like to see, many theatre operators will allow their theatres to be rented. If a film powerfully explores a Biblical approach to living (*The Blind Side, Fireproof, Chariots of Fire*), why not buy a showing of the film then offer the film at low cost or free to the general public? The average person gets to see a film for free and the Faithful promote Biblical teaching. The same can be done in the context of community theatres and other performance venues.

Petition your local video stores to offer more family-friendly and Biblically informed DVDs. If they can find room for B-grade horror movies, they can probably find room for more uplifting fare.

Film Clubs

Get together outside of church. It is a great way for members of a congregation to deepen their relationships. Book clubs are one way members of churches get together. The group selects a list of books to read then discusses the books from a biblical perspective.

You can start a film club. Members select a number of films, one or two a month, then get together to discuss the biblical perspective of the films.

When you begin to view movies through a biblical lens, you may be surprised at what you see. To share perspectives and opinions in a group setting can make even a film you have seen a hundred times seem new and interesting.

My suggestion is to meet in small groups and keep the films neutral at first. Pick from well-known classics (*The Sound of Music, The Hiding Place, Casablanca, Strangers on a Train*) or modern, Hollywood blockbusters (*The Lord of the Rings: The Fellowship of the Ring, The Pursuit of Happyness, WALL-E, Night at the Museum*). Since these films can be easily digested and have little questionable content (depending on each member's tolerances) the discussions can start simple. As the group gains experience and gets to know each other's tastes and perspectives, they can move toward complex films with challenging content and subjects (*The Pawnbroker, The Decalogue, There Will Be Blood*).

Your group should have a designated facilitator for each session who will drive the discussion and keep things on topic. Identify the story structure, character archetypes, and the Central Question and Answer (moral of the story). Note the film's purpose and question the truths and messages presented. Locate Scriptures that support or contradict the film's morality points. The group can look for Christian symbolism, Biblical references, and product placements within the film and decide how other aspects of the film and its characters track with Biblical teaching.

Support Your Local Filmmakers

With Hollywood's disposable paradise constantly in sight, it is easy to be distracted from the Lord's purposes for us. Every aspect of our existence should be in tune with His will—easier said than done. To help us, He has provided the tools necessary for us to stay on track with Him. One of these tools is the artistic impulse. It is our job to employ our invention and labor to express both His glory and our desire to be with Him.

As audience members, we do the Lord's work when we support and spread the word regarding works that rightly show a universe commanded by the one true Lord, works of Art that express Scriptural truth.

When you find a filmmaker or artist who consistently delivers Biblically-accurate work, support them. Go to their films, buy their DVDs, buy DVDs for other people, talk it up. Go online, visit their official website and drop them a line. A simple e-mail of support from a stranger can mean the world to a struggling artist—and it does not cost you a thing.

Support for excellence in the Arts does not include only encouraging professionals. Many teenagers enjoy expressing themselves. Many love to make short movies. Why not hold a festival for short films at your church? Perhaps have a short-film competition? Criterion and judging could include, "Storyline includes heroic portrayal of truth conquering deception" or "Film encapsulates a realistic depiction of . . ."—insert your preference here.

If members of your church are budding filmmakers or desire to pursue other Arts, support them. Help them produce films of heroic integrity, write poetry which introduces hope into pathos, compose a piano concerto which thrills with the excitement of God's grace, paint cloudscapes which capture hints of the awesome power of our Creator. Any person can offer work space, time, or money. Once the piece is completed, incorporate the work into a worship service or study time, have a premiere or a showing at your church, or, better yet, rent out the local theatre and make their message available to the general public.

This can all be done online, as well. Most churches have their own websites. Why not allow teens the opportunity to mentor under a gifted, Christ-following professional within your congregation to produce YouTube videos for your site?

Artists do not grow on trees in full flower. They must develop their craft, hone their skills; it requires time, and every artist needs that initial support.

Professional Christian artists appreciate every kind word and all the support we can give. The Arts are overpopulated by secularists, and it will be good for the Christ-follower who has chosen to take a stand for Him in the milieu to be reminded they are not alone in their struggle for excellence and integrity.

The difference between secular members of our culture and those of us who live to serve Christ is that our goal is to not hold our enemies down. We hope to lift them up—up to Jesus for the glory of God. Through effective artistry and the core intellect of our faith we can regain our rightful place at the forefront of our culture. Through the example of Christ, this society can change. We only need to stand up for Him.

We can provide a path for cultural change. We can develop a fruitful and resilient artistic community which speaks to Truth. Beginning today, we can demonstrate there *is* a more noble way.

And I will show you a
still more excellent way.[2]
— Paul

---

2   1 Corinthians 12:31b

32

I Screwed Up. Now What?

"Every judgment of conscience, be it right or wrong,
be it about things evil in themselves or morally indifferent, is obligatory,
in such wise that he who acts against his conscience always sins."[1]
—— Saint Thomas Aquinas

I KNOW HOW FILMS WORK. I CAN WATCH MOST FILMS AND NOT BE IMPACTED by what I see because I can usually discern the intents of the filmmaker. I liken it to a magician watching another magician perform. If you know where the rabbit is hidden, it takes the illusion out of the trick and becomes a matter of enjoying the mechanics in another person's work. Yet there are times, even with someone as calloused as I am, that we see something that unsettles us.

One of the most difficult films I have ever seen is *Silent Hill,* an adaptation of the popular and influential video game. Rose Da Silva's troubled young daughter, Sharon, disappears. Rose tracks her daughter to a remote, desolate town named Silent Hill and discovers the town has been cast into hell—the local townspeople are religious zealots holed up in the church. Periodically, the town shifts in tone, turns darker and stranger. World War II air sirens, attached to the belfry of the church, wail. Everyone still in town quickly retreats to the church as demons descend upon the town and attempt to drag the citizens to their damnation. The film is a vibrant display of demonic imagery, suffering, and anti-Christian bigotry.

It is also poorly thought-out and stupid—quite simply, it is a bad movie. However, I have to admit it is a deeply demonic film and I found it quite

1. Saint Thomas Aquinas. *Philosophical Texts.* Labyrinth Press. 1982. 291.

disturbing on many levels. There was something too authentic about the demonic imagery. It disturbs me even now as I write these words.

Why did I sit through something that disturbed me? I am a film reviewer, and in order to critique movies, I have to sit through them. In many cases I wish there was another way. To this day, there are still images I have seen that I wish I could erase.

The biggest warning I can ever give to anyone who exposes them self to our culture is that **you cannot unwatch something**. Once it enters your head, it stays there for the rest of your life. Even the smallest, most seemingly inconsequential triviality can linger in your subconscious for decades.

This can work for both bad and good. A scene in a film can inspire you for years, just as another can darken your spirit. What is important is to keep in mind that when you choose to sit down and watch a film or television show, or even play a video game, you invite the content into your life, into your soul. Restraint and caution are not only prudent, they are vital. Your body is a temple—and that includes your mind.

> Or do you not know that your body is a temple of the Holy Spirit within you, whom you have from God? You are not your own, for you were bought with a price. So glorify God in your body ?" — Paul (1 Cor. 6:19–20)

Even when we heed that warning and are careful to keep to the straight and narrow, we still slip. I hear it repeatedly as I talk to Christians about culture: A man is watching television, flips through the channels and stops on a show. He is not sure about the show but it draws him in. He watches it. Once it is over, he is flushed with guilt. The show was too coarse. It was dark and foul. There was violence or nudity. He is left thinking, "Why did I sit through that? Why did I open myself to such lurid content?"

Life is not fair. The good news is, neither is salvation.

I have met people all along the continuum: from someone troubled by a questionable blip once seen on television, to someone burdened with pornography addiction. Any Christian actively engaged in film, television, or any part of mainstream culture will eventually encounter something that leaves them unsettled. If you decide to be part of modern culture, you will be tempted. Most of us will fail at some point.

When that happens to you, it is important to remember that you are not unique. Humans are weak, fallen, sinful creatures. We all experience moments where we fail, we trip over our own sinful natures. This is a part of life. Life is not fair. The good news is, neither is salvation.

Jesus Christ died for your sins. That means all of them—your sinful nature. It is easy for us to assign the big ticket items to Jesus then wrestle with the small stuff on our own. If the blood of Christ covers cheating on a spouse, robbing a bunch of banks, or murdering some guy in Reno, it covers the sins committed on the couch with a remote control in hand.

If you watch something that sticks in your craw, pray. Ask for direction, ask for forgiveness. God knows:

> For He knows how we are formed; He remembers that we are dust — David (Psa 103:14).

Too often Christ-followers torment themselves over past actions. Your response should be to pray and to consider *why* you watched the scene in the first place. This is the step many people forget to take.

Examine

When we sin, it does not happen in a vacuum. Events, ungodly attitudes, errant behaviors, unresolved problems, or past injuries led to that decision. The best way to keep from falling into a trap more than once is to identify causal factors and resolve them.

Ask God to reveal patterns in your life of disregard for His ways or of carelessness in your thought life. Be alert to those times you make decisions without thinking them through.

Ask God to uncover hurts, attitudes, or wrong-thinking that may cause you to repeat destructive behaviors. Ask Him to provide friends who will care enough about you to hold you to higher standards.

And again, pray (1 Thess. 5:17). Christ-followers find mercy, forgiveness, grace, and strength at the foot of the cross. Jesus said, "Go, and from now on sin no more" (Jn. 8:11).

Research

To avoid certain types of troubling films and television, be as informed as possible up front. If you identify films with questionable content before you see them, you can protect yourself.

One tool to keep in your arsenal is the Internet Movie Database (IMDb) (http://www.imdb.com)—an online database covering almost every film and television show ever produced.

Type the name of the film in the search box and you are taken to the film's page. There you will find a section listing Plot Keywords, words or simple phrases that describe key components within the film—a simple, effective tool for knowing what is actually in that movie.

Keywords for *The Bourne Supremacy* include "Shot in the Chest," "Shot in the Face," "Gash in the Face," "Suicide," and "Strangulation." Some Plot Keywords for *Old School* include "Premarital Sex," "Male Frontal Nudity," and "Sexual Arousal."

Wait

Despite what the advertising says, you do *not* need to see any movie on opening weekend. There is no reason for the rush. Wait a week and read up on a film before you see it. Read what the critics have to say. Go online, check out the reviews and comments.

In the interest of full disclosure, remember I am a film critic, so I have some interest in this suggestion. It is one of the reasons I began critiquing films—I could find no reviewer who spoke from both a moral and an artistic perspective. Even were I not a film critic, I would believe this to be an important step in protecting yourself and your family.

Read Reviews and Stay Informed

A Christ-follower does not need to be immersed in every aspect of the world around them. Many areas of our society are ones we should actively avoid. What is important is that we stay informed about the events and trends within our culture, know who pushes the envelope and in what direction—not only in Hollywood but across the entire cultural landscape.

It does not take much time or effort to remain informed. The Internet is loaded with websites which cover entertainment news. Many of these sites are secular, however, and tend to have explicit images and promote amoral behavior. If you follow the entertainment pages from more mainstream sites such as USAToday.com, Reuters.com, FoxNews.com, or any of the sites from the network broadcasters, your local paper, or IMDb.com, you should have enough information to keep in touch with what is happening in the mainstream. You can also use your search engine to locate sites that cover any area of the culture which interests you.

Find a few film critics and entertainment journalists you trust, preferably those who base observations on the content and spiritual issues you deem important. Track their RSS feeds. I always suggest reliance on more than one critic since no critic is always right. If you put all your cinematic eggs into one critic's basket, you risk following their advice on the day they happen to write their worst review. Compare opinions from two or more critics and you get a better perspective of the quality of a film.

When you can find a critic you trust, they can be a valuable component in your decision-making. Refer to them often, even on films you may not be interested in watching—so you can converse with other movie-goers about the pros and cons of that weekend blockbuster everyone's dying to see.

Avoid it Altogether

Despite the importance popular critics place on the latest smash hit, and no matter how much fun your friends and family claim it was when they saw it, you do not ever have to see any movie.

An obvious statement? Maybe. But in this marketing culture, we are urged, encouraged, pushed to see every latest film and to see it while it is still fresh. Exert your own peer pressure—stay informed and engaged at all times. Films can be wonderful things. They can be entertaining and enlightening, even educational and character-building. One thing they are not, however, is vital to your existence.

If you ever have any question or hesitation about a film, skip it. Like I said earlier, you can never unwatch it.

If it Does Not Grab You, Leave

Also, you are never required to finish any film or television show. A good story should sweep you away, grab your attention, engage your mind. If a show or film does not work for you or makes you uncomfortable, then turn it off or leave the theatre.

People complain that a film was boring or confusing or insulting or pointless. If it stinks, why watch it? I review films, I study them. I *have* to sit through the lousy ones. I *have* to suffer. You do *not*.

33

Honor Christ in What You See

*"So whether you eat or drink or whatever you do,
do it all for the glory of God."*[1]

ONE OF THE BIGGEST PROBLEMS WITH BEING A CHRISTIAN WHO participates in this world is, well, being a Christian who participates in this world. Being a Christ-follower reveals an intention to do more than merely put in your time on this earth. We are, literally, held to a higher standard, both by God and hopefully by our own self as well as faithful brothers and sisters around us.

A Christian whose actions are no different than those of a non-believer is not a Christ-follower, is he? He is someone with something to do on Sunday morning.

The Faithful have a life beyond this present, terrestrial existence to consider, which leads us to be more concerned with life's realities such as discipleship. We should be concerned with not only following Christ—

> If you abide in my word, you are truly my disciples, and you will know the truth, and the truth will set you free. — Jesus (Jn. 8:31–32)

—but also that our lives under Christ be as productive as possible:

> I am the vine; you are the branches. If a man remains in me and I in him, he will bear much fruit; apart from me you can do nothing. If anyone does not remain in me, he is like a branch that is thrown away and withers; such branches are picked up,

---

1. 1 Corinthians 10:31

> thrown into the fire and burned. If you remain in me and my words remain in you, ask whatever you wish, and it will be given you. This is to my Father's glory, that you bear much fruit, showing yourselves to be my disciples. — Jesus (Jn. 15:5–8)

We must lift up the light of Christ to the world around us whenever possible. A faith walk with Jesus must be active to be alive, must involve what is best for others as well as our family and ourselves.

A real-life example of this type of Christian service is seen in the life of former-pornography-producer-now-Christian Donny Pauling.[2] Donny not only turned his broken life over to Christ but he now speaks and offers advice to those enslaved by the viewing or production of pornography.

You can flap your lips all day long to recite Bible verses, but it is not enough. Your hands must be as active as your lips, then your life in Christ is revealed. I like to think of it as helping to pick up the litter along the side of the highway to heaven.

What does this have to do with watching movies? Well, we are to put all things to the service of Christ—all things.

To be a Christ-follower is difficult. My flesh would love to be able to mindlessly sit around all day and watch whatever it wanted, no matter how low and disgusting it would take me. Who does not long for the freedom to consume whatever they please without considering the consequences? That is the nature of sin and the flesh and is what got us into this mess.

Living with definitive standards can be hard. To give up the addictions of a material lifestyle can be uncomfortable and complex. I think that is one of the biggest reasons people stumble early in their Christian walk.

For some of you reading this book, a change in how you consume media will be difficult to accomplish. We were raised to believe films and television are meaningless and that to worry about their impact is foolishness. It often seems easier to go with the flow, and it is easy to want to segregate your spiritual life, your quiet time, from the rest of who you are. Who wants to know God looks over their shoulder while they watch a movie?

To those who compartmentalize their spirituality and faith, I say that your faith life is more critical during moments when you are alone than during your time within a church building. While in church, you are involved in a social event, a planned, specific, faith-centered experience. It is easy to be Christian, to behave and speak as a Christian when you are surrounded by others doing the same. When we are alone or within a more passive environment, we relax. Our grasp on our faith can also relax.

---

2. Donny Pauling's blog can be found at http://www.donnypauling.com/blog.

It is easy to stop thinking altogether and consider your "me time" to be about you. It is not. What we do in our leisure time is often as important in defining us as what we do when we are at work.

Down times can define
our relationship with God.

We spend our snippet of time on this planet to live for the glory of God. This can be an easy concept to grasp when we are at work. It is common to hear Christians claim they do X, Y, and Z "for the glory of God," whether it is going to work in the morning, doing chores around the house, or helping someone in need.

What we often forget is that we are to dedicate our whole life to Him, not just the productive times. This includes when you recline on your couch, munch Doritos, and watch a new release on DVD.

Jesus Christ does not call you for only a moment of your life. He is not interested in merely a portion of your attention. When it comes to your salvation, Jesus is downright selfish about you. He wants all of you. That was the biggest lesson of my death.

Advice from a Former Corpse

I have spent time in heart clinics, surrounded by people who face their own mortality. I have seen hospital roommates with their families during the moments before complicated, life-threatening bypass surgery. I know firsthand what it is like to look at your small children and say what you think could be your final words to them. Hang around the borderlands of the Valley of Death long enough and the reality of existence is plain to see.

But the dying are more alive than anyone else you will ever meet.

Dying men are without machinations, without schemes. The world has shrunken to precious, final morsels of existence, and that is all they need. A dying man will not care about meaningless things but will tenaciously grip the important—family, friends, God and His love.

If you want to see the dead, look outside. People allow their lives to be stuffed with hollow moments, meaningless tasks, fruitless labors. A person who throws their time away without a thought is a chronological glutton. They are a lottery ticket winner who spends and spends because they assume their jackpot will never dry up.

Pay attention, I speak from experience: Do not waste your life.

I died. For all we know, you are next.

Do not dismiss relaxation as inconsequential. We have more leisure time than any other generation in human history. We also have more avenues down which we can travel to temptation and sin.

To live the life of a Christ-follower, you must evaluate all aspects of how you live, which includes those times you appear to do nothing at all. To sit around "doing nothing" is less possible than you think. Unless you are dead, you are always doing something.

When you sit down for a two hour movie, you literally spend a portion of your precious existence on that film. You are not doing nothing; you are expending valuable time.

Life should be active, not dormant. I implore you to take control of your spare time and turn those moments of relaxation into something of value—a life with no meaningless moments, a faith that never fades into the background; rather, your faith in Christ Jesus should always be something you actively rely on and turn to. All aspects of your life should be lived in the light of Christ—even the parts you think are of little consequence.

From this day forward, begin to see your choices in entertainment not only as a way to pass the time but as a way to impact your culture. Your choices may not amount to much on their own, but if Christ-followers begin to act consciously in the choices they make, if we act more assertively in the marketplace, we can initiate a movement. In order for there to be a movement, each of us must continue to move in the right direction.

You have now been given tools to understand the stories found in film. Let people in on that secret. Teach your children, grandchildren, parents, and friends that there is meaning to be found in movies. The more we expose how lies are propagated by cinema, the more people will want the truth.

Write filmmakers and let them know what you want to see. Confront movie reviewers (myself included, if need be) when they praise products that undermine our society. When you find a film that promotes morality, life, love, or Christ, let everyone know. Everyone.

Trust me, when you get to the end of your life, you are going to want two things: first, more life; second, for your life to have had meaning. Your time is precious, even the time you waste. Do not fritter it away doing nothing. When you choose to watch a movie, make it a good choice. Once you have watched it, let your actions make it worth the time you have been given.

> So teach us to number our days
> that we may get a heart of wisdom.
> — Psalm 90:12

"Art requires philosophy, just as philosophy requires art. Otherwise, what would become of beauty?"[3]

—— Paul Gauguin

3. Paul Gauguin. *Gauguin's Intimate Journals*. Courier Dover Publications. 1997. 109. Used by permission.

Appendix A: The Structure of *Pulp Fiction*

Quentin Tarantino opens his unsettling film with a silent title board:

> **Pulp** n. **1.** A soft, moist, shapeless mass of matter. **2.** A magazine or book containing lurid subject matter and being characteristically printed on rough, unfinished paper.

The dictionary definition above is a perfect description of Quentin Tarantino's film. *Pulp Fiction* consists of four interwoven tales of underworld mobsters, hit men, drug dealers, and a wayward boxer on the run. The film, highly praised by film critics and historians, is certainly vivid and memorable. The film is also a formless, ultimately meaningless mass of narrative slathered in a veneer of cool. For the most part it gets by on its personality rather than its brains.

The film is broken down into four parts. [***Warning***: plot spoilers and plain retelling of graphic film content are contained in the following plot breakdown.]

The film opens with a prologue and ends with an epilogue. Both take place in a diner and show a young couple "Honey Bunny" and "Pumpkin" (Amanda Plummer and Tim Roth) robbing the joint. The prologue centers on the couple as they impulsively conspire to hold up the diner. At the end of the film the epilogue focuses on the robbery itself.

Next, we are introduced to Vincent Vega (John Travolta) and Jules Winnfield (Samuel L. Jackson), two hit men who work for the grumbling kingpin Marsellus Wallace (Ving Rhames). Vincent is nervous because in addition to his regular assignment he has been ordered by Marsellus to take Marsellus's beautiful wife, Mia, on a date. Vincent understands that Marsellus's jealousy is easily triggered. Marsellus is not the kind of man who is known for his evenhandedness and mercy.

Vincent and Jules get to their job. They stop at an apartment where Brett lives—Brett and his roommates have apparently crossed Marsellus. Jules and Vincent have come to retrieve a briefcase and kill the young men in the apartment. Jules quotes Ezekiel 25 to Brett then shoots him. Vincent grabs Marsellus' briefcase which, when opened, shines with a heavenly glow from within.

On their way out, Vincent and Jules are ambushed by a roommate hidden in the apartment. Instead of being gunned down, the bullets, fired at point blank range, miss the two assassins. After they dispatch their would-be killer, the hit men fall into an argument. How could they have survived that ambush? Was it a miracle? Vincent is unmoved by the sheer statistical chance that he survived the attack while Jules spots the hand of God. From this point forward Jules is a changed man.

The film then turns to its first story, *Vincent Vega and Marsellus Wallace's Wife*. Prior to heading out on the town, Vincent stops at his drug dealer's house and buys some rare, expensive, and potent heroin. Following a detailed scene of Vincent shooting up the heroin, he takes Mia (Uma Thurman) on a date. They banter over milkshakes and a burger at a retro-'50s restaurant. They dance at Jack Rabbit Slim's, then they head home. At Mia's place she snorts Vincent's powerful heroin and overdoses. In a panic, Vincent rushes her to his drug dealer's home and they shoot adrenaline directly into her heart. She survives and Vincent takes her home.

The second story, *The Gold Watch*, opens with a masterfully written monologue performed by Christopher Walken. It is the early 1970s and Butch, a little boy, is watching cartoons. Butch is interrupted and introduced to Captain Koons (Walkn). Koons delivers Butch's birthright, a dingy, gold watch that has been passed down from generation to generation. Each holder of the watch has been killed in military action. Butch's father, a P.O.W. in Vietnam, concealed the watch in his rectum for years to spare it for his son.

Fast forward to today, Butch (Bruce Willis) is now a grown man and a professional boxer. Earlier we witnessed Butch being ordered by Marsellus Wallace to throw a fight. Instead, Butch not only fails to throw the fight, he kills his competitor in the ring. Butch goes on the lam with his girlfriend, Fabienne. Marsellus orders Butch to be hunted down.

The following morning Butch learns that Fabienne has left his treasured gold watch behind in his apartment. It is his heirloom, his future son's birthright. He has no choice but to leave Fabienne behind and retrieve his watch regardless of the risk.

Butch goes to his apartment and finds Vincent waiting for him. Actually, Vincent is on the toilet reading a book. Butch kills Vincent, then retrieves the watch and begins his journey back to the hotel.

Driving back, Butch comes across Marsellus passing a crosswalk. He runs Marsellus down but crashes his car in the process. Butch tries to hide out in a pawn shop but Marsellus finds him. The two begin to fight but are interrupted by the shop's owner who captures the two men.

The owner of the shop along with his cop friend and a leather-bound creep called "The Gimp" hold the men in the basement where they intend to rape and torture their victims. The perverts rape Marsellus. Butch manages to escape. Instead of running, he returns to save Marsellus. Butch kills the men with a samurai sword (it makes some sense in the context of the scene.) In exchange for saving his life, Marsellus forgives Butch and exiles him from Los Angeles.

The final story, *The Bonnie Situation,* begins with Vincent (before he is killed by Butch) and Jules surviving the rain of bullets at the apartment. They argue the inherent meaning of their survival as they drive hostage Marvin, one of the roommates from the apartment, to Marsellus. Vincent accidentally shoots Marvin in the face, exploding the young man's head all over the interior of the car.

Jules stops off at a friend's house. The friend, Jimmie (Quentin Tarantino), is incensed over the two criminals dropping by first thing in the morning with a bleeding corpse in their car. Jimmie complains that his wife, Bonnie, will be home soon and when she finds the thugs and the dead body in their house she will divorce him. Jules calls The Wolf (Harvey Keitel), a fixer. The Wolf shows up, pays off Jimmie, has Jules and Vincent cleaned up, and has them take the car to the junkyard. Apparently, the Wolf is not the world's most clever fixer.

The film ends with the epilogue. Back in the diner, Vincent and Jules continue their argument over the theological aspects of their survival. Having witnessed God's mercy, Jules is unable to continue as a criminal and chooses to put his sin aside. [*language warning*]:

> **JULES:** . . . Whether or not what we experienced was an According to Hoyle miracle is insignificant. What is significant is that I felt the touch of God. God got involved.
>
> **VINCENT:** But why?
>
> **JULES:** That's what f*****g with me. I don't know why. But I can't go back to sleep.

Suddenly, Honey Bunny and Pumpkin hold up the diner, including Vincent and Jules. When Pumpkin comes to Jules to collect his wallet, he demands the briefcase. Jules tells him he cannot give him the briefcase since it is not his to give away. He then opens the briefcase and the heavenly, golden light shines in Pumpkin's eyes. Pumpkin is enraptured and mutters, "It's beautiful." Jules pulls his gun out and holds it to Pumpkin's head.

At this point Jules has his gun on Pumpkin and Honey Bunny has hers on Jules. In an attempt to calm the situation down, Jules has Pumpkin sit down across from him. He gives all his money to Pumpkin—who he calls Ringo. Jules then explains why he is giving the money to Pumpkin [*language warning*]:

> **JULES:** I'm buyin' somethin' for my money. Wanna know what I'm buyin' Ringo?
>
> **PUMPKIN:** What?

JULES: Your life. I'm givin' you that money so I don't hafta kill your ass. You read the Bible?

PUMPKIN: Not regularly.

JULES: There's a passage I got memorized. Ezekiel 25:17. "The path of the righteous man is beset on all sides by the inequities of the selfish and the tyranny of evil men. Blessed is he who, in the name of charity and good will, shepherds the weak through the valley of the darkness. For he is truly his brother's keeper and the finder of lost children. And I will strike down upon thee with great vengeance and furious anger those who attempt to poison and destroy my brothers. And you will know I am the Lord when I lay my vengeance upon you." I been sayin' that **** for years. And if you ever heard it, it meant your ***. I never really questioned what it meant. I thought it was just a cold-blooded thing to say to a motherf***** 'fore you popped a cap in his ***. But I saw some **** this mornin' made me think twice. Now I'm thinkin', it could mean you're the evil man. And I'm the righteous man. And Mr. .45 here, he's the shepherd protecting my righteous *** in the valley of darkness. Or it could be you're the righteous man and I'm the shepherd and it's the world that's evil and selfish. I'd like that. But that **** ain't the truth. The truth is you're the weak. And I'm the tyranny of evil men. But I'm tryin'. I'm tryin' real hard to be a shepherd.

Jules lowers his gun and lays it on the table.

Pumpkin and Honey Bunny are free to leave. Once they are gone, Vincent and Jules leave the diner themselves. The end.

A majority of the film is filler. It is entrancing filler, but filler just the same. I am not saying it is not masterfully shot and acted and well-written. What I am saying is that it is essentially inconsequential. Tarantino could have put anything in the middle of his film as long as it was showing criminality. I say this because the three middle stories are ultimately meaningless. The meat of the story comes in the prologue and epilogue.

The prologue and epilogue are used as framing devices for the rest of the film. In the basic structure of all stories, at the opening there is a Central Question posed. In the final moments, the Central Question is answered. In the case of this script, Tarantino is very blunt with this structure. He opens with an Adam and Eve (Pumpkin and Honey Bunny) couple devising sin. In the end their sin is resolved by Jules (think Jesus) paying for their sin, in this case literally. Instead of offering God's Old Testament wrath, Jules overcomes his very human desire for vengeance and offers the sinful couple forgiveness and redemption.

The rest of the film is the machinations of man wallowing in his sinful ways. It is an ugly display. Actually, it is more than just ugly. Tarantino celebrates sin. He presents evil in intricate detail with flashy dialog and cinematography. This is why the film is so gripping. The film commands attention because it showcases the criminality in men's hearts without reservation. We do not want this kind of filth in our private lives but we are entranced when we see it on screen. We effectively all slow down to watch the car crash of the human soul.

When the film was released there was much made about the broken narrative. The timeline of the film is not chronological. Butch kills Vincent, but Vincent is shown later in a time before his death, for example. The distorted timelines make absolute sense in the film since the stories are told from the perspectives of the characters involved. Their chronological order is meaningless because Tarantino is not showing a series of narratively-connected stories; they are connected by the themes of crime and sin. He could have shoved anything in between his prologue and epilogue and it would have made sense. What matters is that the two frames were in order—Question followed by Answer, sin followed by forgiveness.

The structure of the film shows the power of the Great Story structure. The film's scenes break down as follows:

Prologue

» Honey Bunny and Pumpkin plot crime at a cafe

» Vega and Jules on the way to Brett and Marvin's pad

» Vega and Jules kill Brett; they survive an ambush by Brett's roommate

Vincent Vega and Marsellus Wallace's Wife

» Marsellus orders Butch to take a dive

» Vega stops in at his drug dealer's to buy / shoots up

» Vega picks up Mia

» Vega takes Mia to Jack Rabbit Slim's—dance sequence

» Vega takes Mia home—she snorts the Choco (heroin) and dies

» Vega takes Mia to drug dealer's—shoots adrenaline into her heart—she lives

» Vega takes Mia home

The Gold Watch

- » Butch as child—gets daddy's watch
- » Butch does not throw the match—Marsellus calls for Butch's capture
- » Butch, in cab, is asked "What does it feel like to kill a man?"
- » Butch meets up with Fabienne in hotel
- » Butch/Fabienne—in bed—wants to live with her
- » Butch/Fabienne plan their future–Butch falls asleep
- » Butch/Fabienne the next morning realize she left the gold watch
- » Butch drives to apartment, enters, finds watch, kills Vega
- » Butch runs over Marsellus
- » Fights Marsellus—gets caught by Maynard/Zed
- » Maynard's basement—Marsellus is raped
- » Butch saves Marsellus
- » Butch is forgiven

The Bonnie Situation

- » Jules and Vega survive attack; discuss divine intervention
- » Jules decides to retire—Vega accidentally shoots Marvin as Vega says the words "God came down from heaven and stopped . . ." He doesn't get to say the words "the bullets."
- » They arrive at Jimmy's house
- » Over coffee Jimmie explains that Bonnie is coming home from work
- » Marsellus sends in the Wolf
- » Phase one—Clean the car
- » Phase two—Clean the cons
- » They drive to junkyard

Epilogue:

- » Jules and Vega go into cafe. Jules explains his "moment of clarity"
- » Honey Bunny and Pumpkin hold up the joint

» Jules buys the couple's lives, recites Ezekiel 25:17 as Scripture this time—says it is salvation and not ultimate death—Pumpkin is the weak and tyranny of evil man but Jules is trying real hard to be the shepherd

» Honey Bunny and Pumpkin, then Vega and Jules leave cafe (forgiveness)

The film is broken down easily into the Four-Act Structure:

Opening Question: The problem of sin as presented by Honey Bunny and Pumpkin

End of Act One: Vega reluctantly goes into Jack Rabbit Slim's

Reversal: Butch refuses to throw a fight and goes on the run—from this point forward all of the criminals are hit with bad times. Butch is on the run. Marsellus gets raped. Jules and Vincent deal with killing Marvin. Their criminal lives are closing in on them.

Death/Rebirth: "divine intervention" spares Jules and Vincent

Final confrontation: Jules forgives Honey Bunny and Pumpkin

The Great Story structure works to clarify messages and sort out narrative. The example of *Pulp Fiction* reveals that even when we want to break away from traditional storytelling we cannot help but come back to the essential structure we all inherently know. Even when the timelines are broken and rearranged, the writer still must sort them in a fashion that follows The Great Story in order for them to make sense.

What is even more telling about this film is its display of amorality. Tarantino takes us on a trip into the blackness of men's hearts but fails to make any moral distinctions in a bulk of the film. His criminal world is without morals. People kill one another, do drugs, rape, and steal with abandon. Without right and wrong in the world there is only survival. "Will this keep me safe or will it kill me?" are the only real concerns to the amoral man. This condition is shown consistently throughout the film.

Vincent's concern over taking Marsellus' wife on a date exemplifies this amoral condition. He had no moral quandary over seducing her but focused purely on the potential of Marsellus killing him—his own survival. This missing moral piece at the heart of each of the stories is why they end abruptly without a sense of resolution. The stories become nonsensical when the moral framework is removed—the morality that should be threaded through any well told story.

The only morality presented in the film is done in the prologue and epilogue. In these two segments, Jules is transformed from a brutish hit man who callously quotes Ezekiel to become a reborn Bible quoting man trying to understand his role under God. Jules is the central figure of the film; he is the hero of *Pulp Fiction*. He is the only character who experiences any change. Jules is also the only one who breaks away from the amoral swamp of the world. The rest remain sinful and lost. It is significant that Vincent is killed after his denial of God's miracle that spared his life. He chose the route of the sinner and died for his own sins. Jules chose another path and promised to walk the earth doing good.

Even though he wallows in the sinfulness of the world, Tarantino was compelled to dispense a moral message in order to provide his film with any depth. His morality is shoddy, but it is still there. Tarantino does not strike me as being gifted with wisdom so I'll take what I can get.

The flowering of Jules is the film's heart and the film's only lasting piece of drama. It is the reason why Samuel L. Jackson's performance is so memorable. As an actor he is given the best of all possible roles—a man who finds redemption.

For those who are curious about the film, I must warn that even though there is a kernel of morality to be found within the opening and ending, this is a deeply corrupt film. It is not moral and it not Scriptural. Tarantino loves to show cruelty and crudity in all of its hideous detail. This film is not for the faint of heart or the easily tempted. This is a film not easily forgotten.

Appendix B: The Structure of *The Lord of the Rings* Film Trilogy

J.R.R. Tolkien wrote *The Lord of the Rings* to create a meaningful myth for his modern English culture. His tale of a simple hobbit's quest to destroy the Dark Lord Sauron's One Ring in the fiery depths of Mount Doom stands as one of the most influential works of literature of the twentieth century.

Woven through the tale of the hobbit, Frodo, is a second story—the rise of Aragorn. Aragorn is heir to Isildur who cut the One Ring from Sauron's hand during a previous battle for Middle Earth. Aragorn begins the story as a wayfarer, Strider, who has avoided his place as king of men. He was raised by elves and is now a Ranger, one who helps provide security for Middle Earth. As the story progresses, and as it becomes more likely that Sauron will capture all of Middle Earth, Aragorn reluctantly ascends to the throne and leads men to victory.

The intertwined stories of Frodo and Aragorn create an epic fantasy that has influenced generations of writers and artists. Tolkien knew how stories operated both within a society and within a reader's mind. To create his work, the Oxford professor called on his knowledge of pre-Christian fairytales and Catholicism. He appropriated common icons and motifs from world mythologies and laced his multi-layered story with images and themes that speak to the heart of Western culture and the Western mind.

He was also aware of the theological undertones of his work. His mythological approach to the conflict between good and evil replicated the depictions within religious texts. There are clear lines between the wholesome and the despoiled. Both sides are imbued with supernatural gifts and good ultimately has the upper hand. Tolkien insisted his story was neither analogy nor allegory, but he applied elements of theology and mythology to craft a thoughtful and moving tale which told again the story of man's fall and his ultimate redemption.

In *The Lord of the Rings*, we can see Sauron as the ultimate evil; he is Satan. Frodo can represent us, the common people, the little man in the big world. He is charged with the solemn task of carrying the weight of the One Ring, sin, on his long journey through Sauron's realm.

It may seem that Frodo is the hero of the trilogy since he is the one who moves to destroy the ring. The fact is, though, that Frodo fails in his task. In the end, he falters and succumbs to the One Ring. It is only through Gollum's impulsiveness—he bites off Frodo's finger, retrieves the ring, then slips into the fires of Mt. Doom—that the One Ring is destroyed. The melting of the One Ring, the salvation of Middle Earth, comes as the result of betrayal and misfortune. Aragorn is the beneficiary of this happening and ascends to his kingship following destruction of the foe. It is Aragorn who is the hero of the story.

Aragorn's role is more metaphysical; he is the royal elite. He is essentially the Christ of Middle Earth. It is his rise to the throne that stands as the true triumphant moment over evil. Following the destruction of the One Ring, which was created to rule all other Rings of Power, Aragorn becomes king to rule over all other realms of man. Narratively, the One Ring is replaced by the One King.

When we review the structure of each film individually, Aragorn's importance is muted. He is one more vibrant player on a crowded stage. When we take all three stories and lay them out as one long tale—the way Tolkien intended the original book to be published—the structure moves Aragorn to front and center and reveals him to be the focus of the work. Frodo fades into an important supporting role.

In the films, this heroic duality in the story is rather obvious. Director Peter Jackson was forced to swing back and forth between the two plots of Frodo and Aragorn, and the two characters rarely connect again once they part at the end of the first film.

The Lord of the Rings movie trilogy is a fantastic example of how The Great Story structure will map a full story as well as its segments. We will look at the structure of each of the three stories and then compile them to see how they work together to deliver a fuller theme.

Before we begin, I want to pause to recognize one of the truths of modern life. Tolkien's work has spawned college courses and countless books, articles, and arguments. Many of his fans will squabble endlessly over themes and details. To tell the truth, *The Lord of the Rings* fans, known as Ringers, are like Trekkies who know how to read.

Don't know if you're a Ringer? Let me ask a couple of questions:

» If the One Ring makes the wearer invisible, then why is Sauron not invisible in the opening sequence of the film?

» Why didn't they just ride the eagles to Mount Doom?

If you found yourself answering either of those questions, you are probably a Ringer. You can find a support group if you look online.

Here is a note to all of you Ringers: I am discussing the films not the books. There is a difference between the two. A film that is adapted from a book is still a film. It is a different medium and has different requirements. The details laid out below are not intended to cover any aspect of the books.

Film One—Lord of the Rings: The Fellowship of the Ring

Prologue: The first battle for Middle Earth / Isildur cuts the One Ring from Sauron's hand / Isildur falls to the power of the One Ring—sin enters Middle Earth

End of Act One: Frodo is sent on his journey with the One Ring

Reversal: The Council of Elrond

Death/Rebirth—End of Act Three: Gandalf falls at the Bridge of Khazad-dum

The Final Conflict: Aragon swears to protect Isengard as he comforts the dying Boromir and thereby accepts his role as king

Dénouement: Frodo and Sam leave the Fellowship / Aragon and company go hunt for orcs

The Fellowship of the Ring opens with historical context. The prologue sets up the overarching battle between good and evil and describes in detail the fall of man (as represented in the fall of Isildur to the power of the One Ring).

The original world of the peaceful Shire is shattered by Bilbo's abrupt exit and Gandalf's bestowal of the ring upon Frodo. The tone of the film turns dark and foreboding. Act One closes with Frodo hurried out the front door of his home and into the dangerous world beyond the Shire.

Soon the Ringwraiths descend upon the helpless Shire. Frodo and company are on the run. They are joined by Aragorn, introduced as Strider—a fitting name since he straddles two lives, his current persona as a ranger and his true role as leader of men. The group runs from the ringwraiths and eventually reaches Rivendell.

In Rivendell, the Council of Elrond is conducted. This counts as the reversal scene. At this point Frodo is cemented as the bearer of the One Ring. This is also where the focus of evil falls squarely on the little hobbit. He is the target for the enemy.

The Fellowship begins their journey and is forced to enter the Mines of Moria. This dank, dead place is location for the Death/Rebirth scene. Gandalf sacrifices himself to spare the rest and is dragged into shadow beneath the Bridge of Khazad-dum by the Balrog. While he is not reborn immediately, Gandolf's fall serves as the central death that spurs the hero forward.

The film closes as Saruman, the real villain of this first film, releases his minions, the Uruk-hai, onto the remaining Fellowship. Pippin and Merry are kidnapped, Boromir is killed, and the Fellowship is broken.

Frodo ends the story by leaving the Fellowship to alone take the ring to its destruction; though he is joined by Samwise. Aragorn has his moment as well when he promises the dying Boromir that he will help save Isengard, thus he accepts his responsibility to become king.

In this first installment of the story, Frodo is the clear hero; he is the one who grows and changes. The plot focuses tightly on his path. Aragorn is heroic but has yet to take a lead position. His acceptance of his heritage combined with Frodo's disbanding of the Fellowship marks the transfer of the heroic position from the hobbit to the future king.

Film Two—Lord of the Rings: The Two Towers

Prologue: Gandalf battles the Balrog

End of Act One: Gandalf is revealed as Gandalf the White. He tells his companions, "One stage of your journey is over, another begins."

Reversal: Saruman reveals his army and sparks the war for Middle Earth

End of Act Three: The wall of Helm's Deep is breached / Aragon is thrown to the ground, possibly dead

The Final Conflict: The knights of Rohan ride to the rescue with Gandalf

Dénouement: The battle of Helm's Deep is over. Gandalf states, "The battle for Middle Earth is about to begin. All our hopes lie with two little hobbits, somewhere in the wilderness."

The second film opens with a prologue—Gandalf battles the Balrog as they descend into the deep chasms beneath Middle Earth. The name Middle Earth comes from the German *Midgard*. In Germanic mythology Midgard lay between Asgard (heaven) and Hel (hell). With this in mind, Gandalf falling with the Balrog can be interpreted as his following the beast into hell.

In Act One, Aragorn, Gimli, and Legolas trail the orcs who carry Pippin and Merry to Saruman. In Fangorn Forest the trio are shocked to find Gandalf, now "Gandalf the White," an angelic, reborn Gandalf sent back to Middle Earth to complete his work of battling the evil that threatens to consume Middle Earth. He announces to his companions that "One stage of your journey is over, another begins." This marks the end of Act One.

Act Two is consumed by the poor conditions in Rohan. Théoden, King of Rohan, is a shell of a man, lulled into Saruman's spell by Grima Wormtongue. Théoden's niece, Eowyn, and nephew, Éomer, are distressed by the condition of their enfeebled king. Gandalf arrives, exorcises Saruman's influence, and restores Théoden.

The reversal reveals Saurman's army of tens of thousands of Uruk-hai to Grima Wormtongue. Saruman sends this army to overrun Helm's Deep. This is the opening salvo in the battle for Middle Earth.

Act Three focuses entirely on the battle for Helm's Deep. The Death/Rebirth scene comes with the dramatic breaching of the Deeping wall. A mining orc carries a flaming torch like an Olympic runner, casts himself into the drain in the base of the wall, and ignites explosives placed in casks beneath the wall. The wall is decimated. Aragorn, atop the wall, is thrown down and possibly killed. He is found lying in the rubble surrounded by the dead and dying. He gets his bearings and leads a heroic stand against the invading Uruk-hai which ends with the death of a beloved elven friend. The forces of men fall back into the keep and Helm's Deep is overrun by Saruman's forces.

The final Act shows the fall of Helm's Deep. The Uruk-hai have breached the wall and the men inside struggle to stay alive. On the other side of Middle Earth, Pippin and Merry have joined forces with the Ents who attack Saruman's headquarters at Isengard. In the end, the knights of Rohan, led in part by Gandalf the White, come to the rescue of Helm's Deep. The Uruk-hai are routed. Saruman's defeated is shown at Isengard.

At the end of the film, Helm's Deep has been spared, but it is clear the larger war has begun. Gandalf, weary from the battle, sternly admits, "The battle for Middle Earth is about to begin. All our hopes lie with two little hobbits, somewhere in the wilderness." This final statement acts as a bridge to the final film.

The hero of the second film becomes Gandalf. Frodo fades into the background almost completely. Aragorn also fails to command the plot; he acts in a supporting role to the character of Gandalf who drives the story forward. Gandalf opens the film and remains a key figure at every major point in the structure.

This move away from the more easily identifiable hero is not unique to this trilogy. This can also be seen in *Star Wars: The Empire Strikes Back* where Luke remains the hero but Han Solo's role is inflated to make up for Luke's lack of character development. In middle films such as these, the hero is often weighed down by numerous conflicts and troubles and, therefore, does not grow. His development is seen in the third film, after he survives his trials.

To compensate, a secondary character must step up during the middle portion of the trilogy to fill the void.

Film Three—Lord of the Rings: The Return of the King

Prologue: Sméagol kills Déagol and steals the One Ring / Sméagol morphs into Gollum

End of Act One: The beacons are lit to alert Rohan they are needed

Reversal: Anduril, Flame of the West, is bestowed upon Aragorn

Death/Rebirth—End of Act Three: The Oath-Breakers from the Paths of the Dead are freed from their bondage / Aragon heals Éowyn / Merry also appears to cheat death / Frodo awakens from being poisoned by Shelob

The Final Conflict: The One Ring is destroyed / Sauron is defeated / Aragorn takes his throne

Dénouement: The elves and ring-bearers leave Middle Earth—the Age of Men begins

The final film opens with another prologue—the discovery of the One Ring by Sméagol's cousin, Déagol. Once Sméagol sights the magical ring, he is obsessed with possessing it. He murders his relative in order to have it. Sméagol becomes Gollum.

Act One opens with Gollum as he leads Frodo and Sam on their way into Mordor.

Aragorn, Gandalf, and company discover Merry and Pippin at Isengard. They also find Saruman and Grima Wormtongue lurking atop the wizard's tower. Saruman and Grima are killed. Gandalf retrieves a palantír, a magical seeing glass that looks like a crystal ball, and takes it with him from Isengard. The group travels to Rohan.

In Rohan, Pippin peers into the palantír and is spotted by Sauron, himself. Pippin identifies the city of Minas Tirith in Gondor as the place Sauron plans to strike. Gandalf rushes to that city with Pippin in tow. In Minas Tirith, they meet the Steward of Gondor, Boromir's father, who seems to be insane with grief at the loss of his son. As Sauron's army approaches the city, the Steward insists on ignoring the threat at his doorstep.

Gandalf and Pippin secretly light the beacons which travel to Rohan with the message that Gondor needs their aid.

Act Two presents the growing stress which Gollum is able to create between the exhausted Frodo and Sam. The trio claw their way through the brutal landscape of Mordor. In secret, Gollum plots to lead the pair to the lair of the giant spider Shelob. There the ever-hungry beast will snare the hobbits and feast on their quivering bodies. Once she discards the hobbit's empty husks, Gollum can then scavenge for the One Ring in their remains.

As the orc armies close on Minas Tirith, they overrun the defensive city of Osgiliath. From there, the orcs and their leader, the Witch-king of Angmar, are able to organize their offensive.

Act Two ends with the ill-fated ride of Faramir and his men to attack the fallen city of Osgiliath. The knights are slaughtered by the orcs.

In Mordor, Frodo sends Sam home. Gollum has caused doubt in Frodo's mind and friction between the two hobbits. All Gollum needs to do now is lead Frodo to his death at the stinger of Shelob and he will have his prize.

The Reversal comes with Elrond's dramatic revealing of the reforged shards of Arundiel—the sword used by Isildur to cut the One Ring from Sauron's hand. The elf lord presents the heirloom to Aragorn. Just as wielding Excalibur proved Arthur's worth, so Aragorn's ability to wield the sword Anduril, Flame of the West, will prove his right and position as king.

Knowing their small numbers could never defeat the massive army preparing to take Gondor, Aragorn rides the Paths of the Undead, accompanied by Gimli and Legolas, to raise the army of the undead Oath-Breakers, an army of restless souls cursed to languish in the mountainside until the true King of Gondor releases them. Aragorn tells the Undead they will be freed if they take up arms with him against Sauron. They agree.

Act Three shows the battle for Gondor. It also contains the torment of Frodo in the lair of Shelob. The giant spider hunts the frightened hobbit. She strikes him with her stinger and coils him in her webbing. He will be a fine meal. Sam returns to find Frodo dead (he thinks) and fights off the ugly beast with Frodo's sword, Sting, and the vial of the Light of Elendil given to Frodo by Galadriel.

At Minas Tirith, the knights of Rohan come to the aid of Gondor and win an initial defeat of the orc armies but are overrun by the Westerlings and their elephants. Aragorn arrives with the Undead army under his control. The Undead quickly defeat the horrified armies of Sauron.

The Death/Rebirth scene comes in a string of resurrections. The Oath-Breakers from the Paths of the Dead are freed from their bondage. Aragon heals Éowyn who was injured while dispatching the Witch-King. The hobbit Merry also cheats death in the aftermath of the battle. Finally, Frodo wakes from his venom-induced coma.

In the final conflict, Frodo enters Mount Doom but succumbs to the power of the One Ring. He is attacked by Gollum, who bites off Frodo's finger, retrieves the ring, and, in his jubilation, falls into the steaming lava of the fires of Mount Doom. Gollum and the One Ring are destroyed.

Without his essence contained within the One Ring, Sauron and his kingdom are destroyed and his armies are swallowed up by chasms within the earth. The war for Middle Earth is complete and goodness has won.

Aragorn is crowned King of Gondor—King of Men. The hobbits return to the Shire. Frodo chooses to join his uncle Bilbo and Gandalf as they sail from the Grey Havens (think going to heaven).

This final film belongs to Frodo. He is the hero of the tale. It is his struggle with the ring and with Sam and Gollum that gives the film much of its dramatic depth. Aragorn's fight for Gondor and his assumption of the crown is critical but, in the context of this film, he is a side player.

Each of the three films is self-contained and forms a distinct tale on their own. Obviously, though, they are meant to be enjoyed together. While each film has its own structure with its individual themes and arcs, when melded together to create the one massive film they are intended to be, we see a new structure emerge.

The *Lord of the Rings* Trilogy of Films

Prologue: The first battle for Middle Earth/ Isildur cuts the One Ring from Sauron / Isildur falls to the power of the One Ring—sin enters Middle Earth

End of Act One: Aragon swears to protect Isengard as he comforts the dying Boromir—and, thereby, accepts his role as king

Reversal: The wall of Helm's Deep is breached /Aragon is thrown to the ground, possibly dead

Death/Rebirth—End of Act Three: Anduril, Flame of the West is bestowed upon Aragorn

The Final Conflict: The One Ring is destroyed / Sauron is defeated / Aragorn, now king, takes his throne

Dénouement: The elves and ring-bearers leave Middle Earth—the Age of Men begins

When we combine the three films into a single narrative, the focus of the story turns from little Frodo to King Aragorn. The story is no longer about a hobbit's quest to destroy the One Ring and thereby exorcise sin from the world.

Aragorn begins the story as Strider. He avoids his ultimate responsibilities as king. He attempts to blend in with the Fellowship, to be one of many but it does not work. By story's end, he must step into his proper role as king. Aragorn promises the dying Boromir that he will protect Minas Tirith—that he will accept his responsibilities as king. At this point, Aragorn begins to lead. From this point forward he moves, is proactive, and works to undo Sauron's grasp upon Middle Earth.

Throughout the second act Aragorn chases the orcs in his hope to save Merry and Pippin. He also collects his allies including Gandalf the White, Théoden, King of Rohan, Eowyn, Éomer, and the elves who arrive to help defend Helm's Deep.

The Reversal of the story comes with the breaching of the wall at Helm's Deep. Aragorn has a brief death and rebirth at this moment. More importantly, it stands as Sauron's first physical break in their defenses. It is at this point that the defenders of Middle Earth are put on the defensive. They will remain in this position until the end of the story.

Following his failure at Helm's Deep, Sauron presses his assets against the unprepared city of Minas Tirith. This phase of the war begins with a small engagement with Faramir's men at Osgiliath. Faramir's troops are routed and return to Minas Tirith to help defend the great city. The Steward of Gondor, displeased with Faramir, his son, for leaving Osgiliath unguarded, sends Faramir and his men back to Osgiliath on a suicide mission.

The desperate ride of Faramir and his men into the certain doom that awaits them is the story's main death and rebirth. This is a very dramatic sequence in the film. As Faramir and his men are cut down by orc arrows, Pippin sings a sweeping and sad song for the Steward who sits in his great hall consuming a rich meal.

The riders represent all of mankind. They are the defenses of man against the inhuman, overwhelming armies of evil. With the decimation of Faramir's men it appears that all hope for humanity is lost.

Elrond appears to Aragorn and bestows upon him his birthright, Anduril, Flame of the West. By wielding Anduril, Aragorn proves his right to Gondor's throne, for only Isildur's heir is able to command it. Wielding Anduril also reveals Aragorn's authority, as Isildur's heir, to command the army of Undead Oath-Breakers.

The battle for Middle Earth comes to conclusion when Aragorn leads the joined armies to the Black Gate. This act distracts Sauron and his remaining armies and gives Frodo and Sam the time they need to slip into Mount Doom and destroy the One Ring.

Following the destruction of the One Ring and the fall of Sauron, Aragorn returns to Gondor and claims his throne. He takes his elven love, Arwen, as his bride and queen.

Man has a new king, a singular leader. Middle Earth is healed. The age of the elves is over and the age of men begins.

Tolkien originally wrote *The Lord of the Rings* as a single story. The stark change in focus that occurs when we place the three films together is the difference between enjoying the glory of the whole forest versus the details of one tree. Tolkien may or may not have considered Frodo his hero. Either way, I believe it is clear that it is Aragorn who takes on that role. Frodo is no slacker, but he does not carry the same weight as the future king of Gondor.

Index

AUTHOR BIO

Film critic Scott Nehring's reviews are found on GoodNewsFilmReviews.com and on ChristianCinema.com. His movie reviews have also been seen on the websites for *USAToday*, Reuters, *The Chicago Sun-Times*, *The India Times*, and FoxNews along with numerous local television station websites across the U. S.

Scott is a speaker, instructor, screenwriter, and fiber artist. For the past decade, Scott has focused on teaching Christians about film and culture. It is Scott's belief that one of the biggest reasons for the gulf between American Christianity and modern culture is that Christians have unwisely abandoned the Arts and artists. Shunning of the Arts has caused Christians to fall out of step with culture and too often left them ill-equipped to understand or criticize culture in a productive way.

Through his film reviews and classes Scott hopes to educate readers to the world of Story and story progression, to open up the world of cinema and, by extension, the Arts to the average Christian.

Scott lives outside Minneapolis, Minnesota, with his wife, Andrea, their three children, and the family dog, Clementine. In his off-hours, Scott enjoys his family, gardening, beekeeping, and watching films.

ACKNOWLEDGMENTS

Special thanks go to my editor, Christine Hunt. Without your boundless patience and endless supply of red ink this book would have remained an unreadable heap.

I would also like to thank Tim Porter, Jeff Burton, Ken Hunt, Julie Davis, Andrew Turonie, Jacob Nehring, Andrew Nehring, Evelyn Nehring, Ron Nordin, Brandy Dopkins, Jay and Ernestine Covington, Kristi Noser, Sybil Thon, Gregg Heinsch, Leticia Velasquez, Troy A. LaFaye, John Turonie, Renee Turonie, Kendre Turonie, Christopher Stephan, Jim Zimmerman, Michael Norman, and all the poor souls who ever had to listen to me ramble on and on about film—for your support, encouragement, correction, and friendship.

Appreciation also goes out to Tim Challies, Judy Davis, Craig Detweiler, Joan Graves, Curtis Hanson, Bruce Marshall, John Mellencamp, Bob Merlis, John Ottinger, Jeffrey Overstreet, Paul Taylor, Dover Publications, the Libreri Editrice Vaticana, Peter Lang Publishing, New Directions Publishing, Brad Bird of Pixar Animation Studios, Princeton University Press, Random House, Stanford Magazine, and Taylor & Francis Group for their generous permission to use their creativity and words within this publication.

LaVergne, TN USA
13 June 2010
185794LV00006B/4/P